D0856952

Bloom's Modern Critical Interpretations

The Adventures of
Huckleberry Finn
The Age of Innocence
Alice's Adventures in
Wonderland
All Quiet on the
Western Front
As You Like It
The Ballad of the Sad
Café
Beowulf
Black Boy
The Bluest Eye
The Canterbury Tales
Cat on a Hot Tin
Roof
The Catcher in the
Rye
Catch-22
The Chronicles of
Narnia
The Color Purple
Crime and
Punishment
The Crucible
Darkness at Noon
Death of a Salesman
The Death of Artemio
Cruz
Don Quixote
Emerson's Essays
Emma
Fahrenheit 451
A Farewell to Arms
Frankenstein

The Grapes of Wrath
Great Expectations
The Great Gatsby
Gulliver's Travels
The Handmaid's Tale
Heart of Darkness
I Know Why the
Caged Bird Sings
The Iliad
Jane Eyre
The Joy Luck Club
The Jungle
Lord of the Flies
The Lord of the Rings
Love in the Time of
Cholera
The Man Without
Qualities
The Metamorphosis
Miss Lonelyhearts
Moby-Dick
My Ántonia
Native Son
Night
1984
The Odyssey
Oedipus Rex
The Old Man and the
Sea
On the Road
One Flew Over the
Cuckoo's Nest
One Hundred Years of
Solitude
Persuasion

Portnoy's Complaint
A Portrait of the Artist
as a Young Man
Pride and Prejudice
Ragtime
The Red Badge of
Courage
The Rime of the
Ancient Mariner
The Rubáiyát of Omar
Khayyám
The Scarlet Letter
Silas Marner
Song of Solomon
The Sound and the
Fury
The Stranger
A Streetcar Named
Desire
Sula
The Tale of Genji
A Tale of Two Cities
The Tempest
Their Eyes Were
Watching God
Things Fall Apart
To Kill a Mockingbird
Ulysses
Waiting for Godot
The Waste Land
White Noise
Wuthering Heights
Young Goodman
Brown

Bloom's Modern Critical Interpretations

J. D. Salinger's

The Catcher in the Rye
New Edition

Edited and with an introduction by
Harold Bloom
Sterling Professor of the Humanities
Yale University

BLOOM'S
LITERARY CRITICISM
An imprint of Infobase Publishing

Editorial Consultant, John Unrue

Bloom's Modern Critical Interpretations:
J. D. Salinger's *The Catcher in the Rye*—**New Edition**
Copyright ©2009 by Infobase Publishing

Introduction ©2009 by Harold Bloom

Bloom's Literary Criticism
An imprint of Infobase Publishing
132 West 31st Street
New York NY 10001

Library of Congress Cataloging-in-Publication Data

J.D. Salinger's The catcher in the rye / edited and with an introduction by Harold
Bloom.—New ed.
    p. cm.—(Bloom's modern critical interpretations)
Includes bibliographical references and index.
ISBN 978-1-60413-183-3 (alk. paper)
1. Salinger, J. D. (Jerome David), 1919– Catcher in the Rye. 2. Caulfield, Holden
(Fictitious character) 3. Runaway teenagers in literature. 4. Teenage boys in literature.
I. Bloom, Harold.

PS3537.A426C3292 2009
813'.54—dc22

                        2008045784

Contents

Editor's Note

My Introduction raises—but declines to answer—the question of any lasting aesthetic value of *The Catcher in the Rye*.

The baker's dozen of essays tend to merge in an appreciation of Salinger's narrative. I would choose Sanford Pinsker, David Castronovo, Jane Mendelsohn, and Carl Freedman as making their critical responses more agile than are most reactions to Salinger.

HAROLD BLOOM

Introduction

J. D. SALINGER (1919–)

I

It is more than a half-a-century since the publication of *The Catcher in the Rye* (1951), and the short novel has gone through hundreds of printings. Authentic popular fiction of authentic literary distinction is rather rare. Does *The Catcher in the Rye* promise to be of permanent eminence, or will it eventually be seen as an idealistic period-piece, which I think will be the fate of Harper Lee's *To Kill a Mockingbird* and Toni Morrison's *Beloved,* works as popular as *Catcher* continues to be.

The literary ancestors of Holden Caulfield rather clearly include Huck Finn and Jay Gatsby, dangerous influences upon Salinger's novel. *The Adventures of Huckleberry Finn* remains Mark Twain's masterwork, central to Faulkner, Hemingway, Scott Fitzgerald, and the other significant novelists of their generation. *The Great Gatsby* endures as Fitzgerald's classic achievement, capable of many rereadings. Rereading *The Catcher of the Rye* seems to me an aesthetically mixed experience—sometimes poignant, sometimes mawkish or even cloying. Holden's idiom, once established, is self-consistent, but fairly limited in its range and possibilities, perhaps too limited to sustain more than a short story.

And yet Holden retains his pathos, even upon several rereadings. Manhattan has been a descent into Hell for many American writers, most notably in "The Tunnel" section in Hart Crane's visionary epic *The Bridge*. It becomes Holden's Hell mostly because of Holden himself, who is masochistic, ambivalent towards women, and acutely ambivalent in regard to his father. Holden's psychic health, already precarious, barely can sustain the stresses of

1

Manhattan. He suffers both from grief at his younger brother Allie's death, and from the irrational guilt of being a survivor.

Holden is seventeen in the novel, but appears not to have matured beyond thirteen, his age when Allie died. Where Holden's distrust of adult language originates, Salinger cannot quite tell us, but the distrust is both noble and self-destructive. To be a catcher in the rye, Holden's ambition, is to be a kind of secular saint, willing and able to save children from disasters.

Faulkner remarked that Holden's dilemma was his inability to find and accept an authentic mentor, a teacher or guide who could arouse his trust. The dilemma, being spiritual, hurts many among us, and is profoundly American. Holden speaks for our skepticism, and for our need. That is a large burden for so fragile a literary character, and will turn out eventually to be either aesthetic salvation for *The Catcher in the Rye,* or a prime cause for its dwindling down to the status of a period piece.

II

The pleasures of *The Catcher in the Rye* adequately are revealed by its famous first paragraph:

> If you really want to hear about it, the first thing you'll probably want to know is where I was born, and what my lousy childhood was like, and how my parents were occupied and all before they had me, and all that David Copperfield kind of crap, but I don't feel like going into it, if you want to know the truth. In the first place, that stuff bores me, and in the second place, my parents would have about two hemorrhages apiece if I told anything pretty personal about them. They're quite touchy about anything like that, especially my father. They're *nice* and all—I'm not saying that—but they're also touchy as hell. Besides, I'm not going to tell you my whole goddam autobiography or anything. I'll just tell you about this madman stuff that happened to me around last Christmas just before I got pretty run-down and had to come out here and take it easy. I mean that's all I told D.B. about, and he's my *brother* and all. He's in Hollywood. That isn't too far from this crumby place, and he comes over and visits me practically every week end. He's going to drive me home when I go home next month maybe. He just got a Jaguar. One of those little English jobs that can do around two hundred miles an hour. It cost him damn near four thousand bucks. He's got a lot of dough, now. He didn't *use* to. He used to be just a regular writer, when he was home. He wrote this terrific book of short stories, *The Secret Goldfish,* in case you never heard of him. The best one in it was "The Secret Goldfish." It was about

this little kid that wouldn't let anybody look at his goldfish because he'd bought it with his own money. It killed me. Now he's out in Hollywood, D.B., being a prostitute. If there's one thing I hate, it's the movies. Don't even mention them to me.

The ear, inner and outer, is certainly evident, and the tone is alive and consistent. What we miss, as we age into rereaders, is surprise, even when Holden signs off with some grace:

> D.B. asked me what I thought about all this stuff I just finished telling you about. I didn't know what the hell to say. If you want to know the truth, I don't *know* what I think about it. I'm sorry I told so many people about it. About all I know is, I sort of *miss* everybody I told about. Even old Stradlater and Ackley, for instance. I think I even miss that goddam Maurice. It's funny. Don't ever tell anybody anything. If you do, you start missing everybody.

One thinks of Huck Finn's evenhanded mode of narration, with its constant undersong of fellow-feeling and compassion, and of Nick Carraway's fair-mindedness, and even of Jake Barnes's rueful affection for almost anyone whose story he has told. Holden Caulfield has added a certain zany zest, but little else. Yet that is to grant Salinger's best book rather less than it merits, since no book can touch the universal, even for a time, without a gift of its own for the receptive reader.

Holden is derivative, but still highly likeable, and for all his vulnerability he remains an attractive survivor, who has returned from illness as his narrative ends. Survival is his entire enterprise, even as freedom was Huck Finn's enterprise. This regression from freedom to survival is what gives Salinger's one novel its curious pathos, which is also its principal aesthetic virtue. Endlessly honest with the reader, Holden wistfully keeps revealing that his outcast condition is only partly a voluntary one. He is potentially self-destructive, very nearly masochistic in his psychosexuality, and religiously obsessed, to the extent that he admires poor Legion, the madman and tomb-haunter, trapped by many demons. The most unpleasant sentence in the novel is surely Holden's declaration: "If you want to know the truth, the guy I like best in the Bible, next to Jesus, was that lunatic and all, that lived in the tombs."

Any aesthetic judgment of *The Catcher in the Rye* turns finally upon its most famous passage, which is what might be called its title-passage:

> I'm not too sure old Phoebe knew what the hell I was talking about. I mean she's only a little child and all. But she was listening, at least. If somebody at least listens, it's not too bad.

"Daddy's going to *kill* you. He's going to *kill* you," she said.

I wasn't listening, though. I was thinking about something else—something crazy. "You know what I'd like to be?" I said. "You know what I'd like to be? I mean if I had my goddam choice?"

"What? Stop *swearing*."

"You know that song 'If a body catch a body comin' through the rye'? I'd like—"

"It's 'If a body *meet* a body coming through the rye'!" old Phoebe said. "It's a poem. By Robert *Burns*."

"I *know* it's a poem by Robert Burns."

She was right, though. It *is* "If a body meet a body coming through the rye." I didn't know it then, though.

"I thought it was 'If a body catch a body,'" I said. "Anyway, I keep picturing all these little kids playing some game in this big field of rye and all. Thousands of little kids, and nobody's around—nobody big, I mean—except me. And I'm standing on the edge of some crazy cliff. What I have to do, I have to catch everybody if they start to go over the cliff—I mean if they're running and they don't look where they're going I have to come out from somewhere and *catch* them. That's all I'd do all day. I'd just be the catcher in the rye and all. I know it's crazy, but that's the only thing I'd really like to be. I know it's crazy."

Old Phoebe didn't say anything for a long time. Then, when she said something, all she said was, "Daddy's going to kill you."

From "meet" to "catch" is Holden's revision, and Salinger's vital epiphany, as it were. Huck Finn's story, on this basis, might have been called *The Meeter in the Rye*. To meet is to be free; to catch is to aid survival, and somehow to survive.

ALAN NADEL

Rhetoric, Sanity, and the Cold War: The Significance of Holden Caulfield's Testimony

If, as has been widely noted, *The Catcher in the Rye* owes much to *Adventures of Huckleberry Finn*[1], it rewrites that classic American text in a world where the ubiquity of rule-governed society leaves no river on which to flee, no western territory for which to light out. The territory is mental, not physical, and Salinger's Huck spends his whole flight searching for raft and river, that is, for the margins of his sanity. A relative term, however, "sanity" merely indicates conformity to a set of norms, and since rhetorical relationships formulate the normative world in which a speaker functions, a fictional text—whether or not it asserts an external reality—unavoidably creates and contains a reality in its rhetorical hierarchies, which are necessarily full of assumptions and negations.[2] This aspect of fiction could not be more emphasized than it is by Holden Caulfield's speech, a speech which, moreover, reflects the pressures and contradictions prevalent in the cold war society from which it was forged.

I
Caulfield's Speech

An obsessively proscriptive speaker, Caulfield's essay-like rhetorical style— which integrates generalization, specific examples, and consequent rules— prevails throughout the book, subordinating to it most of the description,

The Centennial Review, Volume 32, Number 4 (Fall 1988): pp. 351–371. Copyright © 1988.

5

narration, and dialogue by making them examples in articulating the principles of a rule-governed society. In one paragraph, for example, Caulfield tells us that someone had stolen his coat (example), that Pency was full of crooks (generalization), and that "the more expensive a school is, the more crooks it has" (rule) (4). In a longer excerpt, from Chapter 9, we can see how the details Caulfield sees from his hotel window—"a man and a woman squirting water out of their mouths at one another"—become examples in a series of generalizations, rules, and consequent evaluations:

> The trouble was, [principle] that kind of junk is sort of fascinating to watch, even if you don't want it to be. For instance, [example] that girl that was getting water squirted all over her face, she was pretty good-looking. I mean that's my big trouble. [generalization] In my *mind*, I'm probably the biggest sex maniac you ever saw. Sometimes [generalization] I can think of *very* crumby stuff I wouldn't mind doing if the opportunity came up. I can even see how it might be quite a lot of fun, [qualification] in a crumby way, and if you were both sort of drunk and all, [more specific example] to get a girl and squirt water or something all over each other's face. The thing is, though, [evaluation] I don't *like* the idea. It [generalization] stinks, if you analyze it. I think [principle arrived at deductively through a series of enthymemes] if you really don't like a girl, you shouldn't horse around with her at all, and if you *do* like her, then you're supposed to like her face, and if you like her face, you ought to be careful about doing crumby stuff to it, [specific application] like squirting water all over it. (62)

Caulfield not only explains his world but also justifies his explanations by locating them in the context of governing rules, rendering his speech not only compulsively explanatory but also authoritarian in that it must demonstrate an authority for *all* his statements, even if he creates that authority merely through rhetorical convention.

With ample space we could list all the rules and principles Caulfield articulates. Here are a few: it's really hard to be roommates with people if your suitcases are better than theirs; "grand" is a phony word; real ugly girls have it tough; people never believe you; seeing old guys in their pajamas and bathrobes is depressing; don't ever tell anybody anything, if you do you start missing everybody. We could easily find scores more, to prove the book a virtual anatomy of social behavior. The book, however, also anatomizes Caulfield's personal behavior: he lies; he has a great capacity for alcohol; he hates to go to bed when he's not even tired; he's very fond of dancing, sometimes; he's a pacifist; he always gets those vomity kind of cabs if he goes anywhere late at night, etc.

As the author of the two anatomies, Caulfield thus manifests two drives: to control his environment by being the one who names and thus creates its rules, and to subordinate the self by being the one whose every action is governed by rules. To put it another way, he is trying to constitute himself both as subject and as object; he is trying to read a social text and to write one. When these two drives come in conflict, there are no options left.

Although reified in the body of Holden Caulfield—a body, like the collective corpus of Huck and Jim, that longs for honesty and freedom as it moves more deeply into a world of deceit and slavery—this lack of options reveals an organization of power which deeply reflects the tensions of post-WWII America from which the novel emerged. The novel appeared in 1951, the product of ten years' work. Especially during the five years between the time Salinger withdrew from publication a 90-page version of the novel and revised it to more than double its length, the "cold war" blossomed.[3]

Richard and Carol Ohmann have related *Catcher*'s immense success to the political climate of the Cold War by trying to show that Caulfield provides a critique of the phoniness "rooted in the economic and social arrangements of capitalism and their concealment" (29). Although they tend, unfortunately, to oversimplify both the text and the relationship between literature and history,[4] *Catcher* may indeed reveal what Fredric Jameson has termed the political unconscious, a narrative in which "real social contradictions, unsurmountable in their own terms, find purely formal resolution in the aesthetic realm" (79). As we shall see, Caulfield not only speaks the speech of the rule contradictions embedded in the voice of his age but also displaces it by internalizing it. He thus converts his rhetoric into mental breakdown and becomes both the articulation of "unspeakable" hypocrisy and its critic. Finally, he becomes, as well, for his audience a sacrificial escape from the implications of such an articulation.[5]

II
The Search for Phonies

Victor Navasky describes the cold war as a period having

> three simultaneous conflicts: a global confrontation between rival imperialisms and ideologies, between capitalism and Communism . . . a domestic clash in the United States between hunters and hunted, investigators and investigated . . . and, finally a civil war amongst the hunted, a fight within the liberal community itself, a running battle between anti-Communist liberals and those who called themselves progressives. . . . (3)

These conflicts took not only the form of the Korean War but also of lengthy, well-publicized trials of spies and subversives, in ubiquitous loyalty oaths, in Senate (McCarthy) and House (HUAC) hearings, in Hollywood and academic purges, and in extensive "anti-Communist" legislation. Even three years before Senator Joseph McCarthy's infamous speech alleging 57 Communists in the State Department, President Truman had created a Presidential Commission on Employee Loyalty and the Hollywood Ten had been ruined by HUAC.[6] Constantly, legislation, hearings, speeches and editorials warned Americans to be suspicious of phonies, wary of associates, circumspect about their past, and cautious about their speech. A new mode of behavior was necessary, the President's Commission noted, because America was now confronted with organizations which valorized duplicity: "[these organizations] while seeking to destroy all the traditional safeguards erected for the protection of individual rights are determined to take unfair advantage of those selfsame safe-guards."

Since uncovering duplicity was the quest of the day, in thinking constantly about who or what was phony, Caulfield was doing no more than following the instructions of J. Edgar Hoover, the California Board of Regents, *The Nation,* the Smith Act, and the Hollywood Ten, to name a very few. The President's Loyalty Commission, for example, announced as its purpose both to protect the government from infiltration by "disloyal persons" and to protect loyal employees "from unfounded accusations." The Commission's dual role, of course, implied dual roles for all citizens: to be protected *and* exonerated. Potentially each citizen was both the threat and the threatened. Because the enemy was "subversive," furthermore, one could never know whether he or she had been misled by an enemy pretending to be a friend; without a sure test of loyalty, one could not sort the loyal from the disloyal and therefore could not know with whom to align. The problem—elevated to the level of national security and dramatized most vividly by the Hiss case—was to penetrate the duplicity of phonies.

This problem manifests itself in Caulfield's rhetoric not only in his diatribe against "phonies" but also through a chronic pattern of signifiers which indicate the truthfulness of Caulfield's testimony. He regularly marks his narration with such phrases as "it (he, she, I, they) really does (do, did, didn't, was, wasn't, is, isn't, can, had, am)," "if you want to know the truth," "I (I'll, I have to) admit (it)," "if you really want to know," "no (I'm not) kidding," "I swear (to God)," "I mean it." The word "really" additionally appears at least two dozen more times in the narration, often italicized. These signifiers, along with those which emphasize the intensity of an experience (e.g. "boy!") or the speaker's desire for clarity (e.g. "I mean. . . .") make Caulfield's speech one which asserts its own veracity more than once for every page of narration.[7]

Because it is so important to Caulfield that the reader not think he is a phony, he also constantly provides ample examples and illustrations to prove each assertion, even his claim that he is "the most terrific liar you ever saw in your life" (16). Examples of such rhetorical performances abounded in the media during the novel's five-year revision period. Like many of the ex-Communist informers of the period, Caulfield's veracity rests on the evidence of his deceitfulness. This paradox is especially foregrounded by a discussion Caulfield has on the train with Mrs. Morrow, the mother of another boy at Pency. In that discussion, he convinces the reader of his truthfulness with the same signifier he uses to make Mrs. Morrow believe his lies. Although Caulfield feels her son, Ernie, is "doubtless one of the biggest bastards that ever went to Pency," he tells her, "'He adapts himself very well to things. He really does. I mean he really knows how to adapt himself.'" Later he adds: "'It really took everybody quite a while to get to know him.'" Having used "really" as a false signifier, Caulfield in confessing to the reader italicizes part of the word: "Then I *real*ly started chucking the old crap around." The evidence which follows should thus convince the reader that the italicized "real" can be trusted, so that the more he demonstrates he has duped his fellow traveler, the more the reader can credit the veracity of the italicized "real". The *real* crap is that Ernie was unanimous choice for class president but wouldn't let the students nominate him because he was too modest. Thus Caulfield proves his credibility to the reader: he *is* a good liar, but when he italicizes the "real" he can be trusted. In trying to convince Mrs. Morrow, however, he adds: "'Boy, he's *really* shy'" and thus destroys the difference between italicized and unitalicized signifier (54–57).

III
The Meaning of Loyalty

Although presented as a trait of Caulfield's character formalized in his speech, these inconsistencies reflect as well the contradictions inherent in a society plagued by loyalty oaths. Swearing that something is true doesn't make it true, except at the expense of anything not-sworn-to. There exists, in other words, some privileged set of "true" events marked by swearing. The swearing, of course, marks them not as true but as important to the speaker—the things that he or she wants the audience to believe, cares about enough to mark with an oath. In this way, Caulfield creates a rhetorical contract—the appeal to ethos—which legitimizes the discourse. It does so, however, at the cost of all those items not stipulated: they reside in the margins by virtue of being so obvious that they can be taken for granted or so unimportant that they need not be substantiated. Thus grouped together as the "unsworn," the taken-for-granted and the not-*necessarily*-so become indistinguishable parts of the same unmarked set. This is exactly what, as

Americans were discovering, loyalty oaths did to the concept of loyalty. For all constitutions bind those loyal to them, and the failure to take that for granted becomes the failure to grant a group constituted by a common social contract. It leaves the "we" of "We the People" without a known referent and makes it impossible to distinguish the real American from the phony—the one so disloyal that he or she will swear false allegiance, will italicize *real* commitment in order to dupe others.

Since social contracts rely upon rhetorical contracts, the problem then is one of language. But Communism according to its accusers acknowledged neither the same social nor rhetorical contracts. According to a major McCarthy witness, ex-Communist Louis Budenz, Communists often used "Aesopean" language so that, "no matter how innocent the language might seem on its face, the initiate understood the sinister underlying message" (Navasky 32). Because no court recognizes a contract binding on only one party, in dealing with those outside the social and rhetorical contracts, the traditional constitutional rules no longer applied. In his 1950 ruling upholding the Smith Act, under which eleven leaders of the American Communist Party were sentenced to prison, Judge Learned Hand indicated that when challenged by an alternative system, "Our democracy . . . must meet that faith and that creed on its merits, or it will perish. *Nevertheless,* we may insist that the rules of the game be observed, and the rules confine the conflict to the weapons drawn from the universe of discourse" [emphasis added]. Because the Communists do not function in the same universe of discourse, the same rules do not apply to them. But, as the need for loyalty tests proved, it was impossible to distinguish those for whom the rules did not apply from those for whom they did.

To do so requires a position outside the system, from which to perceive an external and objective "truth." In other words, one needs a religion, which as Wayne Booth implies is the only source of a truly reliable narrator.[8] All other narration must establish its credibility rhetorically by employing conventions. One of Caulfield's conventions is to acknowledge his unreliability by marking specific sections of the narration as extra-reliable. As we have seen, however, marked thus by their own confessions of unreliability, Caulfield's oaths become one more series of questionable signs, indicating not reliability but its myth. Roland Barthes has astutely demonstrated that a myth is an empty sign, one which no longer has a referent but continues to function as though it did, thus preserving the status quo. The loyalty oath is such a myth in that it preserves the idea of a "loyalty" called into question by its own presence, and in that it is executed at the expense of the field in which it plays—the constituted state to which the mythical loyalty is owed.

Like Caufield's oaths, loyalty oaths in the public realm also proved insufficient. In a truly Orwellian inversion, the "true" test of loyalty became betrayal. Unless someone were willing to betray friends, no oath was credible.

With the tacit and often active assistance of the entire entertainment industry, HUAC very effectively imprinted this message on the public conscience through half a decade of Hollywood purges. As has been clearly shown, investigating the entertainment industry was neither in the interest of legislation nor—as it could be argued that an investigation of the State Department was—in the interest of national security. It was to publicize the ethic of betrayal, the need to name names.[9]

IV
The Importance of Names

If the *willingness* to name names became the informer's credential, furthermore, the *ability* to do so became his or her capital. Thus the informer turned proper nouns into public credit that was used to purchase credibility. Caulfield too capitalizes names. The pervasive capitalization of proper nouns mark his speech; he compulsively names names. In the first three chapters alone, the narration (including the dialogue attributed to Caulfield) contains 218 proper nouns—an average of nine per page. They include people, places, days, months, countries, novels, cars, and cold remedies. Many of the names, moreover, are striking by virtue of their unimportance. Does it matter if "old Spencer" used "Vicks Nose Drops" or read *Atlantic Monthly?* Is it important that these items are named twice? Caulfield's speech merely mirrors the convention of the Hollywood witness by demonstrating the significance of his speech lay in alacrity, not content:

> A certain minimum number of names was necessary; those who . . .
> could convince HUAC counsel that they did not know the names
> of enough former comrades to give a persuasive performance . . .
> were provided with names. The key to a successful appearance . . .
> was the *prompt* recital of the names of a few dozen Hollywood
> Reds [emphasis added]. (Ceplair and Englund 18)

Nor was the suspicion of Hollywood one-sided. Suspected by the right of being potentially subversive, it was suspected by liberals of being inordinately self-censored. Carey McWilliams, writing in *The Nation*, in 1949, bemoans the effects of the "graylist." Intimidated out of dealing realistically with social issues, the movies, McWilliams fears, were becoming more and more phony.

Not surprisingly, Caulfield too equates Hollywood with betrayal and prostitution. The prostitute who comes to his room, furthermore, tells him she is from Hollywood, and when she sits on his lap, she tries to get him to name a Hollywood name: "'You look like a guy in the movies. You know. Whosis. *You* know who I mean. What the heck's his name?'" When Caulfield refuses to name the name, she tries to encourage him by associating it with that of another actor: "Sure you know. He was in that pitcher with Mel-vine Douglas. The one that was Mel-vine Douglas's kid brother. *You* know who I mean" (97). In 1951, naming that name cannot be innocent, because of its associations. Douglas, a prominent Hollywood liberal (who in 1947 supported the Hollywood Ten and in 1951 distanced himself from them) was, more importantly, the husband of Helen Gahagan Douglas, the Democratic Congresswoman whom Richard Nixon defeated in the contest for the California Senate seat. Nixon's race, grounded in red-baiting, innuendos, and guilt by association, attracted national attention and showed, according to McCarthy biographer David Oshinsky, that "'McCarthyism' was not the exclusive property of Joe McCarthy" (177).

If Caulfield is guilty by virtue of his association with Melvyn Douglas, then guilty of what? Consorting with prostitutes? Naming names? Or is it of his own hypocrisy, of his recognition, also inscribed in his rhetoric, that he hasn't told the truth in that he actually loves the movies, emulates them, uses them as a constant frame of reference. The first paragraph of the book begins "if you really want to know the truth" and ends with the sentences: "If there's one thing I hate, its the movies. Don't even mention them to me." Despite this injunction, Caulfield's speech is full of them. He acts out movie roles alone and in front of others, uses them as a pool of allusion to help articulate his own behavior, and goes to see them, even when he believes they will be unsatisfactory.[10]

This marked ambivalence returns us again to the way historical circumstances make Caulfield's speech, like all public testimony, incapable of articulating "truth" because the contradictions in the conditions of public and private utterance have become visible in such a way as to mark all truth claims "phony." In their stead come rituals of loyalty, rituals which do not manifest truth but replace it. In presenting advertised, televised, confessionals, which were prepared, written, and rehearsed, and then were performed by real-life actors, the HUAC Hollywood investigations not only replicated the movies, but they also denied the movies distance and benignity, in short their claim to artificiality. The silver (and cathode-ray) screen is everywhere and nowhere, presenting an act of truth-telling hard to distinguish from its former fabrications, stories for the screen which may or may not have been encoded, subversive messages. So too in "real life"—the viewers of these confessions may have been duped, made inadvertently to play a subversive role, followed an encoded script produced by a secret conspiracy of the sort they're used to seeing in the movies. And of course the movies *can* be believed, for if they cannot what is all the worry about? Why bother investigating the harmless? This was the mixed message of the HUAC hearings: movies were dangerous because they *could* be believed, and movies were dangerous because they *could not*. One cannot escape such a message by discovering the "truth," but only by performing the ritual that fills the space created by the impossibility of such a discovery. In this light, perhaps, Phoebe Caulfield's role in her school play should be read. When Caulfield asks her the play's name she says:

> "'A Christmas Pageant for America'. It stinks but I'm Benedict Arnold. I have practically the biggest part . . . It starts out when I'm dying. This ghost comes in on Christmas Eve and asks me if I'm ashamed and everything. You know. For betraying my country and everything. . . ." (162)

The passage accurately summarizes the ideal HUAC witness. The former traitor now starring in a morality play that honors the state through a form of Christian ritual, the goal of which is not the discovery of truth, but the public, "educational" demonstration of loyal behavior, in which the fiction's paragon of innocence and the nation's historical symbol of perfidy validate one another by exchanging roles.

V
Simple Truth and the Meaning of Testimony

Phoebe's play unites the two central loci for phonies in Caulfield's speech, the worlds of entertainment and of education. In questioning the phoniness of all the schools and teachers he has seen, Caulfield again articulates doubts prevalent in the public consciousness, especially as he is most critical of the Eastern Intellectual Establishment. That establishment, with Harvard as its epitome, came to represent for the readers of *Time*, for example, a form of affluence and elitism that could not be trusted. In their education section, the week of June 5, 1950, for example, *Time* quoted I. A. Richards at length on college teaching:

> "You are never quite sure if you are uttering words of inspired . . . aptness, or whether you are being completely inept. Often you will find yourself incompetent enough to be fired at once if anybody was intelligent enough to see you as you are. . . ."
>
> "'Am I, or am I not, a fraud?' That is a question that is going to mean more and more to you year by year. At first it seems agonizing; after that it becomes familiar and habitual." (65–66)

Again we have the same confessional paradigm. Richards gains credibility by confessing he was a fraud. He also suggests an encoded language meant to deceive the average person—anybody *not* "intelligent enough to see you as you are"; by implication, those who *were* intelligent enough participate in the conspiracy to keep the fraudulence hidden.

This issue becomes particularly germane in a period when teachers and professors were being forced to sign loyalty oaths and/or were being dismissed because of present or past political beliefs. The central issue, many faculty argued, was that academic personnel were being judged by non-academic standards.[11] Yet Richards' statement could suggest that "true" academic standards were really a myth created by those intelligent enough to know better. Intelligence thus signified the capacity for fraud: only someone intelligent enough to see them as they are had something to hide. Because they knew more, intellectuals were more likely to know something they should confess, and not confessing hence signified probable disloyalty rather than innocence.

Time (1/23/50) made the same inferences about the psychiatrists who testified in Alger Hiss's defense, pointing out that Dr. Murray (like Dr. Binger and Hiss) was a Harvard graduate: "He backed up his colleague, Binger. Chambers . . . was a psychopathic personality. . . . He had never seen Chambers but this did not faze him. He had psychoanalyzed Adolph Hitler *in absentia*, correctly predicting his suicide" (14).

If, filtered through *Time*'s simplifying voice, these doctors seemed foolish accomplices, Hiss himself came to stand for everything that needed exposure and rejection. About his conviction, *Time* (1 /30/50) wrote: "[Hiss] was marked as a man who, having dedicated himself to Communism under a warped sense of idealism, had not served it openly but covertly; a man who, having once served an alien master, lacked the courage to recant his past, but went on making his whole life an intricate, calculated lie" (12). Thus the past existed to be recanted, not recounted. The recounted past—the truth of one's past—became living a lie, while recanting revealed Truth, discovered not in past actions but in ideological enlightenment, enlightenment which reveals that one's life was a lie. Analysis is intellectualized lying. *Time* had suggested in its treatment of Hiss's "authorities," part of the Intellectual conspiracy that did not revere the Truth but rather suggested that facts could be contravened by an unseen, subversive presence, knowable only to a trained elite whom the general population had to trust without evidence. For *Time*, truth was less ambiguous, existing in a transparent connection between physical phenomena and accepted beliefs, and with its authority lying outside the speaking subject. Hiss had transgressed by seeking to intervene, to analyze, to apply principles not grounded in Truth but in the trained intellect of a fallen mortal, fallen because he believed in the power of human intervention, the ability of the intellect to discern and interpret.

This too is Caulfield's failing, and he must recognize the error of locating himself as the discoverer, interpreter and arbiter of truth and phoniness.

In other words, if his speech constitutes him both as subject and as object, it also constitutes him as testifier and judge, accuser and accused. It has the quality of testimony—the taking of oaths and the giving of evidence to support an agenda of charges. And like much of the most publicized testimony of its day, it has no legal status. As Navasky pointed out about the Hollywood hearings:

> [T]he procedural safeguards . . . were absent: there was no cross examination, no impartial judge and jury, none of the exclusionary rules about hearsay or other evidence. And, of course, the targets from the entertainment business had commited no crime. . . . (xiv)

In such a context, it was hard to regard testimony as a form of rhetoric in a forensic argument. Although sometimes masked as such, it rarely functioned in the way Aristotle defined the concept. Rather it more often resembled testimony in the religious sense of confessing publicly one's sins. Caulfield's speech thus simultaneously seeped in conventions of both forensic testimony and spiritual, reveals the incompatibility of the two, in terms of their intended audience, their intended effect, and their relationship to the speaker. Most important, forensic testimony presumes truth as something arrived at through the interaction of social and rhetorical contract, whereas spiritual testimony presumes an external authority for truth; its rhetoric *reveals* the Truth, doing so in such a way as to exempt the speech from judgment and present the speaker not as peer but as paragon.

These distinctions apply particularly to the concept of incrimination. A witness giving forensic testimony always risks self-incrimination; recognizing this, our laws allow the witness to abstain from answering questions. The paragon, who gives spiritual testimony, however, is above such self-incrimination; the paragon knows the Truth and has nothing to fear. Exercising the legal protection against self-incrimination (as many HUAC witnesses chose to do) meant the speaker was offering forensic testimony not spiritual, had thus not found the Truth, and therefore could not be trusted. Designed to protect the individual from self-incrimination, the Fifth Amendment then became the instrument of that self-incrimination. In a society that determined guilt not by evidence but by association and/or the failure to confess, people often found that the only way not to incriminate others was to claim they would be incriminating themselves. Since that claim became self-incriminating, they purchased silence by suggesting guilt. They thus internalized the dramatic conflict between social contract and personal loyalty, with the goal not of catharsis but silence. Autobiography, always potentially incriminating, had become recontextualized as testimony, but testimony itself had been freed of its evidenciary contexts and become an unbound truth-of-otherness. It potentially revealed the other—the subversive—everywhere but in the place he or she was known to be, even in the audience of investigators and/or in the speaker. The speaker, by virtue of testimony's two voices and self-incrimination's merger with its own safeguard, was as much alienated in the face of his or her own speech as in the face of his or her silence.

VI
The Case for Silence

The battle waged internally by so many during the Cold War, between spiritual and forensic testimony, public and personal loyalty, recounting and recanting, speech and silence, created a test of character. No matter how complex and self-contradictory the social text, the individual was supposed to read it and choose correctly. This is exactly the dilemma Caulfield's speech confronts from its first words:

> If you really want to hear about it, the first thing you'll probably want to know is where I was born, and what my lousy childhood was like, and how my parents were occupied and all before they had me, and all that David Copperfield kind of crap, but I don't feel like going into it, if you want to know the truth. In the first place, that stuff bores me, and in the second place, my parents would have about two hemorrhages apiece if I told anything pretty personal about them. (1)

Caulfield will try to tell the truth to this "hearing" without incriminating himself or his parents. But at every turn he fails, constantly reflecting rather than negotiating the contradictions of his world. Against that failure weighs the possible alternative, silence, in the extreme as suicide. The memory of James Castle's suicide haunts the book. Castle, the boy at Elkton Hills, refused to recant something he had said about a very conceited student, and instead committed suicide by jumping out a window. Caulfield too contemplated suicide in the same manner after the pimp, Maurice, had taken his money and hit him (104). This image of jumping out the window not only connects Caulfield with Castle but also epitomizes the fall from which Caulfield, as the "catcher in the rye," wants to save the innocent.

The image of jumping out the window also typified, as it had during the stock market crash of 1929, admission of personal failure in the face of unnegotiable social demands. In 1948, for example, Lawrence Duggan fell or threw himself from the window of his New York office. Immediately Congressman Karl Mundt announced the cause was Duggan's implication in a Communist spy ring; along with five other men, his name had been named at a HUAC meeting. The committee would disclose the other names, Mundt said, "as they jump out of windows."

On April 1, 1950, F. O. Matthiessen, "at the time," in the words of William O'Neill, "the most intellectually distinguished fellow traveler in America" (173), jumped to his death from a Boston hotel window. In his suicide note, he wrote: " . . . as a Christian and a socialist believing in international peace, I find myself terribly oppressed by the present tensions" (Stern 31). Although Matthiessen did not commit suicide solely for political reasons, for the general public his death symbolized the culpability and weakness of the Eastern Intellectual Establishment. His powerful intellect, his political leanings and, especially, his longstanding affiliation with Harvard identified him clearly as the kind of analytic mind that typified the intellectual conspiracy *Time*, Joseph McCarthy, et al. most feared and despised. Like Hiss, he was led astray by his idealism which, in true allegorical fashion, led to deceit and ultimately the coward's way out. *Or:* like many dedicated progressives, he was hounded by witch hunters forcing him to choose between the roles of betrayer and betrayed, and leading him ultimately to leap from melodrama into tragedy. Hero or coward, Christ or Judas—in either case, in the morality drama of his day, he graphically signified the sort of fall from innocence against which Caulfield struggles.[12]

But, in the end, Caulfield renounces this struggle, allowing that one cannot catch kids: ". . . if they want to grab for the gold ring, you have to let them do it *and not say anything*. If they fall off, they fall off, *but it's bad if you say anything to them*" [emphasis added] (211). Thus the solution to Caulfield's dilemma becomes renouncing speech itself. Returning to the condition of utterance, stipulated in his opening sentence, which frames his testimony, he says in the last chapter—"If you want to know the truth . . ." (213), this time followed not with discourse but with the recognition that he lacks adequate knowledge for discourse: " . . . I don't *know* what I think about it" (213–214). From this follows regret in the presence of the named names:

> I'm sorry I told so many people about it. About all I know is, I sort of *miss* everybody I told about. Even old Stradlater and Achley, for instance. I think I even miss goddam Maurice. It's funny. Don't ever tell anybody anything. If you do, you start missing everybody. (214)

These last sentences of the book thus replace truth with silence. The intermediary, moreover, between Caulfield's speech—deemed unreasonable—and his silence is the asylum, and we could say that the whole novel is speech framed by that asylum. It intervenes in the first chapter, immediately after Caulfield asks "if you want to know the truth" and in the last, immediately before he says he does not know what to think. In this way, the asylum functions in the manner Foucault has noted—not to remove Caulfield's guilt but to organize it "for the madman as a consciousness of himself, and as a non reciprocal relation to the keeper; it organized it for the man of reason as an awareness of the Other, a therapeutic intervention in the madman's existence" (247).

> Incessantly cast in this empty role of unknown visitor, and challenged in everything that can be known about him, drawn to the surface of himself by a social personality silently imposed by observation, by form and mask, the madman is obliged to objectify himself in the eyes of reason as the perfect stranger, that is, as the man whose strangeness does not reveal itself. The city of reason welcomes him only with this qualification and at the price of this surrender to anonymity. (249–250)

In this light, we can see that the asylum not only frames Caulfield's speech but also intervenes throughout as an increasing awareness of his otherness, marked by such phrases as "I swear to God, I'm a madman." Given the novel's frame, it is not astonishing that Caulfield's speech manifests traits of the asylum. In that his speech also manifests the contradictions of McCarthyism and the Cold War, the novel more interestingly suggests that the era in many ways institutionalized traits of the asylum. To prove the validity of his "madman" oaths, Caulfield again must assume the dual roles of subject and object, for as Foucault demonstrates, the intervention of the asylum (and, by extension we can say the Cold War) functioned by three principal means: perpetual judgment, recognition by the mirror, and silence.[13]

Notes

1. Heiserman and Miller make this connection. Others examining the book's relationship to *Adventures of Huckleberry Finn* include: Aldridge (129–131), Branch, Fiedler, Kaplan, and Wells.

2. The relationship between reality and rhetoric has been most fully developed, of course, by Auerbach and, in some ways, modified and extended by Iser's concept of the "implied reader" who is lead by an author's strategies of omission to complete the text's implied reality. It is important to note, therefore, that I am not using the word "negation" here in the sense that Iser does, but rather to suggest the "blanks" of Lacanian discourse—something akin to the "blindness" of a text which, for de Man, its rhetoric signifies. For Lacan, de Certeau notes, "'literary' is that language which makes something else heard than that which it says; conversely psychoanalysis is a literary practice of language. . . . At issue here is rhetoric, and no longer poetics" (53).

3. Grunwald (20) and French (26) mention this shorter 1946 version.

4. Miller's response demonstrates that their reading tends to be reductive and ignores much significant textual evidence.

5. For discussion of Caulfield as Christ figure, surrogate, saint or savior, see: Barr, Baumbach 55–67, French 115–117, and Rupp 114–118.

6. See Oshinsky's discussion of "The Red Bogey in America, 1917–1950" (85–102). The literature on American history and politics in the five-year period following WWII is, of course, extensive. Caute provides an excellent bibliography (621–650) for additional references beyond my necessarily selective citations.

7. Approximately one third of the novel is dialogue rather than narration.

8. As a result, the voice-of-God narrator, as typified in the Book of Job, serves as the paradigm of authority against which Booth analyzes other forms of narrative.

9. See Navasky, Ceplair and Englund 254–298, 361–397; Caute 487–538.

10. Oldsey discusses the movies in the novel.

11. See Caute 403–445.

12. Stern: "Those were years in which a person searching for a community of shared socialist and Christian concerns needed the greatest personal support and fortitude to keep from the bottle, from an ignominious abandonment of all previous social concerns, or from the window ledge. Matthiessen chose to end his life, but others of his contemporaries I have known who shared his ideas at some point gave up lifelong commitments to socialism for goals far less honorable during the period" (30).

13. See Foucault 241–278.

Works Cited

Aldridge, John W. *In Search of Heresy: American Literature in an Age of Conformity.* New York: McGraw-Hill, 1956.

"Am I A Fraud?'" *Time* 5 June 1950: 65–66.

Auerbach, Eric. *Mimesis: The Representation of Reality in Western Literature.* Trans. Willard R. Trask. Princeton: Princeton University Press, 1953.

Barthes, Roland. *Mythologies.* Trans. Annette Lavers. New York: Hill & Wang, 1978.

Baumbach, Jonathan. *The Landscape of Nightmare: Studies in the Contemporary American Novel.* New York: New York University Press, 1965.

Booth, Wayne. *The Rhetoric of Fiction.* Chicago: University of Chicago Press, 1961.

Branch, Edgar. "Mark Twain and J. D. Salinger: A Study in Literary Continuity." *American Quarterly* 9 (1957): 144–158.

Caute, David, *The Great Fear: The Anti-Communist Purge under Truman and Eisenhower.* New York: Simon and Schuster, 1978.

Ceplair, Larry. and Steven Englund, *The Inquisition in Hollywood: Politics in the Film Community 1930–1960.* Garden City, NY: Doubleday-Anchor, 1990.

de Certeau. Michel. *Heterologies: Discourse on the Other.* Trans. Brian Massumi. *Theory and History of Literature,* vol. 17. Minneapolis: University of Minnesota Press, 1986.

Fiedler, Leslie. "The Eye of Innocence." *Salinger.* Ed. Henry Anatole Grunwald. New York: Harper, 1962.

Foucault, Michel. *Madness and Civilization: A History of Insanity in the Age of Reason.* Trans. Richard Howard. New York: Random-Vintage, 1973.

French, Warren. *J. D. Salinger.* New York: Twayne, 1963.

Galloway, David D. *The Absurd Hero in American Fiction.* Revised edition. Austin: University of Texas Press, 1970.

Grunwald, Henry Anatole. "The Invisible Man: A Biographical Collage." *Salinger.* Ed. Grunwald. New York: Harper, 1962.

Hassan, Ihab. *Radical Innocence: Studies in the Contemporary American Novel.* Princeton: Princeton University Press, 1961.

Heiserman, Arthur, and James E. Miller. "J. D. Salinger: Some Crazy Cliff." *Western Humanities Review* 10 (1956): 129–137.

Iser, Wolfgang. *The Implied Reader: Patterns of Communication in Prose Fictions from Bunyan to Beckett.* Baltimore: Johns Hopkins University Press, 1974.

Jameson, Fredric. *The Political Unconscious: Narrative as a Socially Symbolic Act.* Ithaca: Cornell University Press, 1981.

Kaplan, Charles. "Holden and Huck: The Odysseys of Youth." *College English* 18 (1956): 76–80.

Lacan, Jacques. *Speech and Language in Psychoanalysis.* Trans. Anthony Wilder. Baltimore: Johns Hopkins University Press, 1968.

Lundquist, James. *J. D. Salinger.* New York: Ungar, 1979.

McWilliams, Carey. "Graylist." *The Nation* 19 Oct. 1949: 491.

de Man, Paul. *Blindness and Insight: Essays in the Rhetoric of Contemporary Criticism.* New York: Oxford University Press, 1971.

Navasky, Victor. *Naming Names.* New York: Viking, 1980.

Ohmann, Carol and Richard Ohmann. "Reviewers, Critics and *The Catcher in the Rye.*" *Critical Inquiry* 3 (1976): 64–75.

Oldsey, Bernard S. "The Movies in the Rye." *College English* 23 (1961): 209–215.

Oshinsky, David M. *A Conspiracy So Immense: The World of Joe McCarthy.* New York: Macmillan-Free Press, 1983.

O'Neill, William L. *A Better World: Stalinism and the American Intellectuals.* New York: Simon and Schuster, 1982.

Rupp, Richard H. *Celebration in Postwar American Fiction 1945–1967.* Coral Gables, FL: University of Miami Press. 1970.

Salinger, J. D. *The Catcher in the Rye.* 1951. New York: Bantam, 1964.

Stern, Frederick C. *F. O. Matthiessen: Christian Socialist as Critic.* Chapel Hill: University of North Carolina Press, 1981.

"Trials—The Reckoning." *Time* 30 Jan. 1950: 11–12.

"Trials—Some People Can Taste It." *Time* 23 Jan. 1950: 14.

Wells, Arvin R. "Huck Finn and Holden Caulfield: The Situation of the Hero." *Ohio University Review* 2 (1960): 31–42.

SANDRA W. LOTT AND STEVEN LATHAM

"The World Was All Before Them": Coming of Age in Ngugi wa Thiong'o's Weep Not, Child and J. D. Salinger's The Catcher in the Rye

According to Robert G. Carlsen, adolescents readily identify with works which relate to the quest for identity and which address problems of the social order (118–119). Their strong interest in these themes perhaps reflects the need of young readers in many cultures for increased understanding of themselves and of others, and for heightened awareness of their own individual identity in the context of family and society. In oral folk literature, this need has been met by tales in which the quest theme follows a familiar pattern which satisfies the needs of young readers for independence, competence, and self-worth and which often depicts the young person as a savior figure who rights the wrongs of his or her society. As Elaine Hughes and Cynthia Gravlee note in their bibliographic essay on the hero, characters such as Aladdin, Scheherazade, Robin Hood, Jack the Giant Killer, Sundiata, and Momotaro are among the many folk heroes whose stories demonstrate these characteristics. As Gravlee and Hughes suggest, the journey motif in such stories often depicts the young protagonists venturing out into unknown territory, going beyond their own safe and familiar worlds, and thus attaining increased knowledge and understanding. This knowledge can take the form of increased understanding of self (*The Uses of Enchantment*, Bruno Bettelheim, 1976), increased and often critical understanding of the society (*Breaking the Magic Spell: Radical Theories of Folk and Fairy Tales*, Jack

Global Perspectives on Teaching Literature: Shared Visions and Distinctive Visions. Eds. Sandra Ward Lott, Maureen S. G. Hawkins, and Norman McMillan. (Urbana, IL: National Council of Teachers, 1993): pp. 135–151. Copyright © 1993 National Council of Teachers.

Zipes, 1984), and even increased understanding of new perspectives beyond those known and approved of by their own cultures (*Old Tales and New Truths*, James Roy King, 1992). Kenneth Donelson and Aileen Pace Nilsen, in their *Literature for Today's Young Adults*, identify modern-day books with these characteristics as belonging to a genre called the adventure/accomplishment romance, which they suggest "has elements applicable to the task of entering the adult world." The story pattern they describe includes "three stages of initiation as practiced in many cultures" in which "the young and innocent person is separated both physically and spiritually from the nurturing love of friends and family . . . undergoes a test of courage and stamina" which may be "either mental, psychological, or physical," and "in the final stage is reunited with former friends and family in a new role of increased status" (1989, 126–127).

As Donelson and Nilsen note, there is a strong element of wish fulfillment in such literature (1989, 126). However, many of the best realistic books written for young adults today follow this basic pattern, but overlay it with a sense of the complexity and difficulties of real life in which the young person must inevitably make compromises with his or her ideals and dreams in order to achieve a sense of identity in keeping with the often harsh realities of family and social life. It is a life in which the welfare of his or her immediate family and society is often threatened by the negative impact of other cultural groups. Such books present moving and complex accounts of the inner challenges of coming of age at the same time that they give a good sense of the social and cultural pressures brought to bear on young persons. Many of the most distinctive books which have recently been written for a young adult audience deal with such issues. Good examples are found in the books of noted African American writer Virginia Hamilton. Hamilton's best-known work, *M. C. Higgins, the Great*, tells the story of young Mayo Cornelius Higgins's quest to save his family from the strip miners' spoil heap which threatens to destroy their Appalachian home. M. C.'s world is enlarged through contact with two visitors from the city who help him to overcome his family's prejudice and hostility to the communal style of the life led by their "witchy" neighbors, the Killburns, and who also help him to develop independence and competence within the family setting. Hamilton's *Arilla Sun Down* depicts a young girl's attempt to resolve the conflict between her Native American and her African American family heritage, and her *Sweet Whispers, Brother Rush* shows how a young black girl's encounters with the ghost of her dead uncle help her to understand her mother's neglectful and sometimes abusive treatment of her children. In Katherine Paterson's *Bridge To Terabithia*, country-bred Jess Aarons learns and grows, through his friendship with a privileged girl from a sophisticated and artistic family, and later he learns self-reliance and maturity in facing his grief over his friend's death. All of these works, which show a young person confronting the problems of family and society, deal also with cultural contrasts and conflicts and thus help the young reader not only to develop self-understanding but also to develop increased understanding of others and of the problems of the social order.

Moving beyond such young adult novels, young readers may well turn to contemporary adult literature which focuses on the experiences of adolescents engaged in the process of coming of age. Books such as Harper Lee's *To Kill a Mockingbird* and John Knowles's *A Separate Peace* have become perennial favorites with the young because of their honest and immediate treatment of the struggles of coming of age. Such works challenge readers to come to terms with personal and cultural limits, but they also retain sympathy for youthful idealism and dreams. In Julio Cortazar's story "The End of the Game," three young girls whose lives are restricted by poverty and by the physical handicap of one of the group transform these painful realities by devising a game of statues in which they impersonate famous people and abstract attitudes for the benefit of passengers on the train which regularly passes near their home. Reality intrudes on their game when a young male student, who has watched their performance on his trips to and from his school, arranges one day to get off the train and meet the three girls. His note, thrown from the train window, indicates his special interest in the crippled child, but when he learns of her physical handicap, he loses interest in her and in the game, moving thereafter to the other side of the train where he will not see the girls as he passes their accustomed spot. Thus the end of the game is also the end of the innocent pleasures of childhood, as the girls must now cope with a world which is harsher and more restricted than that created in their fanciful play.

Another work which deals with the interplay of imagination and actuality is Maxine Hong Kingston's *The Woman Warrior*. The title of this work comes from a folktale about a Chinese girl who leaves her home and family and undergoes an extended apprenticeship in preparation for warfare against the wicked barons who oppress her people. Recounting this story as a young girl living in contemporary America, not ancient China, Kingston is painfully aware that her own experiences are quite different from those of the folk tale heroine, but she comforts herself that she couldn't have done as well since, unlike the legendary swordswoman, she has no magic beads and no old people to tutor her, and since, as a Chinese American, she is no longer even sure what her village is. At the end of the story, she concludes that she can emulate the woman warrior by becoming a word warrior. "The reporting is the vengeance—not the beheading, not the gutting, but the words" (1989, 53).

Such a struggle to reconcile dreams and reality is present in much contemporary literature about adolescence. Two works from divergent cultures which present this conflict in an exceptionally memorable and moving fashion are *Weep Not, Child* by Kenyan author Ngugi wa Thiong'o and *The Catcher in the Rye* by J. D. Salinger. Both novels give a strongly realistic account of an adolescent hero's quest for identity in an imperfect adult world. Salinger's Holden Caulfield and Ngugi's hero Njoroge both dream of saving the disadvantaged of their society from suffering and oppression. In pursuing these goals, the heroes follow many of the typical experiences of the adventure/accomplishment romance, including separating themselves from home and familiar surroundings, facing serious and dangerous trials and challenges, and eventually returning with a transformed identity to home and family. However, in these novels, the heroes also experience disillusionment with themselves and with the world around them as they move from the innocent idealism of the very young to a more realistic acceptance of personal limits and social imperfections.

The cultural contexts of these works are strikingly different. Holden's experiences begin in the urban prep school environment of the Atomic Age of the United States, whereas Njoroge's experiences reflect Kikuyu tribal culture during the Mau Mau uprisings in Kenya in the 1950s. In fact, many young readers in today's high schools and colleges may find these worlds almost equally foreign, and they will certainly need some help with contextualizing. For example, African practices of polygamy, the history of colonialism, and the role of Africans in the two world wars are relevant to an understanding of Ngugi's book. However, many of today's readers may find Holden's slang of the forties and fifties and his privileged lifestyle almost as culturally distant from their lives as the Mau Mau revolt in Kenya. Quite possibly, however, young readers will be able to approach the typical challenges of growing up which are raised in both books more openly and objectively just because these challenges are presented in a context different from their own. Juxtaposing these works from such different cultures can lead to a better understanding of the crises of growing up in both worlds and of the place of the individual in the larger community. As Reed Way Dasenbrock notes in an article about teaching multicultural literature, the readers of such works will themselves be changed through the inevitable expansion of their experiences in encountering and interacting with texts which reflect a world which is different from their own (13).

Readers of these books may wish to consider whether or not the differences in the two treatments of coming of age are culturally determined and to explore the degree to which the similarities reflect universally shared challenges of growing up. As Sarah Lawall points out in her introductory essay to this text, some scholars believe that works about the coming of age of the adolescent male hero may privilege the Western, masculine tradition. However, Ngugi's book presents this theme in the context of a traditional African setting, which is, if anything, more patriarchal in many ways than Western society. Thus students and teachers may find it profitable to compare and contrast the effects of male dominance on the experiences of these two adolescent heroes.

Some scholars maintain that the very concept of adolescence is itself the invention of Western societies, which artificially prolong childhood dependency through extended educational programs, thus unnaturally postponing marriage and career. Certainly Holden's dreams about marrying "Old Sally" and running away from school and home might seem to confirm this view, but Ngugi's hero, Njoroge, also dreams of escaping his present problems by leaving his school to marry his girlfriend Mwihaki. Because his school offers a Western-style education, Njoroge's frustrations, which to Westerners typify adolescence, may lead readers to consider whether or not Western influence, particularly in the area of education, may have introduced the trials of adolescence into a non-Western setting or whether these trials are an inevitable part of adolescence. Comparing Ngugi's and Salinger's books with accounts of coming of age from various cultures may also shed light on this question.

In her autobiographical work *Silent Dancing*, Judith Ortiz Cofer writes:

> To a child, life is a play directed by parents, teachers, and other adults who are forever giving directions: "Say this," "Don't say that," "Stand here," . . . If we miss or ignore a cue, we are punished. . . . The world—our audience—likes the well-made play, with everyone in their places and not too many bursts of brilliance or surprises. (1990, 101)

In a similar vein, Ronald Ayling suggests in his essay in this text that childhood in every culture may be compared with the process of colonization. Such comparisons make adolescent rebellion against authority seem a natural stage in which the well-made play described by Ortiz Cofer will inevitably be disrupted by the youthful "brilliance or surprises" which she suggests adults dislike. Certainly many young readers will recognize in these descriptions problems and conflicts inherent in their own struggle for independent identity, as well as in the struggles of the fictional heroes of *The Catcher in the Rye* and *Weep Not, Child*.

For the fictional characters, Njoroge and Holden, the quest for adolescent identity is connected to family and peer relationships; both confront questions about courtship and marriage; both struggle with conflicting religious and ethical values; and both oppose various forms of social and political oppression. However, Njoroge's rebellion takes place in a clearly colonized setting, whereas the objects of Holden's rebellion are more diffuse and less clearly identifiable. In contrast with Njoroge, who has grown up in a communal society, Holden is at first more individualistic, more lonely, and more alienated. Eventually, however, perhaps as a result of the incursion of Western values and conflicts, Njoroge, too, undergoes a process of alienation which can be compared in some ways with that experienced by Holden. And in the final sequences of both books, the heroes begin tentatively to regain a sense of community, of renewed connections with family and peers and, perhaps, with their society at large.

Comparison of the opening sections of the two books clearly shows that Holden is initially much further along the road toward disillusionment than is Njoroge. In the opening pages of *Catcher*, we learn that Holden has experienced a series of academic failures and is about to be expelled from his current preparatory school. Disaffected with himself and the world around him, Holden decides to leave early before the Christmas holidays begin, and the major action of the book concerns his three-day odyssey in New York City.

Salinger underscores Holden's world-weary pseudo-sophistication, revealing Holden's disillusionment with establishment institutions and values through an engaging and intimate first-person narration. Recounting the events which have led to his hospitalization, Holden tells the story of his departure from school, his adventures in New York City, and his earlier family traumas and educational misadventures. Holden's language, liberally sprinkled with profanity, conveys his dissatisfaction with headmasters, ministers, Jesus' disciples, and all "big shots." Such rebellious and irreverent attitudes reflect his fear of being vulnerable, gullible, or "square." Wayne Booth has noted, however, that despite such indications of immaturity, Salinger's hero quickly enlists the sympathy of most readers with his funny commentary on the manifold forms of phoniness which he finds everywhere around him (1964, 161–163). Holden's narration, blending earnest idealism and naivete with self-protective skepticism, establishes his essential innocence and appeals to readers to become allies against all that is false, mean-spirited, and unjust. Holden's academic hopscotch reflects his conviction that there is little of worth in an educational system in which the "grand" people with money and power lord it over the disadvantaged. Holden sympathizes with a wide range of educational misfits, including the boy with cheap luggage, the boy whose sincere, if disorganized, speech about his uncle is interrupted by jeers of "digression," and, perhaps most significantly, the boy named James Castle, who was hounded to his death because he would not acknowledge the hazing rights of older school bullies. Prior to his expulsion from Pencey Prep, Holden visits his history teacher, who expresses disappointment in Holden's academic failure and tells him, "Life *is* a game that one plays according to the rules" (12). Opposing this view, Holden cynically reflects, "Some game. If you get on the side where all the hot-shots are, then it's a game, all right.... But if you get on the *other* side, where there aren't any hot-shots, then what's a game about it?" (12). Holden, who has already taken his place "on the other side," wants no part of an educational system designed to ensure that the game continues to be weighted against the "poor in spirit."

The causes of Holden's disillusionment may in some ways seem insignificant in comparison with the colonial oppression and even torture to which Ngugi's hero Njoroge is subjected with at least the tacit approval of his educators. But Holden, too, is deeply disturbed by his perception that his educators do nothing to protect their innocent charges. One exception, in Holden's view, has been the English teacher Mr. Antolini, who shared Holden's deep concern and sorrow over the death of James Castle. During Holden's sojourn to New York, he goes late at night to the home of Antolini, who unquestioningly takes him in. Antolini displays a sincere interest in Holden's development and advises Holden to resume his education, assuring the boy that he is "not the first person who was ever confused . . . and even sickened by human behavior" (246). Antolini tells Holden that education will enable him to learn from others who have come through similar periods of moral and spiritual anguish.

However, when Holden awakens to find Mr. Antolini patting his head, he interprets this quite possibly innocent gesture as a homosexual pass and leaves in a panicky and bitter frame of mind. Disillusioned about the purity of even the best of educators, Holden sees the educational process as one intended to support the established power structure, inculcating values and attitudes which serve mainly to protect the privileged classes.

This sense of alienation and disaffection is also seen in Holden's relationships with his family, in his view of love and marriage, and in his attitude toward organized religion. From the beginning, Holden is estranged from his family as well as from the larger community. As the son of wealthy New Yorkers, Holden has been given every material advantage, but, saddened and guilty over his academic failures, he seems distanced from all of his family except for his adored younger sister Phoebe. He thinks his older brother D. B. has sold out by going to Hollywood to write movie scripts, and he is at least implicitly critical of his parents for shuffling him around from one "phony" school to another.

For Holden, religious concerns and questions about love and marriage also present difficult ethical and moral issues and serve further to alienate him from those he considers to be phony. Like many young people, he centers dreams, hopes, and illusions around an idealized figure of the opposite sex and thinks of love and marriage as an escape from social pressures. Though evidently quite confused about this area of life, Holden idealizes a girl named Jane Gallagher and wants to protect her from the type of boys he knows at school who would prey upon her innocence. He feels ashamed that he has never "given . . . [a girl] the time" (56), but he cannot bring himself to use girls in the heartless manner of his roommate Stradlater. His sympathy for the outsiders of his society extends to many of the girls he encounters; he feels sorry for ugly girls, for girls who marry "dopey guys" (160), and even for a prostitute, with whom he talks at great length because he cannot bring himself to have sex with her. He exclaims: "Sex is something I just don't understand. I swear to God, I don't" (82). Holden thinks frequently of Jane, but does not contact her, perhaps because he wants to keep the dream of her perfection and innocence intact; however, during his sojourn in New York, he does contact an old girlfriend named Sally Hayes. Though it is clear that he does not care for Sally as he does for Jane, he proposes in desperation that they run away to New England to live on his bank account of $180 "in cabin camps and stuff" (171). He says, "We could live somewhere with a brook and all and, later on, we could get married or something. I could chop all of our own wood in the wintertime and all" (171). When Sally suggests that they wait until after college, Holden's response shows the escapist nature of his attachment to Sally: "I'd be working in some office, making a lot of dough, and riding to work in cabs and Madison Avenue buses, and reading newspapers, and playing bridge all the time. . . . Christ almighty" (173). Realizing that Sally represents the very establishment phoniness he wants to avoid, Holden relinquishes the dream of love and romance as an escape from the inevitable changes of growing up.

Holden is also confused about religion. Though Holden claims to be "sort of an atheist" (99), he admires Christ, and he wants to protect the two nuns he meets from the corrupting influence of *Romeo and Juliet.* However, he cannot stand the all-too-human disciples, and he has only disdain for organized religions and dogma. Holden's hatred of religious phoniness is evident in his reaction to the Christmas show at Radio City Music Hall: "Old Jesus probably would've puked if He could see it" (137). Holden can tolerate only those religious figures who seem totally innocent, pure, and childlike. But perhaps realizing how far he himself is from this standard of purity, he turns his destructive impulses inward against himself, invites his roommate Stradlater and the pimp Maurice to hit him, and even imagines his own funeral. Toward the end of the book he plans to run away and live a reclusive life in the wilderness, pretending to be a deaf-mute. Such fantasies are sadly amusing, but they highlight Holden's unwillingness to seek community with ordinary people or to adjust his ideals to the requirements of his society.

The contrast between Salinger's alienated protagonist and Ngugi's trusting and hopeful hero are striking. Ngugi's narrative provides a moving account of Njoroge's attempt to fulfill himself through serving his community. Depicting Njoroge's passage to adulthood amidst the turmoil of the Mau Mau independence movement, the events of the novel recount the impact on Njoroge and his family of years of this political and economic upheaval.

Commenting on the colonial context of Ngugi's book, Ndiawar Sarr observes that in East Africa, as in Southern Africa, the colonial settlers wanted
more than raw materials and trade. These settlers, who came to stay, captured
the best land and pushed out the Africans born on that land. The Mau Mau
were the Kikuyu militants, whose blood oaths symbolized the people's eter-
nal unity with the land. Though many, like Njoroge's father Ngotho, did not
join the movement, the colonial powers tended to regard all Kenyans as Mau
Mau, whose main goal was to recapture the land. Although Njoroge's family
is divided over whether to take the oath, all of the family suffer from the British attempts to suppress revolt. In 1952, the British rulers began four years of
military operations against the rebels. The struggle was a bloody one in which
thousands of rebels were killed, and thousands more, including their leader
Jomo Kenyatta, were put in detention camps. Sarr points out, however, that
Ngugi's book is not a mere catalogue of political events, nor is it a propagan-
distic work. Everything is concentrated on the family level, on the impact of
these historical events on individual human beings (Sarr, 1988).

Ngugi's simple and direct style of narration reflects the serious-minded
and hopeful attitude of the hero in the first part of the book, and it also serves
toward the end of the novel to convey the depths of Njoroge's sorrow when
his dreams are shattered. At the beginning of the novel, Njoroge, who is about
to enter school for the first time, is excited about the opportunity to attain a
European education, which he sees as the key to success. Sarr has pointed out
that as the Mau Mau rebellion challenges Europeanization and control, the
tangle of history overtakes Njoroge and his family, and he sees everything he
believes in scrambled. These events, which affect the entire society, are filtered
through the consciousness of Njoroge, who at first does not understand what
is going on (Sarr, 1988).

Perhaps the heroes' contrasting relationships to the community may be
seen most clearly by looking at the educational experiences of the two protagonists. Unlike Holden, Njoroge initially demonstrates an innocent faith
that a Western education promises him a bright future, as evidenced in his
enthusiastic and childlike response when his mother first asks if he would like
to attend school. As the years pass, he excels academically, while his family,
indeed the whole of Kenya, begins to experience civil unrest as the Kikuyu
attempt to reclaim their sacred land from the European settlers. His youthful
idealism creates within him a messianic vision of the purpose of his education: "He knew that for him education would be the fulfillment of a wider
and more significant vision, a vision that embraced the demand made on him,
not only by his father, but also by his mother, his brothers, and even the village" (39). Only after the emergency intensifies is Njoroge's dream lost. In the
village school, the Mau Mau leave notes threatening students and teachers;
and his teacher, Isaka, is later killed by white police who blame the murder

on the Mau Mau. Shocked, Njoroge exclaims, "I thought Mau Mau was on the side of the black people" (83). He thinks of leaving school at this point but takes his brother Kamau's advice to remain in school. Kamau tells him he would be no safer at home than in school: "There's no hiding in this naked land" (83). Njoroge does continue his schooling and later leaves home to attend the Siriana Secondary School.

When Njoroge goes to live at the mission secondary school, his hopes are at first renewed by the white missionaries' earnest efforts to teach their African charges. At first, the school seems "like a paradise . . . where children from all walks of life and of different religious faiths could work together without any consciousness" of difference (115). Njoroge eventually realizes, however, that the paternalistic spirit of colonialism exists in the school as well. The headmaster, for example, "believed that the best, the really excellent, could only come from the white man. He brought up his boys to copy and cherish the white man's civilization as the only hope of mankind and especially of the black races" (115). The headmaster makes no protest when the colonial authorities come to take Njoroge from the school for "questioning" about his family's alleged connections with the Mau Mau uprising.

Police officers take Njoroge away to his village, where the boy discovers that his father Ngotho has been tortured and castrated during an interrogation about the murder of a black collaborator, Jacobo. Ngotho has falsely confessed to this crime in order to protect his older son, also a suspect. Njoroge is accused of having sworn the Mau Mau oath and is also threatened with emasculation. As the young man sees his father die, he realizes that his dream is also perishing. The difference between Holden's cynicism about his schooling and Njoroge's innocent and romantic expectations that education will solve all of his problems is initially strong. But Njoroge's faith in a Westernized education turns bitter when he begins to realize the effects of this colonial system on his people. If we accept Ayling's premise that all children are in some sense colonized by the power structures of family and society, Njoroge's and Holden's disillusionments are parallel in the sense that school, for both, is a colonial power which socializes children to accept the rule of the powerful—whether of their own race or another.

If both boys are viewed as struggling against the effects of colonization, a significant difference is that in an obviously colonized situation, as in Kenya, it is easier to develop and maintain a sense of community because there is an oppressive "other," against which to rebel; in Holden's situation, on the other hand, it is more difficult to find a clear enemy. As a result, Holden lashes out almost indiscriminately against pervasive forms of "phoniness."

Thus another initial contrast is seen in Njoroge's idealization of his family and in his dreams of playing an important role in his community. Unlike Holden, Njoroge has few material advantages, but his entire extended family—including, in this polygamous society, not only his biological parents and siblings but also his father's second wife and her sons—all work together to provide money and other support for Njoroge's schooling. Eventually, however, Njoroge, like Holden, is estranged from or disappointed with family members whom he nevertheless loves very much.

As a young boy, Njoroge surprises himself with the thought that parents may not always be right. Later, he begins to doubt his father's infallibility as a family leader and to see him instead as somewhat ineffectual in dealing with the economic and political crisis which threatens the family's well-being. Njoroge's older brother, Boro, wants the father, Ngotho, to take a more militant stance, swearing allegiance to the Mau Mau cause, but Ngotho is reluctant to do so, especially as he would have to take the oath from his son. As a result, Ngotho loses his traditional role as unquestioned head of the household. Njoroge tries to retain his faith in his father, but he cannot help acknowledging the change in his father's stature: "He was no longer the man whose ability to keep home together had resounded from ridge to ridge"(81). Unlike the American Holden, for whom irreverence for family authority is almost an expected norm, Njoroge laments the tragic effects of colonialism in undermining his culture's traditional family structure.

Njoroge's romantic attachment to the daughter of his father's enemy, Jacobo, undermines family authority from another direction. Like Holden, Njoroge seeks relief from his growing loneliness and isolation through fantasies of love. Njoroge's childhood affection for the daughter of his rich neighbor, Jacobo, turns to romance as he moves into adolescence, and Njoroge dreams of running away to marry Mwihaki. He knows their families, who have taken opposing sides in the political crisis, will not bless the match. Mwihaki's father, Jacobo, works for the white landowner, Mr. Howlands, a role which many of the Kikuyus regard as that of collaborator and spy. At a protest meeting where Jacobo appears to oppose a general strike, Njoroge's father, who is moved for once to stand up for the cause his sons espouse, attacks Jacobo. As a result, Ngotho loses his home and his job, and he and Jacobo, are clear enemies: "Jacobo on the side of the white people and Ngotho on the side of the black people" (59).

Because of this family rift, the friendship of Njoroge and Mwihaki must thereafter be conducted in secret, and, as with Shakespeare's Romeo and Juliet, their love may hold out the possibility of reconciliation for a strife-torn community. Even after one of Njoroge's brothers kills Jacobo in retaliation for the death of Ngotho, Njoroge dreams of escaping with Mwihaki from the calamity which surrounds them. Njoroge's shocking experiences have shown him "a different world from that he had believed himself living in" (120). Disillusioned, he turns to Mwihaki as his last hope, proposing that they run away to Uganda. Mwihaki dispels this last dream, telling Njoroge, "We are no longer children" (133). She suggests to Njoroge that they will have to face the future, though it will be different from Njoroge's childhood visions: "We better wait. You told me that the sun will rise tomorrow. I think you were right" (133).

Ngugi also traces the process by which his hero becomes confused about and disillusioned with religion. Njoroge's youthful vision consolidates his Christian faith and education with the traditional beliefs of the Kikuyu people: "His belief in a future for his family and the village rested then not only on a hope for sound education but also in a belief in a God of love and mercy, who long ago walked on this earth with Gikuyu and Mumbi, or Adam and Eve" (49). He thinks that the Kikuyu people, "whose land had been taken by white men, were no other than the children of Israel" and that the freedom leader, Jomo Kenyatta, is the Black Moses (49). He himself is to be the David who slays the Goliath of colonialism. Eventually, however, Njoroge's experiences teach him that the Christian religion is not a placebo for the ills that have befallen his people; the revivalist Isaka is slain by Europeans, the very people who brought the religion to his people, despite Isaka's vain attempts to assure the assassins that he is devoutly Christian and not a Mau Mau guerrilla. And Jomo Kenyatta, the Black Moses, is imprisoned by the colonial government.

The religious questions which trouble both Njoroge and Holden reflect their essentially idealistic natures, but their ideals about coming of age are quite different. Holden resists growing up; he wants to protect innocence even at the cost of stopping the passage of time; Njoroge, however, longs to grow up and become the savior of his people. Holden dreams of escaping to go out West and become a deaf-mute; Njoroge dreams of leading his society to a "better tomorrow."

Reminiscent of the typical folk tale or of the adventure/accomplishment romance described by Donelson and Nilsen, both do see themselves as savior figures for groups which they perceive to be disadvantaged and threatened by a corrupt social system. Holden wants to be "the catcher in the rye," to protect all innocent children from falling from the cliffs of life, and Njoroge wants to be the leader of his people who will save them from colonial oppression.

Both look back nostalgically to an earlier period when life was better. Deeply disturbed by present conditions, Njoroge dreams of a time when his people held their land in an innocent, Eden-like state without the corrupting and exploitative presence of white Europeans. Holden, the less communally oriented hero, looks back, not to the childhood of his race, but to his personal experiences in childhood. He thinks of childhood—his own, that of his dead brother Allie, and that of his sister Phoebe—as a time of innocence which he would like to recapture or to perpetuate.

At the end of both works, the two young adults must tentatively begin the process of coming of age by relinquishing some of their dreams about their own messianic roles and by beginning to accept the inevitable imperfections, even corruption and brutality, of the worlds they inhabit. Toward the end of Salinger's novel, Holden's sister Phoebe scolds him about his refusal to participate in life. When Phoebe challenges Holden to name something he likes, the only people he can list are nuns or dead people, and the only occupation he can think of which would really please him is that of "a catcher in the rye." Later, when Holden realizes his little sister Phoebe plans to go with him when he leaves to go out West, he gives up his plans and takes her back home. He also begins to wonder if he was too hard on Mr. Antolini, who after all had tried to help, and he admits he misses everybody he left behind at school. Holden experiences a kind of epiphany when he sees Phoebe riding the carousel in Central Park. He realizes he cannot protect her from the risks and dangers of life but must affirm life despite these dangers:

> All the kids kept trying to grab for the gold ring, and so was old Phoebe, and I was sort of afraid she'd fall off the goddam horse, but I didn't say anything or do anything. The thing with kids is, if they want to grab for the gold ring, you have to let them do it, and not say anything. (273–274)

This realization makes Holden euphorically happy, at least for the moment. Of this key moment in the text, Wayne C. Booth writes:

> Though he cannot protect her from knowledge of the world, though he cannot, as he would like, put her under a glass museum case and save her from the ravages of the sordid, time-bound world, he can at least offer her the love that comes naturally to him. He does so and he is saved. Which is of course why he is ecstatically happy. (Booth, 1964,163)

At the end of the book, Holden is in a mental institution, but is preparing to return to school. His recovery, however, is still quite tentative. To his psychiatrist's questions about whether or not he is ready to apply himself in school next fall, he replies, "I *think* I am, but how do I know?" (276). His final words reflect his awareness of the dangers and pains which inevitably accompany involvement in life, but he recognizes that the very act of telling his story has committed him to just such involvement: "About all I know is, I sort of miss everybody I told about. . . . It's funny. Don't ever tell anybody anything. If you do, you start missing everybody" (277).

Like Holden, Njoroge must relinquish his dreams of escape in order to face the harsh realities of life. After his father's death, he returns home to care for his father's two wives. His job as shop assistant for an Indian merchant is a far cry from his earlier dreams; and when he is fired from even this job he decides to end his life. His suicide attempt, however, is aborted when his mother Nyokabi and her co-wife Njeri find him. Though he feels himself to be a coward for not following through with his intentions, he also feels "a strange relief." The torch his mother carries appears as "a glowing piece of wood which she carried to light the way" (135). He knows he has tried to evade "the responsibility for which he has prepared himself since childhood," but he also accepts the indictment of the inner voice which tells him, "You are a coward. Why didn't you do it?" (136).

The last sentence of the story, however, suggests an acceptance of his responsibilities to the living and a gritty determination to live in the world as it is: "And he ran home and opened the door for his two mothers" (136). The hopefulness which is implicit in the last sentence will be accentuated for young readers when they learn that, although the book ends before Njoroge's people achieve independence, the movement spearheaded by the Mau Maus eventually culminated in majority rule for Kenya. Information which will be helpful includes the fact that in 1961, the Mau Mau leader, Jomo Kenyatta, was released from prison; in 1962, the terms of independence were negotiated; in 1963, the new nation celebrated its independence with Kenyatta as prime minister and one year later became a republic with Kenyatta as president. Thus the "tomorrow" for which Njoroge has longed does eventually come to his people. (Useful resources for providing such contexts are Elizabeth Gunner's *A Handbook for Teaching African Literature* and G. D. Killam's *An Introduction to the Writings of Ngugi.*)

For Njoroge, however, as the individual within this political context, the process of coming of age may truly begin when he relinquishes his dreams of personal glory, but also when he recognizes his obligations to his family and community, despite their very human flaws. In this respect, the parallels with Holden Caulfield are significant. Both Njoroge and Holden are, in a sense, victims of social corruption: Holden is victimized by the commercialism, snobbery, and shallowness of a privileged but empty world in which he cannot find meaningful values or traditions. Njoroge is victimized by the effects of colonialization on the values and traditions of his people. However, in coming of age, each hero must move beyond the role of victim to work toward personal identity and a renewed sense of community in a world which will yield slowly, if at all, to the forces of change. Ultimately, however, both heroes must realize that the lines between enemy and self are not clearly drawn: family and friends may be "collaborators" or "rebels," and a part of Holden's problem may be that he at first perceives his parents solely as "collaborators."

Young readers will find here an honest account of the agonies and uncertainties of growing up in a troubled world. Both books end in a realistically indeterminate manner, as the heroes begin to accept their own flaws and limitations and to acknowledge their interdependence with other equally flawed human beings. The lesson in Mr. Antolini's words to Holden is one which both heroes are beginning to learn: "The mark of the immature man is that he wants to die nobly for a cause, while the mark of the mature man is that he wants to live humbly for one" (244). Both heroes have contemplated their own deaths as a possible escape from their painful realities, but, unlike tragic figures such as Romeo and Juliet, they draw back from the final step. They begin instead, reluctantly and uncertainly, to define their world and themselves in more realistic terms. Young readers who have encountered the vividly recreated worlds of Holden and Njoroge, so different from their own, and who have identified with the struggles of these fictional heroes may be led to repeat this process in their own lives.

Though neither Holden nor Njoroge yet has a comfortable spot in the literary canon, teachers can point to numerous literary parallels within the traditional canon. For example, both heroes experience the stages of innocence, experience, and higher innocence defined by English romantic poet William Blake and both are in need of the comforting lines of Walt Whitman's "On the Beach at Night" which Ngugi uses as his epigraph: "Weep not, Child / . . . . The ravening clouds shall not be long victorious, / They shall not long possess the sky . . . " One is reminded also of Milton's Adam and Eve, who must also relinquish their hold on an idealized realm and take up residence in the fallen world of human and natural imperfection:

Some natural tears they dropped but wiped them soon;
The world was all before them, where to choose
Their place of rest. . . .
They hand in hand with wandering steps and slow
Through Eden took their solitary way.
(*Paradise Lost*, Book XII, Lines 645–649)

Works Cited

Bettelheim, Bruno. *The Uses of Enchantment*. New York: Alfred A. Knopf, 1976.

Booth, Wayne, C. "Censorship and the Values of Fiction." *The English Journal* (March 1964): 155–164.

Carlsen, Robert. "For Everything There Is a Season." In *Literature for Adolescents: Selection and Use*, edited by Richard A. Meade and Robert C. Small. Columbus, OH: Charles E Merrill, 1973.

Cofer, Judith Ortiz. *Silent Dancing: A Partial Remembrance of a Puerto Rican Childhood*. Houston: Arte Publico Press, 1990.

Cortazar, Julio. "End of the Game." Translated by Paul Blackburn. In *The Eye of the Heart*, edited by Barbara Howes. New York: Avon Books, 1973.

Dasenbrock, Reed Way. "Understanding Others: Teaching Multicultural Literature." *Multicultural Readings*. Urbana, IL: NCTE, n.d.

Donelson, Kenneth and Aileen Pace Nilsen. *Literature for Today's Young Adults.* New York. Scott Foresman, 1989.

Gunner, Elizabeth. *A Handbook for Teaching African Literature.* London: Heinemann Educational Books, 1984.

Hamilton, Virginia. *Arilla Sun Down.* New York: Greenwillow, 1976.

———. *M. C. Higgins, the Great.* New York: Collier Books, 1987.

———. *Sweet Whispers, Brother Rush.* New York: Putnam Publishing Group, 1982.

Killam, G. D. *An Introduction to the Writings of Ngugi.* London: Heinemann Educational Books, 1980.

King, James Roy. *Old Tales and New Truths.* Albany: State University of New York Press, 1992.

Kingston, Maxine Hong. *The Woman Warrior.* New York: Vintage International, 1989.

Knowles, John. *A Separate Peace.* New York: Bantam, 1985.

Lee, Harper. *To Kill a Mockingbird.* New York: Warner Books, 1988.

Milton, John. *Paradise Lost and Other Poems.* New York: New American Library, 1961.

Ngugi, wa Thiong'o. *Weep Not, Child.* Portsmouth, NH: Heinemann, 1964.

Paterson, Katherine. *Bridge to Terabithia.* New York: Harper Trophy, 1977.

Salinger, J. D. *The Catcher in the Rye.* New York: Random House Modern Library, 1951.

Sarr, Ndiawar. Classroom Lecture. University of Montevallo, Spring, 1988.

Zipes, Jack. *Breaking the Magic Spell: Radical Theories of Folk and Fairy Tales.* New York: Methuen, 1984.

SANFORD PINSKER

Go West, My Son

"I figured, I'd go down to the Holland Tunnel and bum a ride, and then I'd bum another one, and another one, and in a few days I'd be somewhere out West."

—Holden Caulfield

Dreams of the West have always dominated our national consciousness. With its wider hospitality to the values of rugged individuality, self-reliance, and boundless freedom, the West has a deep, mythic appeal. Perhaps Jack Burden, the brooding narrator of Robert Penn Warren's *All the King's Men* (1946), best describes the attraction:

> For West is where we all plan to go some day. It is where you go when the land gives out and the old field-pines encroach. It is where you go when you get the letter saying: *Flee, all is discovered.* It is where you go when you look down at the blade in your hand and see the blood on it. It is where you go when you are told that you are a bubble on the tide of the empire. It is where you go when you hear that that's gold in them-thar hills. It is where you go to grow up with the country. It is where you go to spend your old age. Or it is just where you go.[1]

The Catcher in the Rye: Innocence Under Pressure (New York: Twayne, 1993): pp. 89–97.
Copyright © 1993 Sanford Pinsker.

37

Holden too wants to go West, West to escape the fate of his contemporaries who, he fears, will become "guys that always talk about how many miles they get to a gallon in their goddam cars. Guys that get sore and childish as hell if you beat them at golf, or even just some stupid game like pingpong. Guys that are very mean. Guys that never read books" (123). These guys, in other words, are phonies, and Holden's sometime-date Sally Hayes is typical of their female equivalents.

Sally represents the fashionable Manhattan of Broadway, Rockefeller Center, and upscale apartments, everything Holden is rebelling against and confused about. Salinger provides plenty of testimony to her conventional, phony values—for instance, when they meet for a date, in chapter 17, she immediately gushes, "It's marvelous to see you! It's been *ages*." Holden comments that she has "one of those very loud, embarrassing voices when you met her somewhere. She got away with it because she was so damn good-looking, but she always gave me a pain in the ass." This scene demonstrates nicely Holden's unpredictable behavior, because he can describe her as looking so good "I felt like I was in love with her and wanted to marry her" the line after he states "I didn't even like her much" (124). He can even tell her he loves her. "It was a lie, of course, but the thing is, I meant it when I said it. I'm crazy. I swear to God I am" (125).

Matters become no clearer as the afternoon progresses, when they have seen a musical and done some ice-skating. After Sally presses Holden to join her family for their Christmas Eve tree trimming, what had simmered just beneath the surface suddenly boils over:

> "Did you ever get fed up?" I said. "I mean did you ever get scared that everything was going to go lousy unless you did something? I mean do you like school, and all that stuff?"
> "It's a terrific *bore*."
> "I mean do you hate it? I know it's a terrific bore, but do you *hate* it, is what I mean."
> "Well, I don't exactly *hate* it. You always have to—." (130)

The increasingly agitated, impatient Holden doesn't allow Sally to finish her sentence, but its gist is clear enough: you have to stay in school, boring though it may be, because your prospects are mighty bleak if you don't. No doubt this puts Sally very solidly in the mainstream, and there is a certain truth in what keeps Sally plugging away term after term. From Holden's alienated perspective, however, schools are a prime target for venting his discontent, although they have to share space with other fixtures of life in a crowded speech that serves as a poignant example of the crossed directions his manic phase can take: "'Well, I hate it [school]. Boy, do I hate it,' I said. 'But it isn't just

that. It's everything. I hate living in New York and all. Taxicabs, and Madison
Avenue buses, with the drivers and all always yelling at you to get out at the
rear door, and being introduced to phony guys that call the Lunts angels, and
going up and down in elevators when you just want to go outside, and guys
fitting your pants all the time at Brooks, and people always—'" Obviously,
Holden is badly in need of an alternative, simpler environment, and says as
much to Sally:

> "How would you like to get the hell out of here? . . . I know this
> guy down in Greenwich Village that we can borrow his car for a
> couple of weeks. He used to go to the same school I did and he
> still owes me a couple of bucks. What we could do is; tomorrow
> morning we could drive up to Massachusetts and Vermont, and all
> around there, see. It's as beautiful as hell up there. It really is. . . .
> I have about a hundred and eighty bucks in the bank. I can take it
> out when it opens in the morning, and then I could go down and
> get this guy's car. No kidding. We'll stay in these cabin camps and
> stuff like that till the dough runs out. Then, when the dough runs
> out, I could get a job somewhere and we could live somewhere with
> a brook and all and, later on, we could get married or something.
> I could chop all our own wood in the wintertime and all. Honest
> to God, we could have a terrific time!" (132)

Holden's vision of the idyllic life bears more than a few resemblances to
the one Henry David Thoreau outlines in *Walden*, although Thoreau focused
on the Imperial Self and certainly did not include a Sally Hayes in his version.
Although Thoreau's experiment in living simply also included regular visits to
Mom for tender loving care and home-cooked meals, he, unlike Holden, knew
the essential difference between being lonely and alone. Holden, on the other
hand, would always miss people, even if the affected and conforming Sally Hayes
would not exactly have fit in at his version of Thoreau's Concord retreat.

One person who would fit in is Holden's sister, Phoebe, who represents
everything Sally is not. After all, even if she presses him about his disaffections and points out (on no fewer than four occasions) that "Daddy'll *kill*
you!," how can one not love a person who makes up middle names—the latest
being Weatherfield—or who takes belching lessons from a fellow classmate.
Phoebe is meant to stand for childhood itself, as made plain by the stories—
pure, unaffected, wonderfully artless—that she writes under the pen name
Weatherfield Caulfield, itself a kind of internal rhyme.

On the other hand, there is enough of the practical about Phoebe to
give one pause. In this regard, her school notebook is instructive, not only for
the sort of "secret" notes students of her age generally pass—"*Bernice meet me*

at recess I have something very very important to tell you" (160)—but also for the careful homework entries that suggest Phoebe is a willing student in ways her older brother has long ago abandoned. One can only conclude that she will do quite nicely at whatever version of Pencey Prep she attends in the future, a conclusion hinted toward by her role as Benedict Arnold in the upcoming school pageant. Like that famous Revolutionary traitor and her brother D. B., Phoebe has her nose toward the main chance.

Not to say that her role as Arnold is entirely unproblematic. Much as Phoebe looks forward to her school pageant, her loyalty lies with family, and particularly with her confused, unhappy brother. She is no traitor to Holden, as he discovers when she meets him with her suitcase in hand, fully prepared to join him in his rebellious sojourn. One cannot help but wonder how far the pair would have gotten—the Caulfields of taxicabs and hard cash decidedly lack the guts and savvy that build cabins at Walden Pond.

By now, Holden has replaced his ideal destination of Massachusetts and Vermont with that of the West, where he plans to lead the simple life, pumping gas and pretending he is a deaf-mute.

> I'd build me a little cabin somewhere with the dough I made and live there for the rest of my life. I'd build it right near the woods, but not right *in* them, because I'd want it to be sunny as hell all the time. I'd cook all my own food, and later on, if I wanted to get married or something, I'd meet this beautiful girl that was also a deaf-mute and we'd get married. She'd come and live in my cabin with me, and if she wanted to say anything to me, she'd have to write it on a goddam piece of paper, like everybody else. If we had any children, we'd hide them somewhere. We could buy them a lot of books and teach them how to read and write by ourselves. (199)

This is wishful thinking—such dreams are destined to be shattered, rather like the recording of "Little Shirley Beans" that Holden buys for his sister and that breaks in dozens of unplayable pieces—but notice how the Holden's pipe dream not only moves toward a blissful silence (where the world's rude noise cannot intrude), but also turns his bitter experience with Sunny into a cabin by the woods bathed in perpetual sunshine. In short, this is the West of dreams, as Holden imagines it and as his author, in the sanctity of a New Hampshire hideaway, largely came to live it.

Perhaps the novel's most blissful scene is when Holden feels "so damn happy" as he watches Phoebe going around and around on the carousel: "I don't know why. It was just that she looked so damn *nice*, the way she kept going around and around, in her blue coat and all. I wish you could have been there" (213). In the heyday of myth criticism, it was not unusual for critics to put an enormous emphasis on the color of Phoebe's coat. After all, blue is the color traditionally associated with the Virgin Mary, and in a novel that features Holden as an avatar of Christ, what would make more sense than a Phoebe-as-Madonna? My problem with such arguments is not that I have quarrels with close-reading or that I think that the details Salinger chooses are accidental (quite the contrary), but rather that there is simply not enough textual evidence to support these conclusions. It is, after all, one thing to admire Salinger's artistry, and quite another to impose religious patterns extraneous to the book itself.

It is far better to see the powerful image of Phoebe on the carousel in terms of the larger pattern of stasis and motion. In this case, the motion is circular, moving in one sense, but frozen in another. Granted, the image is destined to change (Phoebe cannot ride on the carousel forever); moreover, it is not only clear that she will reach out for the brass ring, thereby risking a "fall," but also that Holden is now prepared to allow for the possibility. He cannot "save" her from all the risks, and joys, that, taken together, constitute life—nor is he any longer willing to try. Part of the sheer joy in the moment is a newly quiet acceptance (partly born of exhaustion, partly of relief) of the human condition as it is, and must be.

My suggestion is that one's hunches about this or that detail having a larger significance be tested against the collected evidence of the novel itself. For example, in the opening pages Holden mentions that he had "accidently" forgotten the team's fencing foils on the subway because he kept getting up to check the map. His explanation is plausible enough, although one can also understand how members of the fencing team would be exasperated when they arrived without the equipment necessary to compete. Holden, after all, was their manager and he should have been paying more attention. Holden's point, of course, is that they turned him into a social outcast, a pariah. But if one remembers that the word "foil" is also a term indicating a dramatic counterweight, then the notion of a character without foils takes on an additional significance. Did Salinger *intend* such a reading? Perhaps, perhaps not. The point, however, is that *The Catcher in the Rye* explores Holden's life as a character whose monologue—at times defensive, at times self-justifying—keeps counterarguments ("foils") at an arm's length. The Holden of breezy monologue is, of course, quite different from the sadder, wiser one who watches Phoebe riding on the carousel. Of the latter, we may say that the rest is silence, or at least something that seems world's away from the silence Holden once imagined in the woods of his western exile and overheated imagination. For there is a tremendous gap between the silence behind which Salinger has retreated and the vision of playing the deaf-mute Holden projects. Like Stephen Dedalus in James Joyce's *A Portrait of the Artist as a Young Man,* Holden embraces garden varieties of "silence, exile, and cunning"[2] as weapons in the fight

against the world's corruptibility. In Stephen's case, however, the attractive
(and deeply romantic) formula has a bracing ring, especially for those who do
not follow Stephen's subsequent adventures in *Ulysses* (1922). With Holden,
however, invocation of silence, exile, and cunning has a desperate, tinny sound.
For Holden, as the novel's sole "voice," cannot tell his tale *without* language.
It may be all too true that phonies have ruined speech in much the same
way that they spoil everything else, but if Holden is to give an accounting of
himself, he has little choice but to do it in the words we read as *The Catcher in
the Rye*. To be sure, he would insist that expressions such as "Very big deal!"
are authentic and truthful in ways that, say, "Grand!" never are, but there are
also those who might take Holden to task for the essential shallowness of his
slang.

Silence, of course, can have an authority, an integrity, of its own. In this
regard, it is worth pointing out that vows of silence are often as much a part
of the monastic life Holden finds attractive (at least, as a possibility) as vows
of poverty. And there are occasions when silence is both appropriate and
respectful. But more often silence wears a cowardly face. In the face of the
world's evil, for example, silence is a good deal less attractive—and here one
thinks, for example, of the silence that greeted the Nazi Holocaust. Holden,
of course, takes on antagonists of a lesser order: those who talk glibly about
life as a game or who write "fuck you" on the walls of Phoebe's school. In the
former struggle, Holden swallows his tongue; in the latter, he applies as much
elbow grease and cleanser as possible. But either way, what Holden conjoins
in his reverie of moving west is freedom and silence—a chance to construct
an alternative world.

That America has always given rise to a wide variety of dreams is a
commonplace idea. What is less apparent perhaps is the ways in which these
dreams find themselves realized—usually with heavy doses of irony, and often
as nightmares. Call it the peculiarly American shading of the cunning of history. Call it the special consequences, the blessing and curse, of America itself.
In any event, the land founded on a great dream has been the beneficiary,
and the captive, of dreams ever since. It is a part of what Henry James meant
when he called being an American "a complex fate"[3] and what Fitzgerald had
in mind as he wrote the final lines of *The Great Gatsby*.

I belabor these matters because, although Holden's "madman weekend"
ends in the drenching rains of Central Park with Phoebe "going around and
around in her blue coat" (213), the novel itself concludes with Holden in a
very different West from the one he fantasized about. As Holden puts it, "I
got pretty run-down and had to come out here, and take it easy" (1). The *here*
is a rest home not far from Hollywood, where "this one psychoanalyst guy
they have here, keeps asking me if I'm going to apply myself when I go back

to school next September" (213). Not surprisingly, Holden cannot answer such a question.

Whatever else lies ahead, one thing is clear—Holden, the narrator, no longer clings to the same desperate scenarios that defined him as a participant in his story. His life will be neither as a saintly "catcher in the rye" nor will it include masquerades as a deaf-mute pumping gas in an ill-defined West. For better or worse, when the psychoanalyst rattles on about what his patient will be like next September, Holden listens and makes as honest an effort as he can to respond.

More speculation than this is a mug's game, because characters, even ones as vividly rendered as Holden, do not outlive their last page. When Huck Finn finishes the final paragraph of his adventures, he declares himself "rotten glad" (Twain, 214) that there's nothing left to tell. Holden also concludes on a note of sorrow, but one that revolves around the idea that if you "tell" about people, even people like Stradlater and Maurice, you end up missing them. After all, they were the ones who put his uncompromising sense of innocence under pressure, and in his farewell to them is also the hint of an ambivalent farewell to a fondly remembered former self.

Besides, without other people there is no story, no human context, and, more important, no humanity. Once again, the Stephen Dedalus of Joyce's *A Portrait of the Artist as a Young Man* may prove an instructive model. Stephen imagines that he can only become the writer he is destined to be when he flies past the nets of family, church, and state. Only then—when he is at last free of everything that exasperates and confines—will he be able to discover his true subject. What Stephen discovers, however, is that there are *no* subjects for fiction other than family, church, and state—whether it be the tale of how one lived among them, how one wriggled free, or how one learned to accommodate them. That lesson comes in *Ulysses*, as Stephen meets the thoroughly human, thoroughly vulnerable Leopold Bloom and learns something about the power of love.

I read Holden's concluding admission that he "misses" everyone as a similar recognition. Granted, love does not come easily to the Holden who spares no pains when it comes to phonies; but there is a greater chance he will temper his righteous indignation than fulfill Mr. Antolini's ominous prophecies about him. Even more important perhaps, Holden's story—despite his regrets about telling it—makes good on Mr. Antolini's notion about the value of keeping a record of one's trouble, and the way that the resulting work might help someone "learn something from you" (189). The fact is that you were drawn to Salinger's novel, and even to this book about that book, is proof that Holden's voice still speaks to those experiencing similar confusions, as well as to those who still harbor a fondness for him tucked somewhere inside their adult facades.

Notes

1. Robert Penn Warren, *All the King's Men* (New York: Harcourt Brace Jovanovich, 1946), 270.

2. James Joyce, *A Portrait of the Artist as a Young Man* (New York: Viking Critical Edition, 1964), 247.

3. Henry James, *Letters of Henry James*, vol. I. (New York: Scribners, 1920), 13.

Work Cited

Salinger, J. D. *The Catcher in the Rye* (New York: Bantam, 1964).

DENNIS McCORT

Hyakujo's Geese, Amban's Doughnuts and Rilke's Carrousel: Sources East and West for Salinger's Catcher

Zen koans are supra-logical spiritual projects meant to be worked on full-time. Even when the monk is not formally meditating, the koan continues to resonate from the hinterlands of consciousness, suffusing every thought, word and deed with its impenetrable mystery. So, as Holden Caulfield dutifully attends to the wisdom dispensed to him by his history teacher Mr. Spencer upon his dismissal from Pency Prep, in the back of his mind an odd question lingers and asserts itself: "I was thinking about the lagoon in Central Park . . . wondering where the ducks went when the lagoon got all icy and frozen over."[1] Holden, of course, knows nothing of Zen, but Salinger wants the *reader* to think of him as working on a koan. The matter of the Central Park ducks, silly though it be on the surface, is to bedevil Holden throughout his lost Christmas weekend in New York City and, like a good koan, will not leave him alone until he comes to terms with the central problem of his life, that is, with his so-called *life* koan, which the ducks symbolize.

Although the topic of Zen in Salinger's writings has often been addressed, coverage has been limited primarily to the fiction collected and published subsequent to *The Catcher in The Rye*—fiction in which the Zen theme is explicit.[2] Among those few commentators who have searched for traces of Zen in *Catcher* in particular,[3] one finds interesting speculation as

Comparative Literature Studies Volume 34, Number 3 (1997): pp. 260–278. Copyright © 1997 by the Pennsylvania State University.

45

well as enlightening discussion of Buddhism in the broad generic sense, but not a single unequivocal reference to the unique Sino-Japanese form of Buddhism known as Zen. This is especially mystifying in the case of Rosen, ninety percent of whose monograph is devoted to the topic. Alsen, perhaps the most authoritative voice on the subject of Salinger's interest in Eastern religion (123–164), takes the fictive Buddy Glass' self-characterization as reflective of the author, insisting that Zen is far less important in Salinger's work than "the New and Old Testaments, Advaita Vedanta, and classical Taoism" (134).

This is an odd state of affairs. Since Zen figures so prominently in *Nine Stories*,[4] the compositional chronology of which overlaps that of *Catcher*, and so explicitly in the conversational fabric of "Zooey," one would expect to find at least some evidence of it in *Catcher*, the more so since, according to Skow[5] and Lundquist (70–71), Salinger had been immersed in Zen studies at least since the mid 1940s. Yet *Catcher* is apparently Zen-less. I propose, by way of explanation, that there are indeed traces of Zen in *Catcher*, at least two traces that are quite subtle, seamlessly woven as they are into character and narrative. They are hence easily overlooked, but nevertheless unequivocal once they are linked to their proper sources in Zen lore. The remainder of this essay purports to establish this linkage and, in so doing, to evoke our appreciation of the way the scenes in question symbolically enrich Holden's characterization. This, in turn, should significantly modify and deepen our understanding of the shifting circumstances of Salinger's interest in Zen.

Symbolic echoes of other literature in the work of a great writer are usually a matter of deliberate encoding. This, however, does not preclude a significant degree of spontaneity from the process, as such echoes often tend, as it were on their own, to insinuate themselves in clusters, or even to coalesce in the writer's imagination, much in the way of what Freud called the "overdetermined" or condensed imagery of dreams. Analogous to the dreamer, who has his entire personal history to draw upon in shaping his unconscious narrative, the well-read writer in the throes of creation has a vast "inner library" of texts at his disposal, and the particular focus of that writer's interest in any given moment will tend to draw ("check out") certain of these stored texts to itself metonymically and virtually without effort. As a more or less automatic process, then, literary allusions in texts often freely intermingle, paying no heed to a future interpreter's need for discrete thematic taxonomies or stylistic levels.

Such is the case with Salinger's novel, for it turns out that we cannot fully appreciate the symbolic significance of Zen for Holden Caulfield's final spiritual catharsis without noting its fusion in the penultimate chapter with an allusion to a key image from the work, not of an ancient Chinese or Japanese sage, but of a modern German poet, who, though implicitly Zen-like in many ways, yet most likely had no formal acquaintance with that religion. I refer to none other than Rainer Maria Rilke and his renowned *Dinggedicht*,

"Das Karrussell." In Salinger's *Catcher in the Rye*, it would seem that sources East and West not only meet but indeed become mutually determining.

Hyakujo's Geese

The first trace of Zen in Salinger's novel takes us back to the above-mentioned ducks, which appear four times in the narrative, in each instance as a seemingly superfluous preoccupation of Holden's. After their introduction as a "quirky mental distraction" during his farewell talk with Mr. Spencer, they recur as a "spontaneous question" put by Holden to the first cabby in chapter nine, then again in conversation with the second cabby in chapter twelve, and finally in chapter twenty as the object of a desperate nocturnal search. Viewed together the four instances form a kind of *leitmotif* structured by a sense of increasing urgency, very much like the build-up of tension that leads to the sudden breakthrough to solution in koan meditation practice.

It is likely this odd blend, of emotional urgency on Holden's part with a seeming irrelevance of the ducks to the narrative in any logical or figurative sense, that initially calls one's attention to them. If the attending reader should happen to be familiar with Zen folklore, he might suddenly recognize the ducks' symbolic derivation therein, at which point it would become quite obvious that these "extraneous" fowl lie right at the heart of Holden's identity crisis. Salinger's source for the motif is an anecdote contained in D. T. Suzuki's *Essays in Zen Buddhism (First Series)* which initially appeared in New York in August of 1949 while the author was hard at work on the first draft of *Catcher*.[6] In Essay 5, entitled "On Satori—The Revelation of a New Truth in Zen Buddhism," Suzuki relates the following:

> Hyakujo (Pai-chang Huai-hai, 724–814) one day went out attending his master Baso (Ma-tsu). A flock of wild geese was seen flying and Baso asked:
> "What are they?"
> "They are wild geese, sir."
> "Whither are they flying?"
> "They have flown away, sir."
> Baso, abruptly taking hold of Hyakujo's nose, gave it a twist. Overcome with pain, Hyakujo cried aloud: "Oh! Oh!"
> "You say they have flown away," Baso said, "but all the same they have been here from the very beginning."
> This made Hyakujo's back wet with cold perspiration. He had satori.[7]

Here the master is testing his student's insight by means of a *mondo*, that is, a sudden question meant to evoke the latter's delusive view on some significant spiritual matter—in this case, the relationship between change and per-manence. Hyakujo's conventionally one-sided view of the issue, which sees only change (ducks coming and going), is thrown up to him through Baso's carefully timed nasal shock tactic. The master senses that his mature student needs only a little jolt, some deft act of "compassionate cruelty," to precipi-tate in him that final *salto mortale* from ignorance to Wisdom. As Hyakujo cries out in pain, the master suddenly calls his attention to the other side of the issue ("all the same they have been here from the very beginning"): change and permanence, the transitory and the abiding, are one and the same, an inseparable identity of opposites. From the Zen point of view, to resolve one contradiction is to resolve them all (since the distinction between the one and the many is itself a delusion). This instantaneous coalescence in his consciousness of all that has heretofore been separate is Hyakujo's satori or Enlightenment. Having propelled the monk from his long-suffering state of separative dualism into the rarefied atmosphere of Enlightened monism, Master Baso's *mondo* has served its purpose.

Holden's preoccupation with the ducks is clearly a symbolic extension of this traditional Zen anecdote as recounted in Suzuki's *Essays*. Hyakujo's *mondo* becomes Holden's koan, a koan that embodies the core conflict of his life: how can he hang onto the innocence of childhood while moving, inexorably, into the phony world of adulthood, or, how can he discover that changeless, invio-late innocence that never flies away but "all the same has been here from the very beginning." His brother Allie had found a way to preserve it (as Holden sees it): he died. To the living that is, of course, a one-sided solution: a loved one who dies has made himself inaccessible to change in the minds and hearts of the survivors. Such a denouement falls short of the absolutist standards of Zen, in particular of the koan, which demands a solution that somehow in-cludes both terms of the contradiction: both change and permanence, corrup-tion and innocence, in a seamless *coincidentia oppositorum*. In a word, Holden is trying to do the impossible. It will indeed take nothing less than a death to accomplish this, not biological death, but that much more difficult death of the ego, the mystics' "death before death," a conscious and voluntary surrender that is prelude to Enlightenment, the spiritual condition in which all conflicts and contradictions are resolved "suddenly," and forever.[8]

With the ducks' first appearance—in Holden's consciousness during that farewell chat with Mr. Spencer—Salinger makes allusion to an interesting as-pect of koan psychology: even when the aspirant allows the koan to move from the center to the periphery of his attention so that he can take up other tasks, the koan continues to exert its influence. Though the monk has stopped working on it, it continues to work on him. Kapleau says of this subliminal dimension of koan work: " ... once the koan grips the heart and mind ... the inquiry goes on ceaselessly in the subconscious. While the mind is occupied with a particular task, the question fades from consciousness, surfacing naturally as soon as the action is over, not unlike a moving stream which now and again disappears underground only to reappear and resume its open course without interrupting its onward flow."[9] Thus, as Holden tells us:

> The funny thing is, though, I was sort of thinking of something else while I shot the bull [with Mr. Spencer]. . . . I was wondering where the [Central Park] ducks went when the lagoon got all icy and frozen over. I wondered if some guy came in a truck and took them away to a zoo or something. Or if they just flew away.
>
> I'm lucky, though. I mean I could shoot the old bull to old Spencer and think about those ducks at the same time. It's funny. You don't have to think too hard when you talk to a teacher.(13)

Since Holden is only half-listening to Mr. Spencer's sage counsel, the thing that is really on his mind is able to surface in consciousness.

In the three subsequent duck-episodes there is, as noted, a pattern of growing tension as the issue takes on for Holden the tightening grip of an obsession. As one Rinzai master put it in terms of *Mu*, the fundamental Zen koan: "[You must reach the point where you feel] as though you had swallowed a red-hot iron ball that you cannot disgorge despite your every effort."[10] This sense of entrapment by the issue, of feeling utterly unable either to advance or retreat from it, while at the same time compelled to do something, is fertile ground for the lightning flash of insight. During his first cab ride through Central Park in chapter nine, Holden puts the question to the surly cabby: "You know those ducks in that lagoon right near Central Park South? That little lake? By any chance, do you happen to know where they go, the ducks, when it gets all frozen over? Do you happen to know, by any chance?" (60). In verbalizing his concern Holden begins to experience the unsettling ubiquity of the koan as it spreads from the private inner to the outer social domain. At the same time he is becoming aware of its frustrating imponderability. For a koan to be effective, the meditator must at some point come up against its diamond-hard resistance to reason, otherwise he will not be driven to arouse his own latent supra-rational resources: "I realized [in asking the cabby] it was only one chance in a million" (60).

Later on, this time in Horwitz's cab, Holden presses the issue further: "Hey, Horwitz. . . . You ever pass by the lagoon in Central Park? . . . Well, you know the ducks that swim around in it? In the springtime and all? Do you happen to know where they go in the wintertime, by any chance?" (81). Unlike his predecessor who dismissed Holden's question with contempt, this cabby engages him in a mock-comic round of what is known in Zen as "dharma duelling," defined by Kapleau as "a verbal joust or battle of 'wit' as respects the dharma, usually between two enlightened persons" (363). Here Horwitz takes the role of Holden's/Hyakujo's enlightened master whose task it is to pry his student loose from a one-sided view of things: whereas Holden continues to brood obsessively on the ephemeral (the vanished ducks, with their unconscious associations to his brother's death and to the impending "death" of his own innocence), Horwitz aggressively calls his attention to the fish frozen in the lagoon which embody constancy:

> "The *fish* don't go no place. They stay right where they are, the fish. Right in the goddam, lake."
> "The fish—that's different. The fish is different. I'm talking about the ducks," I said.
> "What's different about it? Nothin's different about it," Horwitz said. . . . "Use your head, for Chrissake."(82)

Unlike the mature Hyakujo who teeters on the brink of insight, needing only a sharp tweak of the nose to transcend the logical boundaries of his own mind, Holden stays mired in his "Dark Night," continuing to struggle and resist the master's Truth: "'You don't think them fish just *die* when it gets to be winter, do ya?' 'No, but—'" (83).

The fourth and final duck-episode, occurring several hours (and drinks) later, finds Holden wandering around Central Park in half-drunken confusion as he presses on with the quest: "I figured I'd go by that little lake and see what the hell the ducks were doing, see if they were around or not" (153). After much fruitless groping and stumbling, "Then, finally, I found it. What it was, it was partly frozen and partly not frozen. But I didn't see any ducks around. I walked all around the whole damn lake—I damn near fell *in* once, in fact—but I didn't see a single duck" (154).

There are in this sequence several allusions to the traditional ordeal of the spiritual path, allusions that are subtle yet unmistakable when viewed in a Zen context. For example, just as the masters warn of sorely testing periods of melancholy, so Holden complains, "I was feeling so damn depressed and lonesome. . . . I wasn't tired or anything. I just felt blue as hell" (153–154). Also, as one would expect, the motif of darkness is emphasized: "Boy, was it dark. . . . I kept walking and walking, and it kept getting darker and darker and spookier and spookier" (154). Kapleau points out that "In Zen it is said that 'the grand round mirror of wisdom is as black as pitch'" and quotes his teacher Yasutani Roshi's version of St. John's "Dark Night of the Soul": "To renounce such conceptions [i.e., what one presumes to know of the way the world works] is to stand in 'darkness.' Now, satori comes out of this 'darkness,' not out of the 'light' of reason and worldly knowledge" (118).

In its subjective aspect, the darkness motif embodies the anguish of being utterly lost. As another master, Shibayama, has it: "the koan will mercilessly take away all our intellect and knowledge. In short, the role of the koan is not to lead us to satori easily, but on the contrary to make us lose our way and drive us to despair" (qtd. in Kapleau 71). Thus Holden, even in the park's familiar surroundings: "I had the most terrific trouble finding that lagoon that night. I *knew* right where it was—it was right near Central Park South and all—but I still couldn't find it" (154).

Finally, there is Holden's eventual discovery of the duckless lagoon, "partly frozen and partly not frozen." The qualities of frozenness and fluidity echo Holden's life koan, that is, the painful contradiction between permanence and change, symbolically played out earlier in Holden's duck/ fish "dharma duel" with Horwitz. The half-and-half or neither/nor aspect of the lagoon's state alludes to the prickly razor's-edge nature of koan work which prevents the meditator from lapsing into either (or, for that matter, *any*) logical position suggested by the koan. Only the Middle Way, a central tenet of Buddhism, leads by its very a-positional "narrowness" to the promised land of Enlightenment, to the ineffable *coincidentia oppositorum* in which all dualities are transcended, all contradictions resolved. Holden has not yet arrived at the promised land ("But I couldn't find any [ducks]" [154]), but he is, at this point, well along the path.

Although Salinger nowhere mentions Suzuki's *Essays* by name as his source for the ducks, the circumstantial evidence for his having worked with this well-known introductory text during the writing of *Catcher* is compelling. As Hamilton tells us, "From summer 1949 to summer 1950 he seems to have worked flat out on the novel" (113). The British Rider edition of the *Essays in Zen Buddhism* came out in both London and New York in August of 1949. The first American edition of the book appeared in New York City on May 10, 1950, published by HarperCollins (then called "Harper Brothers").[11] The publication of *Catcher* by Little, Brown and Co. just over a year later, on July 16, 1951, means that Suzuki's book was available to Salinger in its earlier British edition during his writing of the novel's first draft and, in its American edition, during his completion of the draft in spring and summer 1950. This is not to mention the all-important months of revision extending through winter and spring 1951 preceding publication in July.

I say "all-important months of revision" because it was Salinger's working style not simply to revise and edit his stories but virtually to rewrite them again and again, often incorporating in the rewriting, as suggested earlier, new elements culled from various interesting books that came his way (Hamilton 167–168). When one considers that Salinger fancied himself a Zen bibliophile,[12] that he makes several references to D. T. Suzuki in the Glass stories, revealing his affinity for this renowned transmitter of Zen culture, and that he can be definitely linked to at least *one* other early 50's book of Suzuki's,[13] it seems virtually certain that a copy of the *Essays* lay not far from the typewriter during his completion of the first draft and revisions of *Catcher*.

Amban's Doughnuts

The second reference in *Catcher* to a specific Zen source occurs only once, in chapter 25, as Holden walks uptown from Grand Central Station the next morning looking for a place to have breakfast. In the wake of his tearful reunion with Phoebe and traumatic encounter with Mr. Antolini, Holden's spirits have reached their lowest ebb ("I think I was more depressed than I ever was in my whole life" [194]). Beset by morbid hypochondriacal thoughts ("So I figured I was getting cancer" [196]), he thinks he might feel better with something in his stomach:

> So I went in this very cheap-looking restaurant and had doughnuts and coffee. Only, I didn't eat the doughnuts. I couldn't swallow them too well. The thing is, if you get very depressed about something, it's hard as hell to swallow. The waiter was very nice, though. He took them back without charging me. I just drank the coffee. (196)

Holden's gagging on the doughnuts is an allusion to the forty-ninth and final koan contained in the *Mumonkan* (Ch., *Wu-men-kuan: The Gateless Gate*), the renowned medieval Chinese collection assembled in 1228 by Master Mumon Eikai (Wu-men Hui-k'ai). The koan is entitled "Amban's Addition" because a lay student, so-named, later attached it to Mumon's original edition of forty-eight. In it Amban gives a mock portrayal of himself as seeking revenge on old Master Mumon for foisting those forty-eight undigestible koans on any passerby willing to swallow them. The added koan is Amban's "priceless opportunity" to give Mumon a taste of his own medicine:

> Mu-mon has just published forty-eight koans and called the book *Gateless Gate*. He criticizes the old patriarchs' words and actions. I think he is very mischievous. He is like an old doughnut seller trying to catch a passerby to force his doughnuts down his mouth. The customer can neither swallow nor spit out the doughnuts, and this causes suffering. Mu-mon has annoyed everyone enough, so I think I shall add one more as a bargain. I wonder if he himself can eat this bargain. If he can, and digest it well, it will be fine, but if not, we will have to put it back into the frying pan with his forty-eight also and cook them again. Mu-mon, you eat first, before someone else does:

Buddha, according to a sutra, once said: "Stop, stop. Do not speak. The ultimate truth is not even to think."[14]

Undigestible doughnuts are an apt comic image for the psycho-spiritual impasse that koans are designed to produce. Unaided reason does not equip man to comprehend ("swallow") the freedom from, indeed *within*, contradiction (permanence/change, innocence/corruption, childhood/adulthood) promised by Enlightenment. He simply cannot "take it in." Unless he be driven by an intolerable suffocation to summon up from the abyss of consciousness a power equal to this Truth, he will choke on it. Perhaps instinctively sensing this, Holden backs away from the doughnuts before getting completely "stuck." But stuck he is and, at least for a while longer, stuck he will remain between child and grown-up.

Holden's doughnuts echo Amban's doughnuts, and both echo *Mu*, mentioned earlier as the koan of koans or meta-koan. As the signature koan of Rinzai Zen, *Mu* is placed first in the *Mumonkan*. Its wording is as follows:

A monk asked Joshu [a master], "Has a dog Buddha nature?"
Joshu answered, "Mu."[15]

This *Mu*, variously "nothing, not, nothingness, un-, is not, has not, not any,"[16] is assigned by the *roshi* (master) to most Zen novices as an object of meditation (*zazen*). Like any koan, it is not an intellectual exercise, nor does it have any "correct" answer or interpretation. Any answer, verbal or non-verbal, presented by student to master is correct that demonstrates the former's clear intuitive grasp of the main issue: nothing (no thing) is real, all is emptiness; and hence, by virtue of the *coincidentia oppositorum* portended by the Middle Way of the koan, everything is real, all is fullness. Net result: *Mu* is absolute Freedom, ineffable Mystery, ground zero Truth. Hence its traditional representation in Japanese ink-brush calligraphy as a thick doughnut-shaped cipher. (We noted above *Mu*'s similar characterization by Hakuun Yasutani as a half-swallowed "red-hot iron ball that you cannot disgorge despite your every effort.") Doughnut or iron ball, *Mu* is what nearly chokes Holden.

Salinger's most likely source for the doughnut interlude is Nyogen Senzaki and Paul Reps's 1934 edition of *The Gateless Gate*, published by John Murray in Los Angeles. This likelihood is increased by the compilers' inclusion of Amban's "49th koan," in contrast to its omission by "purist" editors of most other English translations. Salinger is also linked to Reps by Alsen (160, n. 21–22), who cites another Reps collection, *101 Zen Stories* (1939), as a probable source for the Zen motifs in *Nine Stories* and "Raise High the Roof Beam, Carpenters." The point of emphasis here, of course, is that Salinger was already interpolating specific elements of Zen lore into the creative process as early as *Catcher*.

Rilke's Carrousel and Holden's Enlightenment

It has been shown that the aim of a koan is, by dint of its logical absurdity, to frustrate the binary either/or structure of ordinary consciousness; in Western terms, to straitjacket the conventional rationalist Aristotelian viewpoint so that something akin to the mystical Platonic can break through. This is why so many koan and anecdotes in the ancient collections feature the imagery of impasse: a monk hanging from a lofty branch by his teeth, or facing the master's bamboo stick no matter what he says or does, or being challenged to take one step forward from atop a 100-foot flagpole. The more oppressive the dilemma, the more favorable the conditions for inner revolution. Clearly the damned-either-way gallows humor of Zen appealed strongly to Salinger's sense of irony. The missing ducks, the half-frozen pond and the gagging doughnuts are intended, as symbolic echoes of classical Zen situations, to lend an aura of both gravity and, in Balzac's sense, comedy to the situation of a youth mired deep in crisis. The novel is all about Holden's weekend at the crossroads. As the reader approaches the climactic scene at the carrousel, the question verily burns: what will Holden *do?* Similarly, the old Zen masters often put this nakedly terrifying question to their spiritual charges for whom they had just devised some intolerable bind.

What Holden does in fact "do" at the carrousel is resolve his life koan. His subsequent "illness" and therapeutic confinement in no way cast doubt on this. Zen literature is replete with accounts of Enlightenment experiences (*kensho* or *satori*) that are so shattering to the individual's conditioned world view that the rush of emancipation they bring is initially experienced as a kind of nervous breakdown. Kapleau reports the case of one Zen student, a Japanese business executive, who, in his own words, one night

> . . . abruptly awakened. At first my mind was foggy. . . . Then all at once I was struck as though by lightning, and the next instant heaven and earth crumbled and disappeared. Instantaneously, like surging waves, a tremendous delight welled up in me, a veritable hurricane of delight, as I laughed loudly and wildly: "Ha, ha, ha, ha, ha, ha! . . . "
> My son told me later he thought I had gone mad. (216)

What one might call Holden's Divine Madness commences with his sudden announcement of his decision to "go home," made to Phoebe at the carrousel: "'Yeah,' I said. I meant it too. I wasn't lying to her. I really did go home afterwards" (212). Perhaps here too Salinger had in mind Suzuki, who describes Enlightenment in lapsarian-mythical terms as the return of conscious will to its "own original abode where there was yet no dualism, and therefore peace prevailed. This longing for the home, however, cannot be satisfied without a long, hard, trying experience. For the thing [consciousness] once divided in two cannot be restored to its former unity until some struggle is gone through with" (*Essays* 131).

However that may be, there can be little doubt of the Zen reference contained in the rain that then begins to fall, as Holden says, "[i]n *buckets*" (212; Salinger's emphasis). Holden's cliché is an "inside" Zen allusion to this shattering or explosive quality that often ushers in an Enlightenment experience. The bucket or pail or barrel that has its bottom smashed through, thus releasing the flow of water heretofore "confined," is a traditional Rinzai metaphor for the aspirant's longed-for breakthrough to spiritual freedom. The image may have its origins in the biography of the medieval Japanese master Bassui by his student Myodo who describes the moment of the former's Enlightenment as a feeling of having "lost his life root, like a barrel whose bottom had been smashed open" (qtd. in Kapleau 166). However, Salinger's source for the image is more likely to have been an anecdote in Senzaki and Reps's *101 Zen Stories* recounting the sudden awakening of the nun Chiyono, who "one moonlit night . . . was carrying water in an old pail bound with bamboo. The bamboo broke and the bottom fell out of the pail, and at that moment Chiyono was set free!" (Reps 31). Of course, in narrating the climactic event of Holden's spiritual breakthrough, Salinger works some deft displacements on the image to avoid obviousness: the water does not rush out through bottomless buckets, rather it is the buckets (of rain) themselves that come pouring down. Similarly, the analogous onrush of tears expressive of the aspirant's emancipation that usually accompanies the bucket image (Myodo says of Bassui that the tears overflowed, "pouring down his face like rain" [qtd. in Kapleau 166]) is truncated in Holden's case to: "I was damn near bawling, I felt so damn happy, if you want to know the truth" (213).

However, what is truly arresting about Salinger's rendering of *Catcher*'s denouement is the particular way he uses the German poet Rilke's *Dinggedicht*, "Das Karussell" (1908), to say the unsayable, that is, to convey through oblique symbolic allusion the essence of Holden's solution to his life koan. Salinger's veneration of Rilke is well known.[17] Rilke is one of very few poets mentioned by name in the fiction.[18] Also, some preliminary scholarship has been done showing influence,[19] but no one has as yet nearly done justice to the profound connection between Rilke's and Salinger's carrousels.

Both poem and novel are about the loss of innocence marking the passage from childhood to maturity. This, as noted above, is precisely the issue (koan) at the root of Holden's crisis: "How can I possibly move on to a world teeming with phonies [change] without becoming one myself [permanence]?", as it were. The reference to "Das Karussell" as a reflection of the miraculous solution at long last welling up in Holden is contained in the blue coat worn by Phoebe as she rides the carrousel. Giddy with delight, Holden exclaims, "I felt so damn happy, . . . I don't know why. It was just that she looked so damn *nice*, the way she kept going around and around, in her blue coat and all" (213). Blue-clad Phoebe alludes to the "kleines, blaues Mädchen" ["little girl in blue"][20] who rides the stag in Rilke's lyric and stands for innocence, that is, the child's capacity for complete absorption in the moment of play. In counterpoint, the older girls in "Karussell" riding nearby already have, like Holden, one foot in adulthood and thus are afflicted, as is he, with that relentless self-consciousness that breeds phoniness, the bane of Holden's existence: " . . . Mädchen, helle, diesem Pferdesprunge/fast schon entwachsen; mitten in dem Schwunge/schauen sie auf, irgendwohin, herüber—" [" . . . girls, so fair, having all but outgrown such play; in mid-ride they look up, at something, over this way—"] (Rilke 228). These girls on Rilke's carrousel, one a child, the others no longer quite, dramatized for Salinger the collision of world views that bedevils Holden.

The solution to any koan is some realization of a dialectical synthesis that shifts the aspirant to a phase of consciousness deeper and more comprehensive than the logico-rational, one that can effortlessly accommodate both terms of the conflict. This realization must be more than intellectual (in fact, intellect need hardly be involved at all); it must have the immediacy of an insight grounded in experience and must take one well beyond the pairs of opposites that are forever dogging the human mind. In Rilke's poem this is subtly indicated in the line, "Und manchesmal ein Lächeln, hergewendet" ["And now and then a wide grin turned this way"] (Rilke 228).[21] The wide grin is that of some child on the carrousel; it is "hergewendet" ["turned this way"], that is, toward the poet-persona. Poet and child, for a flickering instant locked in each other's gaze. What else can this be but the realization of the *coincidentia oppositorum?* The poet is the one who is somehow able to grow up while yet remaining a child. As Rilke says elsewhere, in response to an imaginary interlocutor, the poet is gifted with the ability to behold all things, good and bad, genuine and phoney, with the celebratory eyes of a newborn: "Oh sage, Dichter . . . / Woher dein Recht, in jeglichem Kostüme, / in j eder Maske wahr zu sein?/—Ich rühme" ["So tell me, poet . . . / Wherefore thy right to be in any mask, in any costume true?'/—'I celebrate'"] (Rilke 230). Indeed, just like a new-born, the poet beholds things by *becoming* them. As Keats has it: "The poet has no self; he is forever filling some other body." This I take to be Salinger's understanding of Rilke's "Das Karussell," and it is this understanding, rather viscerally than intellectually experienced, that now overcomes Holden like an ancient dream fulfilled, releasing him from his long bondage to a worn-out world view.

To be sure, Holden is no poet in the conventional sense, but I believe Salinger takes "poet" in this deeper archetypal sense shaped by the German-Romantic tradition to which Rilke was heir and which he in fact fulfilled: the poet represents the cutting edge of human spiritual evolution, one who has, at least once, been struck by lightning, one who has made, however tentatively, the quantum leap from human to cosmic consciousness. This notion of the poet as spiritual archetype also seems to be what Franny is trying to convey to her boyfriend as she struggles to justify her dislike of the self-styled poets in the English Department:

> I mean they're not *real* poets. They're just people that write poems that get published and anthologized all over the place, but they're not *poets*.[22]

The archetype of the poet as (wo)man-child, as a seamless sacerdotal identity of opposites, and therefore as the solution to Holden's koan, is also hinted at in Holden's repeated references at the carrousel to "old Phoebe," the child who incarnates the wisdom of the ages.

In Salinger's multi-veiled allusion to this Rilkean meeting of eyes, this interlocking glance, it is not only man and child, or experience and innocence, that fuse in Holden's at last emancipated spirit, but also, as it were in miniature, the great Wisdom traditions of East and West. For Holden's character, suddenly becoming in this apocalyptic moment more than itself, is a syncretic expression of their mutual recognition of the universal mystical truth of the *coincidentia oppositorum*. In Zen, the recognition of this truth lies at the heart of any koan; in Rilke, its expression reflects a perennial German spiritual insight the lineage of which can be traced back at least as far as Meister Eckhart's "Single Eye" by which man and God view each other.[23] It is Salinger's particular genius in this climactic scene to have brought these great mystical traditions together in the simple, homey tableau of an older brother happily watching his kid sister as she takes a turn on the local merry-go-round. One need hardly point out that all of this is punctuated, so to speak, by the image of the carrousel itself as a mandala-symbol of the dynamic Eye of Wisdom to which the path of Holden Everyyouth inevitably leads.

A final question suggests itself. The Zen masters tell us that to have solved one koan is, at least for a time, to have solved them all, since every koan, upon solution, vouchsafes a glimpse of the "same" Absolute. If, as is argued here, Holden has accomplished this, if, for the duration of his cheerful repose on that park bench (and doubtless well beyond), he basks in the glow of Enlightenment, then why does Salinger have him end his story on a note of lack or deficit, as if he were still ensnared by what Buddhists call *avidya*, that is, the primal Ignorance that gives rise to desire: "About all I know is,

I sort of *miss* everybody I told about. Even old Stradlater and Ackley, for instance. I think I even miss that goddam Maurice. It's funny. Don't ever tell anybody anything. If you do, you start missing everybody" (214)?

Oddly, the question answers itself when taken paradoxically, that is, when one reads "missing" in the paradoxical context of Enlightenment, wherein all contradictions are resolved, as *itself* a form, even the supreme form, of "having." C. S. Lewis, no mean adept in spiritual matters, makes this point most eloquently in his autobiographical description of the state of "Joy," i.e., Enlightenment considered in its affective aspect. Recalling his experience of a walk during which this sense of Joy had been especially acute, he reflects

> . . . what I had felt on the walk had also been desire, and only possession in so far as that kind of desire is itself desirable, is the fullest possession we can know on earth; or rather, because the very nature of Joy makes nonsense of our common distinction between having and wanting. There, to have is to want and to want is to have.[24]

For Holden at this moment, to miss is to have—fully. As for his missing "even . . . that goddam Maurice" (214), it is another curious fact of Enlightenment that, viewed through Its eyes, all things assume an aura of infinite value, however noble or base they may rank on the valuative scales of ordinary consciousness. Suzuki goes so far as to say:

> But with the realization of Enlightenment, the whole affair [i.e., life] changes its aspect, and the order instituted by Ignorance is reversed from top to bottom. What was negative is now positive, and what was positive now negative. Buddhist scholars ought not to forget this revaluation of ideas that comes along with Enlightenment. (*Essays* 139)

To all appearances, Holden Caulfield is neither a poet nor a Buddhist scholar. Yet he is, by novel's end, an intimate of the Truth both stammer to convey.

Conclusion

Indications are that Salinger's interest in Zen slowly waned in the course of the 1950's as he turned to other Eastern religions and to Christianity for inspiration. In fact, the gradient of this waning interest can be traced in terms of the kind of narrative treatment given the Zen motif from *Catcher* (1950) through *Nine Stories* (1953) to "Zooey" (1957) and "Seymour: An Introduction" (1959). Generally speaking, the movement is from implicit to explicit, or from subtext to text. In *Catcher*, Zen has a clear but strictly covert presence.

It is there *as symbolic* echo and oblique allusion, imbuing the "banal" tale of a modern adolescent's identity crisis with the power and gravity of ancient legend. Its use is, in a word, aesthetic—the more so in view of its subtle but profound resonance, as we have seen, with a spiritually akin yet culturally remote literary echo from the German poet Rilke. In *Nine Stories,* Zen still serves a quasi aesthetic function (e.g., Seymour's semi-implicit banana-fish koan, or Teddy's eccentric "emptying-out" theory of education, a transparent reference to the Buddhist concept of *shunyata*), but the one-hand-clapping koan that prefixes the book signals the emergence of Zen as more an intellectual than a creative issue for Salinger. This is precisely its status in "Zooey," where it is lavishly entertained in the probing religious dialogue of brother and sister, and in "Seymour: An Introduction," which features a longish peroration on Zen given by Buddy near its end. As the author's religious enthusiasms shift away from Zen, Zen becomes in the fiction something that has always been anathema to the masters—a subject of discussion.

Of course, Salinger is not to be faulted for this. Passions wax and wane, interests come and go, for artists no less than mere mortals. An artist's only duty is to follow his daimon wherever it may lead. The matter of waning interest is raised here only as an attempt to account for the peculiar failure of previous critics to identify specific elements of Zen in *Catcher.* The announced presence of Zen in the later fiction seems to have lulled most of them into the assumption that it has little or no presence in *Catcher.* Ironically, just the opposite is the case: the presence of the East in *Catcher* is all the stronger precisely for its being unannounced, not to mention covertly commingled with the strains of the poet from the West. Salinger himself recognized this gradual slackening of his ability to make creative use, not only of Zen, but of religion generally, in his work. He fretted over the question whether he really was following his daimon. Hamilton tells us that Salinger, in an unpublished letter to his friend and confidant, Learned Hand, written in the late 1950's, "admits he is well aware that his new [post-Zen] religious preoccupations might turn out to be harmful to his writing, and that he sometimes wishes he could go back to his old methods. But it seemed to him that there was little he could do about controlling the direction of his work" (154). In contrast to Holden who arrives at Enlightenment at the end of a painful inner struggle, Holden's author seems to have been blessed with a touch of Enlightenment at the beginning, only to have it calcify with the passing years into something not unlike those glass-encased exhibits in his masterly novel.

Notes

1. J. D. Salinger, *The Catcher in the Rye* (1951; Boston: Little, Brown, 1991) 13; hereafter referenced parenthetically in text by page number.

2. Thus the epigraph to *Nine Stories* (1953; Boston: Little, Brown, 1991) quoting the well-known koan of Rinzai master Hakuin: "We know the sound of two hands clapping. But what is the sound of one hand clapping?", and the occasional detailed discussions of Zen philosophy in "Zooey" (1957) and "Seymour: An Introduction" (1959). Eberhard Alsen, *Salinger's Glass Stories as a Composite Novel* (New York: Whitston, 1983) 158–159, lists some nine scholars who, during the years 1957–1971, took up the Zen theme in these post-*Catcher* works. I would add Tom Davis, "The Sound of One Hand Clapping," *Wisconsin Studies in Contemporary Literature* 4 (1963): 41–47; and Sidney Finkelstein, *Existentialism and Alienation in American Literature* (New York: International, 1965) 219–234. Also, by way of updating the list: Thomas Edwin Brinkley, "J. D. Salinger: A Study of His Eclecticism—Zooey as Existential Zen Therapist," diss., Ohio State University, 1976; James Lundquist, *J. D. Salinger* (New York: Ungar, 1979); Katsuhiko Takeda, "Uchi naru Zen v.s. Soto naru Zen," *J. D. Salinger Bungaku no Kenkyu*, ed. Hisashi Shigeo and Ayako Sato (Tokyo: Tokyo Shirakawa Shoin, 1983); and Yasuhiro Tae, "Between Suicide and Enlightenment," *Kyushu American Literature* 26 (1985): 21–27.

3. E.g., Bernice and Sanford Goldstein, "Zen and Salinger," *Modern Fiction Studies* 12 (1966): 313–324 and "Some Zen References in Salinger," *Literature East and West* 15 (1971): 83–95; Gerald Rosen, *Zen in the Art of J. D. Salinger,* Modern Authors Monograph Series 3 (Berkeley: Creative Arts, 1977) throughout; and Lundquist 52–53, 70–74.

4. Lundquist (69–114) views *Nine Stories* as a synthesis of Zen aesthetic principles and the art of the short story.

5. John Skow, "Sonny: An Introduction," *Time* 15 Sept. 1961: 84–90.

6. For more on the compositional chronology of *Catcher,* see Ian Hamilton, *In Search of J. D. Salinger* (New York: Vintage, 1989) 113–116. See also p. 267 above.

7. D. T. Suzuki, *Essays in Zen Buddhism (First Series)* (1949; New York: Evergreen-Grove, 1961) 240.

8. A few commentators have read the ducks as reflecting, in one way or another, Holden's preoccupation with the problems of change (hence, also death) and permanence: e.g., James F. Light, "Salinger's *The Catcher in the Rye,*" *Explicator* 18 (1960): item 59; Lundquist (40); Rosen (23); and John M. Howell, "Salinger in the Wasteland," *Critical Essays on Salinger's "The Catcher in the Rye."* ed. Joel Salzburg (Boston: G. K. Hall, 1990) 85–42. No one, however, has heretofore recognized the Zen source of the episode.

9. Philip Kapleau, ed., *The Three Pillars of Zen: Teaching, Practice and Enlightenment,* rev. ed. (Garden City, NY: Doubleday, 1980) 12.

10. Hakuun Yasurani, as qtd. in Kapleau (76).

11. This according to Donna Slawsky, currently reference librarian for HarperCollins, in a telephone interview with the present author on Oct. 27, 1995.

12. According to Hamilton (126–127), in 1953 Salinger gave a Zen booklist to writer-friend Leila Hadley.

13. As Alsen (130) points out, it is Suzuki's *Manual of Zen Buddhism,* in its 1950 Rider edition, from which Salinger quotes that religion's Four Great Vows in "Zooey." Moreover, Alsen includes the *Essays* as among those works used by Salinger in forming "the basis of Seymour's eclectic religious philosophy" (257–258) in the Glass stories.

14. Paul Reps, ed., *Zen Flesh, Zen Bones: A Collection of Zen and Pre-Zen Writings* (New York: Anchor-Doubleday, n.d.) 128.

15. Katsuki Sekida, ed., *Two Zen Classics: Mumonkan and Hekiganroku* (New York: Weatherhill, 1977) 27.

16. *The Shambhala Dictionary of Buddhism and Zen*, trans. Michael K. Kohn, ed. Ingrid Fischer-Schreiber, et al. (Boston: Shambhala, 1991).

17. See Hamilton (108); also, and esp., Edward Stone, "Salinger's Carrousel," *Modern Fiction Studies* 13 (1967–1968): 521.

18. There is an allusion to the fourth of Rilke's "Duino Elegies" in "Franny." See *Franny and Zooey* (1961; Boston: Little, Brown, 1991) 6.

19. For a comparison of the two carrousels, see Stone (520–523), with whose judgment that "Salinger took the [carrousel] ride itself not for its meaning but merely as a point of departure" (523) I beg to differ. For the Rilke-Salinger connection in the broader sense, see Frederick L. Gwynn and Joseph L. Blotner, *The Fiction of J. D. Salinger* (Pittsburgh: University of Pittsburgh Press, 1958).

20. Rainer Maria Rilke, "Das Karussell," *German Literature since Goethe*, ed. Ernst Feise and Harry Steinhauer, 2 vols. (Boston: Houghton Mifflin, 1958–1959) 2: 228. Translations of Rilke's German are my own.

21. It is interesting to note that, although Rilke was probably not acquainted with Zen, he did have an avid interest in neighboring spiritual practices, such as Hindu yoga, as pathways to expanded consciousness (see Carossa, "Begegnung mit Rilke," *German Literature since Goethe* 2: 330–337). His early *Dinggedichte*, including "Das Karussell," are well known as creative products of some sort of intense sustained contemplation or meditation.

22. *Franny and Zooey* 18. Similarly, the German-Romantic view of the poet as spiritual adept in essence and wordsmith only by accident or convention characterizes Buddy's "rehabilitation" of his brother Seymour's image: " . . . not one Goddamn person . . . had ever seen him for what he really was. A poet, for God's sake. And I mean a poet. If he never wrote a line of poetry, he could still flash what he had at you with the back of his ear if he wanted to." See *Raise High the Roof Beam, Carpenters and Seymour: An Introduction* (1963; Boston: Little, Brown, 1991) 60.

23. The line from Eckhart down to Rilke would include, among others, the "Philosophical Eye" or "Mirror of Wisdom" of the great Baroque mystic Jacob Böhme and the flower-calyx-eye symbolism of such mystically inclined Romantic poets as Novalis and E. T. A. Hoffmann. Contemporary to Rilke is, of course, the archetypal psychology of Carl Jung for whom the Eye signifies the ideal Self that is to be realized, or at least approached, through the psycho-spiritual process of individuation.

24. C. S. Lewis, *Surprised by Joy: The Shape of My Early Life* (New York: Harvest-Harcourt Brace Jovanovich, 1955) 166.

25. The problem of sustaining the creative tension of the dialectic between paradigmatic poles that may be termed variously implicit/explicit, subtextual/ textual or aesthetic/intellectual (as here), immediate/mediate or sudden/gradual (the Zen Enlightenment paradigm), or, in Jacques Derrida's recent parlance, poetic/ rabbinical, without allowing oneself to be pulled too closely to the one pole or the other, is, of course, inescapable, not only for Salinger but for anyone taking a serious interest in Zen, or, for that matter, in the free-flowing quality of consciousness typically associated with creative expression of any kind. Zen has always construed itself as the realization of "immediate experience." Questions from students that engage discriminative thought (e.g., "What is the highest principle of Buddhism?") are usually roundly rebuffed by masters, particularly in the Rinzai tradition, with

a shout ("Kwatz!"), a clout or a nonsensical expletive. Yet even the most sincere intention or effort to "experience immediately" only lands one back in shallow intellectual modeling. The question for us as beings blessed with / condemned to self-reflection is: how can we possibly have immediate experience without, at the same time, suppressing its intellectualization; or, conversely, allowing such intellectualization to occur as it will, how can we "preserve" the immediacy of the experience? This paradox constitutes a koan every bit as challenging as Holden's. (It is, in fact, a variant of it.) One might call it the author's koan and be inclined to judge that Salinger, with his gradual "Fall" into Zen intellectualism, dealt with it rather less successfully than did his protagonist with his. For a most thoughtful reflection on this paradox in terms of the complex relationship that obtains between the writer—be he scholar or novelist—and the religio-cultural tradition about which he writes, see Bernard Faure, *The Rhetoric of Immediacy: A Cultural Critique of Chan/Zen Buddhism* (Princeton, N.J.: Princeton University Press, 1991).

STEPHEN J. WHITFIELD

Cherished and Cursed: Toward a Social History
of The Catcher in the Rye

The plot is brief: in 1949 or perhaps 1950, over the course of three days
during the Christmas season, a sixteen-year-old takes a picaresque journey
to his New York City home from the third private school to expel him.
The narrator recounts his experiences and opinions from a sanitarium in
California. A heavy smoker, Holden Caulfield claims to be already six feet,
two inches tall and to have wisps of grey hair; and he wonders what happens to the ducks when the ponds freeze in winter. The novel was published
on 16 July 1951, sold for $3.00, and was a Book-of-the-Month Club selec-
tion. Within two weeks, it had been reprinted five times, the next month
three more times—though by the third edition the jacket photograph of the
author had quietly disappeared. His book stayed on the best-seller list for
thirty weeks, though never above fourth place.[1]

Costing 75¢, the Bantam paperback edition appeared in 1964. By 1981,
when the same edition went for $2.50, sales still held steady, between twenty
and thirty thousand copies per month, about a quarter of a million copies
annually. In paperback the novel sold over three million copies between 1953
and 1964, climbed even higher by the 1980s, and continues to attract about
as many buyers as it did in 1951. The durability of its appeal is astonishing.
The Catcher in the Rye has gone through over seventy printings and has spread

The New England Quarterly, Volume LXX, Number 4 (December 1997): pp. 567–600.
Copyright © 1997 by The New England Quarterly.

into thirty languages. Three decades after it first appeared, a mint copy of the first edition was already fetching about $200.[2]

Critical and academic interest has been less consistent; and how J. D. Salinger's only novel achieved acclaim is still a bit mystifying. After its first impact came neglect: following the book reviews, only three critical pieces appeared in the first five years. In the next four years, at least seventy essays on *The Catcher in the Rye* were published in American and British magazines. Salinger's biographer explained why: "A feature of the youthquake was, of course, that students could now tell their teachers what to read." Ian Hamilton also notes that by the mid-1950s the novel had "become the book all brooding adolescents had to buy, [and on campuses] the indispensable manual from which cool styles of disaffection could be borrowed."[3] No American writer over the past half-century has entranced serious young readers more than Salinger, whose novel about the flight from Pencey Prep may lag behind only *Of Mice and Men* on public-school required reading lists.[4] And his fiction has inspired other writers as well; the late Harold Brodkey, for example, considered it "the most influential body of work in English prose by anyone since Hemingway."[5]

One explanation for why *The Catcher in the Rye* has enjoyed such a sustained readership came over two decades after the novel was first published—from a middle-aged Holden Caulfield himself, as imagined by journalist Stefan Kanfer: "The new audience is never very different from the old Holden. They may not know the words, but they can hum along with the malady. My distress is theirs. They, too, long for the role of adolescent savior. They, too, are aware of the imminent death in life. As far as the sexual explosion is concerned, I suspect a lot of what you've heard is just noise." Sex "still remains a mystery to the adolescent. I have no cure, only consolation: someone has passed this way before." Objections to schlock and vulgarity and physical decline, and preferences for the pastoral over the machine continue to resonate, "Holden" suspects;[6] and so long as the United States continues to operate very much this side of paradise, a reluctance to inherit what the grown-ups have bequeathed is bound to enlist sympathy. The fantasy of withdrawal and retreat to the countryside ("Massachusetts and Vermont, and all around there . . . [are] beautiful as hell up there. It really is.") is not only a commonplace yearning but also advice Holden's creator elected to take by moving to Cornish, New Hampshire.[7]

But it should be conceded that generally it's the grown-ups who are in charge, and many of them have wanted to ban the widely beloved novel. Why *The Catcher in the Rye* has been censored (and censured) as well as cherished is a curiosity worth examining for its own sake. But how so transparently charming a novel can also exercise a peculiar allure and even emit disturbing danger signals may serve as an entrée into post-war American culture as well.

Bad Boys, Bad Readers

One weird episode inspired by *The Catcher in the Rye* involves Jerry Lewis. He tried to buy the movie rights, which were not for sale, and to play the lead. One problem was that the director did not read the book until the 1960s, when he was already well into his thirties. Playing the protagonist would have been a stretch, but *le roi de crazy* felt some affinity for Salinger (whom Lewis never met): "He's nuts also." Curiously Holden himself mentions the word "crazy" and its cognates (like "mad," "madman," and "insane") over fifty times, more than the reverberant "phony."[8]

Indeed the history of this novel cannot be disentangled from the way the mentally unbalanced have read it. In one instance the reader is himself fictional: the protagonist of John Fowles's first book, which captures the unnerving character of Salinger's only novel as an index of taste, perhaps of moral taste. In the second section of *The Collector*, told from the viewpoint of the victim, the kidnapped Miranda Grey recounts in her diary that she asks her captor, lepidopterist Frederick Clegg, whether he reads "proper books—real books." When he admits that "light novels are more my line," she recommends *The Catcher in the Rye* instead: "I've almost finished it. Do you know I've read it twice and I'm five years younger than you are?" Sullenly he promises to read it. Later she notices him doing so, "several times . . . look[ing] to see how many pages more he had to read. He reads it only to show me how hard he is trying." After the duty has been discharged, over a week later, the collector admits: "I don't see much point in it." When Miranda counters, "You realize this is one of the most brilliant studies of adolescence ever written?" he responds that Holden "sounds a mess to me."

"Of course he's a mess. But he realizes he's a mess, he tries to express what he feels, he's a human being for all his faults. Don't you even feel sorry for him?"

"I don't like the way he talks."

"I don't like the way you talk," she replies. "But I don't treat you as below any serious notice or sympathy."

Clegg acknowledges: "I suppose it's very clever. To write like that and all."

"I gave you that book to read because I thought you would feel identified with him. You're a Holden Caulfield. He doesn't fit anywhere and you don't."

"I don't wonder, the way he goes on. He doesn't try to fit."

Miranda insists: "He tries to construct some sort of reality in his life, some sort of decency."

"It's not realistic. Going to a posh school and his parents having money. He wouldn't behave like that. In my opinion."

She has the final word (at least in her diary): "You get on the
back of everything vital, everything trying to be honest and free,
and you bear it down."

Modern art, she realizes, embarrasses and fascinates Clegg; it "shocks him"
and stirs "guilty ideas in him" because he sees it as "*all* vaguely immoral."
For the mass audience at which William Wyler's 1965 film adaptation was
aimed, Clegg's aesthetic world is made less repellent and more conventional,
and the conversation about *The Catcher in the Rye* is abbreviated.[9]

In a more class-conscious society than is the United States, Fowles's
loner finds something repugnant about the recklessness of the privileged
protagonist. In a more violent society than England, types like Frederick
Clegg might identify with Holden Caulfield's alienation from "normal"
people so thoroughly that they become assassins. To be sure, *The Catcher in
the Rye* is bereft of violence; and no novel seems less likely to activate the
impulse to "lock and load." But this book nevertheless has exercised an eerie
allure for asocial young men who, glomming on to Holden's estrangement,
yield to the terrifying temptations of murder. "Lacking a sense of who he
is," such a person "shops among artifacts of our culture—books, movies, TV
programs, song lyrics, newspaper clippings—to fashion a character." Instead
of authentic individuality, Priscilla Johnson McMillan has written, "all that
is left is a collection of cultural shards—the bits and pieces of popular culture, torn from their contexts."[10]

In December 1980, with a copy of Salinger's novel in his pocket,
Mark David Chapman murdered John Lennon. Before the police arrived,
the assassin began reading the novel to himself and, when he was sentenced, read aloud the passage that begins with "anyway, I keep picturing
all these little kids" and ends with "I'd just be the catcher in the rye and
all" (pp. 224–225). Daniel M. Stashower has speculated ingeniously that
Chapman wanted the former Beatle's innocence to be preserved in the
only way possible—by death (the fate of Holden's revered brother Allie).
Of course it could be argued that the assassin was not a conscientious
reader, since Holden realizes on the carrousel that children have to be left
alone, that they cannot be saved from themselves: "The thing with kids is,
if they want to grab for the gold ring, you have to let them do it, and not
say anything. If they fall off, they fall off" (pp. 273–274). No older catcher
should try to intervene.[11]

Nor was Chapman the only Beatles fan to reify happiness as a warm
gun. John Hinckley, Jr., described himself in his high school days as "a rebel
without a cause" and was shocked to hear that Lennon had been murdered.
A year later Hinckley himself tried to kill President Reagan. In Hinckley's
hotel room, police found, along with a 1981 John Lennon color calendar,

Salinger's novel among a half-dozen paperbacks. Noting the "gruesome congruences between these loners," Richard Schickel wondered whether Chapman and Hinckley could "really believe their disaffections were similar to Holden Caulfield's."[12]

One stab at an answer would be provided in John Guare's play *Six Degrees of Separation*, which opened in New York in 1990 and which he adapted for Fred Schepsi's film three years later. An imposter calling himself Paul insinuates himself into a well-heeled family; he is a perfect stranger (or appears to be). Pretending to be a Harvard undergraduate who has just been mugged, posing as the son of actor Sidney Poitier, Paul claims that his thesis is devoted to Salinger's novel and its odd connections to criminal loners:

> A substitute teacher out on Long Island was dropped from his job for fighting with a student. A few weeks later, the teacher returned to the classroom, shot the student unsuccessfully, held the class hostage and then shot himself. Successfully. This fact caught my eye: last sentence, *Times*. A neighbor described him as a nice boy. Always reading *Catcher in the Rye*.

Paul then mentions "the nitwit—Chapman" and insists that "the reading of that book would be his defense" for having killed Lennon. Hinckley, too, had "said if you want my defense all you have to do is read *Catcher in the Rye*. It seemed to be time to read it again." Paul reads it as a "manifesto of hate" against phonies,

> a touching story, comic because the boy wants to do so much and can't do anything. Hates all phoniness and only lies to others. Wants everyone to like him, is only hateful, and is completely self-involved. In other words, a pretty accurate picture of a male adolescent. And what alarms me about the book—not the book so much as the aura about it—is this: The book is primarily about paralysis. The boy can't function. And at the end, before he can run away and start a new life, it starts to rain and he folds. . . . But the aura around this book of Salinger's—which perhaps should be read by everyone *but* young men—is this: It mirrors like a fun house mirror and amplifies like a distorted speaker one of the great tragedies of our times—the death of the imagination, [which] now stands as a synonym for something outside ourselves.

A smooth liar, Paul later admits (or claims) that a Groton commencement address delivered a couple of years earlier was the source of his insights.[13]

Beloved and Banned

Holden has thus been born to trouble—yet another reminder that, in the opinion of long queues of literary critics, you can't know about him without your having read a book by Mr. Mark Twain called *The Adventures of Huckleberry Finn*, which told the truth mainly about the intensity of the yearning for authenticity and innocence that marks the picaresque quest. Huck and Holden share the fate of being both beloved *and* banned; such reactions were not unrelated. When the Concord (Massachusetts) public library proscribed *The Adventures of Huckleberry Finn* soon after its publication, the author gloated that not even his *Innocents Abroad* had sold more copies more quickly; and "those idiots in Concord" "have given us a rattling tip-top puff which will go into every paper in the country. . . . That will sell 25,000 copies for us sure."[14]

Salinger's novel does not appear to have been kept off the shelves in Concord but did cause enough of a stir to make the short list of the most banned books in school libraries, curricula, and public libraries.[15] In 1973 the *American School Board Journal* called this monster best-seller "the most widely censored book in the United States."[16] It was noted nearly a decade later that *The Catcher in the Rye* "had the dubious distinction of being at once the most frequently censored book across the nation and the second-most frequently taught novel in public high schools."[17] Anne Levinson, the assistant director of the Office of Intellectual Freedom in Chicago, called *The Catcher in the Rye* probably "a perennial No. 1 on the censorship hit list," narrowly ahead of *Of Mice and Men* and *The Grapes of Wrath* and perhaps of Eldridge Cleaver's *Soul on Ice* as well.[18] No postwar American novel has been subjected to more—and more intense—efforts to prevent the young from reading it.

Some examples: The National Organization for Decent Literature declared it objectionable by 1956. Five years later a teacher in a San Jose, California, high school who had included the novel on the twelfth-grade supplementary reading list was transferred and the novel dropped. *The Catcher in the Rye* was excised from the list of approved books in Kershaw County, South Carolina, after the sheriff of Camden declared part of the novel obscene.[19] In 1978 the novel was banned in the high schools of Issaquah, Washington, in the wake of a campaign led by a diligent citizen who tabulated 785 "profanities" and charged that including Holden in the syllabus was "part of an overall Communist plot in which a lot of people are used and may not even be aware of it."[20] Three school board members in Issaquah not only voted in favor of banning *The Catcher in the Rye* but also against renewing the contract of the school superintendent who had explicitly sanctioned the right of English teachers to assign the book. The board members were recalled, however. A school board member also confiscated a copy of Salinger's novel from a high school library in Asheville, North Carolina, in 1973. Several high school teachers have been fired or forced to resign for having assigned *The Catcher in the Rye*.[21]

California was the site of two well-reported incidents. The first erupted in 1962 in Temple City, near Pasadena, at a Board of Education meeting. Salinger's book had been assigned as supplementary reading for the eleventh grade. A parent objected, in the main, to the "crude, profane and obscene" language. For good measure, though, the book was also condemned for its literary assault on patriotism, "home life, [the] teaching profession, religion and so forth." Another vigilant parent, imploring the President of the United States summarily to fire anyone writing such a book, had obviously confused the reclusive novelist with John F. Kennedy's amiable press secretary, Pierre Salinger.[22]

The Catcher in the Rye was also banned from the supplementary reading list of Boron High School, located on the edge of the Mojave Desert. The proscription had an interesting effect. Salinger "has gained a new readership among townspeople," the *New York Times* reported, "and Helen Nelson, the local librarian, has a waiting list of fifteen people for the book that she says has been sitting on the shelf all these years pretty much unnoticed." The campaign against the book had been fueled by its profanity, which aroused the most heated objections. Vickie Swindler, the parent of a fourteen-year-old girl, was startled to see three "goddamns" on page 32. She recalled phoning the school and demanding to know: "How the hell [*sic*] did this teacher [Shelley Keller-Gage] get this book?" Locals who sympathized with the censors offered a curious interpretation of their motives, which they compared to Holden's dream of becoming a catcher in the rye to keep innocence intact; the protagonist and the parents trying to muzzle him shared a desire to exempt children from the vulgarity and corruption of the adult world. Yet, as Mrs. Keller-Gage noted, "Things are not innocent any more, and I think we've got to help them [i.e., children] deal with that, to make responsible choices, to be responsible citizens." Parents were "wanting to preserve the innocence of the children" in vain. The *Times* reported that she offered an alternative assignment for pupils whose parents were opposed to *The Catcher in the Rye:* Ray Bradbury's *Dandelion Wine*.[23]

When the ban took effect in the new term, Mrs. Keller-Gage put her three dozen copies of Salinger's novel "on a top shelf of her classroom closet, inside a tightly taped cardboard box." Raise high the bookshelf, censors. In place of *The Catcher in the Rye*, she announced, she would assign another Bradbury novel, *Fahrenheit 451*,[24] the title referring to the presumed "temperature at which book-paper catches fire, and burns." This dystopian novel about book-burning was published in 1953, though a shorter version, entitled "The Fireman," had appeared in *Galaxy Science Fiction* in 1950. Both versions were too early to allude to Salinger's novel, which is neither shown nor recited in François Truffaut's 1966 film adaptation (though one item visibly consumed is an issue of *Cahiers du Cinéma*).

Efforts at suppression were not confined to secondary schools. A prominent Houston attorney, "whose daughter had been assigned the novel in an
English class at the University of Texas, threatened to remove the girl from
the University," *Harper's* reported. "The aggrieved father sent copies [of the
novel] to the governor, the chancellor of the university, and a number of state
officials. The state senator from Houston threatened to read passages from
the book on the senate floor to show the sort of thing they teach in Austin.
The lawyer-father said Salinger used language 'no sane person would use' and
accused the university of 'corrupting the moral fibers [*sic*] of our youth.'" He
conceded that the novel "is not a hard-core Communist-type book, but it en-
courages a lessening of spiritual values which in turn leads to communism."[25]

In making appointments to the department of English at the University
of Montana, Leslie A. Fiedler recalled that "the only unforgivable thing in the
university or the state was to be 'controversial.'" He nevertheless "began to make
offers to young instructors who had quarreled with their administrators, or had
asked their students to read *Catcher in the Rye*, or had themselves written poetry
containing dirty words, or were flagrantly Jewish or simply Black." The narrator of a recent academic novel, *Mustang Sally*, recalls that "the chairman of the
department has asked us all to use our best judgment in avoiding confrontation
with the evangelicals . . . such as the group who staged a 'pray-in' at the Greens-
burg High School library because *The Catcher in the Rye* was on the shelves. It
has since been removed, along with the principal." No wonder, then, that one
columnist, though writing for the newspaper of record, whimsically claimed to
"lose count of the number of times the book has been challenged or banned."[26]

Such animosity had become a predictable feature of the far right by
the 1980s, when an outfit named Educational Research Analysts, financed
by Richard Viguerie, a leading fundraiser for right-wing organizations, was
formed to examine nearly every textbook considered for adoption anywhere
in the nation. "The group has assembled a list of 67 categories under which a
book may be banned. Category 43 ('Trash') included *The Catcher in the Rye*,"
the *New Republic* reported. Perhaps Salinger should have counted his bless-
ings, since the eclectic Category 44 consisted of the "works of questionable
writers" like Malcolm X, Langston Hughes, and Ogden Nash.[27]

It is more surprising that moral objections surfaced in the pages of
Ramparts, the brashest of the magazines to give a radical tincture to the
1960s. The monthly had begun under Roman Catholic auspices, however;
and though Simone de Beauvoir's *The Second Sex* was deemed a work of depravity on the *Index Librorum Prohibitorum*, Salinger was accorded the same
treatment as Genet, Proust, Joyce, and D. H. Lawrence: omission.[28] But individual Catholics could still get incensed over *The Catcher in the Rye*, as the
new editor of *Ramparts*, Warren Hinckle, discovered one evening. He was

having a conversation with the new fiction editor, Helen Keating, who was married to the magazine's new publisher. Hinckle recalled:

> A great debate somehow began over the rather precious subject of J. D. Salinger. The setting was vaguely Inquisitional. . . . They all listened attentively as [Edward] Keating, suddenly a fiery prosecutor, denounced Salinger for moral turpitude. Keating expressed similar opinions about the degeneracy of writers such as Tennessee Williams and Henry Miller: corruption, moral decay, the erosion of the classic values of Western Civilization, et cetera, ad infinitum. His special contempt for Salinger seemed to have something to do with the fact that he had found his oldest son reading a paperback book by the man.

Keating became enraged enough to make "the hyperbolic assertion, which he later retracted, that if he were President, he would put J. D. Salinger in jail! I asked why. 'Because he's dirty,' Ed said. I barely recalled something in *The Catcher in the Rye* about Holden Caulfield in the back seat unhooking a girl's bra," Hinckle recalled. Despite the lyric, "If a body catch a body," in fact few popular novels are so fully exempt from the leer of the sensualist; and even though Holden claims to be "probably the biggest sex maniac you ever saw," he admits it's only "in my *mind*" (p. 81).

In any case, Hinckle was baffled by Keating's tirade and "unleashed a more impassioned defense of Salinger than I normally would have felt impelled to make of a voguish writer whose mortal sin was his Ivy League slickness." The chief consequence of the argument was Keating's discovery of a "bomb," by which he meant "a hot story. The 'bomb' which exploded in the first issue of *Ramparts* was the idea of a symposium on J. D. Salinger" with Hinckle for the defense and Keating and a friend of his for the prosecution. That friend, Robert O. Bowen, complained in the inaugural issue in 1962 that Salinger was not only anti-Catholic but somehow also "pro-Jewish and pro-Negro." Bowen accused the novelist of being so subversive that he was "vehemently anti-Army" (though Salinger had landed on Utah Beach on D-Day), "even anti-America," a writer who subscribed to "the sick line transmitted by Mort Sahl" and other "cosmopolitan think people." Though Bowen was vague in identifying the sinister campaigns this impenetrably private novelist was managing to wage, alignments with the Anti-Defamation League and "other Jewish pressure groups" were duly noted, and Salinger's sympathy for "Negro chauvinism" was denounced. "Let those of us who are Christian and who love life lay this book aside as the weapon of an enemy," Bowen advised.[29] Such was the level of literary analysis at the birth of *Ramparts*.

The Catcher in the Rye has even taken on an iconic significance precisely because it is reviled as well as revered. What if the Third Reich had won the Second World War by defeating Britain? one novelist has wondered. Set in 1964, *Fatherland* imagines a past in which Salinger is among four foreign authors listed as objectionable to the Greater Reich. Those writers, banned by the authorities, are esteemed by younger Germans "rebelling against their parents. Questioning the state. Listening to American radio stations. Circulating their crudely printed copies of proscribed books. . . . Chiefly, they protested against the war—the seemingly endless struggle against the American-backed Soviet guerrillas." But forget about a history that never happened. One of the two regimes that *had* supplanted the defeated Reich was the German Democratic Republic, whose censors were wary of American cultural imports. In the 1960s, Kurt Hager served as the leading ideologist on the Central Committee of the East German regime. Resisting publication of a translation of Salinger's novel, Hager feared that its protagonist might captivate Communist youth. Though a translation did eventually appear and proved popular among young readers in the GDR, Hager refused to give up the fight. Appropriate role models were "winners," he insisted, like the regime's Olympic athletes, not "losers" like Holden Caulfield.[30]

Yet anti-anti-Communism could make use of the novel too. Its reputation for inciting censorious anxiety had become so great by 1990 that in the film *Guilty by Suspicion,* a terrified screenwriter is shown burning his books in his driveway a few hours after testifying before a rump session of the House Un-American Activities Committee. Shocked at this bonfire of the humanities, director David Merrill (Robert De Niro) categorizes what goes up in flames as "all good books"—though the only titles he cites are *The Adventures of Tom Sawyer* and *The Catcher in the Rye.* The decision of writer-director Irwin Winkler to include Salinger's novel, however, is historically (if not canonically) implausible. When the film opens in September 1951, Merrill is shown returning from two months in France; a hot-off-the-press copy of the bestseller must therefore have been rushed to him in Paris if he could pronounce on the merits of the book on his first evening back in Los Angeles.

The attacks on *The Catcher in the Rye* gathered a momentum of their own and "show no signs of tapering off," one student of book-banning concluded in 1979. The novel became so notorious for igniting controversy "that many censors freely admit they have never read it, but are relying on the reputation the book has garnered."[31] Anne Levinson added: "Usually the complaints have to do with blasphemy or what people feel is irreligious. Or they say they find the language generally offensive or vulgar, or there is a sort of general 'family values' kind of complaint, that the book undermines parental authority, that the portrayal of Holden Caulfield is not a good role model for teenagers." It was judged suitable for Chelsea Clinton, however. In 1993 the First Lady gave her daughter a copy to read while vacationing on Martha's Vineyard. *The Boston Globe* used the occasion to editorialize against persistent censorship, since "Salinger's novel of a 1950s coming of age still ranks among the works most frequently challenged by parents seeking to sanitize their children's school reading."[32]

Assigning Meaning to Growing Up Absurd

Few American novels of the postwar era have elicited as much scholarly and critical attention as *The Catcher in the Rye*, and therefore little that is fresh can still be proposed about so closely analyzed a text. But the social context within which the novel has generated such anxiety remains open to interpretation. If anything new can be said about this book, its status within the cross-hairs of censors offers the greatest promise. What needs further consideration is not why this novel is so endearing but why it has inspired campaigns to ban it. Literary critics have tended to expose the uncanny artistry by which Salinger made Holden Caulfield into the loved one but have been far less curious about the intensity of the desire to muffle him. It is nevertheless possible to isolate several explanations for the power of this novel to affect—and disturb—readers outside of departments of English.

The "culture wars" of the last third of the twentieth century are fundamentally debates about the 1960s. That decade marked the end of what historian Tom Engelhardt has labeled "victory culture," indeed the end of "the American Way of Life," phrased in the singular. The 1960s constituted a caesura in the formation of national self-definition, nor has confidence in *e pluribus unum* been entirely restored. At first glance it might seem surprising for *The Catcher in the Rye* to have contributed in some small fashion to fragmentation. Nevertheless such a case, however tentative, has been advanced. Since nothing in history is created *ex nihilo*, at least part of the 1960s, it has been argued, must have sprung from at least part of the 1950s.

Literary critics Carol and Richard Ohmann, for example, concede that the young narrator lacks the will to try to change society. They nevertheless contend that his creator recorded "a serious critical mimesis of bourgeois life in the Eastern United States, ca. 1950—of snobbery, privilege, class injury, culture as a badge of superiority, sexual exploitation, education subordinated to status, warped social feeling, competitiveness, stunted human possibility, the list could go on." They praise Salinger's acuity "in imagining these hurtful things, though not in explaining them"—or in hinting how they might be corrected. *The Catcher in the Rye* thus "mirrors a contradiction of bourgeois society" and of "advanced capitalism," which promises many good things but frustrates their acquisition and equitable distribution. In this manner readers are encouraged at least to conceive of the urgent *need* for change, even if they're not able to reconfigure Holden's musings into a manual for enacting it.[33]

That moment would have to await the crisis of the Vietnam War, which "converted Salinger's novel into a catalyst for revolt, converting anomie into objectified anger," John Seelye has argued. *The Catcher in the Rye* became "a threshold text to the decade of the sixties, ten years after it appeared at the start of the fifties, [when it was] a minority text stating a minor view." In the axial shift to the left that occurred in the 1960s, the sensibility of a prep school drop-out could be re-charged and politicized: "*Catcher* likewise supplied not only the rationale for the antiwar, anti-regimentation movements of the sixties and seventies but provided the anti-ideological basis for many of the actual novels about Vietnam."[34]

The 1960s mavericks ("the highly sensitive, the tormented") who would brand social injustice as itself obscene were, according to Charles Reich, real-life versions of what Holden had groped toward becoming. Salinger's protagonist may be too young, or too rich, to bestir himself outward. But he was "a fictional version of the first young precursors of Consciousness III. Perhaps there was always a bit of Consciousness III in every teenager, but normally it quickly vanished. Holden sees through the established world: they are phonies and he is merciless in his honesty. But what was someone like Holden to do? A subculture of 'beats' grew up, and a beatnik world flourished briefly, but for most people it represented only another dead end," Reich commented. "Other Holdens might reject the legal profession and try teaching literature or writing instead, letting their hair grow a little bit longer as well. But they remained separated individuals, usually ones from affluent but unhappy, tortured family backgrounds, and their differences with society were paid for by isolation." In making America more green, Holden was portrayed as an avatar of "subterranean awareness."[35]

Daniel Isaacson also reads the novel as seeding later revolt. The narrator of E. L. Doctorow's *The Book of Daniel*, published exactly two decades after *The Catcher in the Rye*, even echoes Holden in self-consciously repudiating Dickens's contribution to Con II: "Let's see, what other David Copperfield kind of crap" should he tell you? But the personal quickly becomes political, when Daniel insists that "the Trustees of Ohio State were right in 1956 when they canned the English instructor for assigning *Catcher in the Rye* to his freshman class. They knew there is no qualitative difference between the kid who thinks it's funny to fart in chapel, and Che Guevara. They knew then Holden Caulfield would found SDS."[36]

Of course Daniel thinks of himself as an outcast and is eager to re-establish and legitimate his radical lineage, and so his assumption that the trustees might have been shrewd enough to foresee guerrillas in the mist must be treated with skepticism. But consider Tom Hayden, a founder of Students for a Democratic Society (and in the 1950s a parishioner of Father Charles Coughlin in Royal Oak, Michigan). As a teenager Hayden had considered

Salinger's protagonist (along with novelist Jack Kerouac and actor James Dean) an "alternative cultural model." "The life crises they personified spawned . . . political activism," which some who had been adolescents in the 1950s found liberating. Hayden remembers being touched not only by Holden's assault on the "phonies" and conformists but by his "caring side," his sympathy for "underdogs and innocents." The very "attempt to be gentle and humane . . . makes Holden a loser in the 'game' of life. Unable to be the kind of man required by prep schools and corporations," Salinger's protagonist could find no exit within American society. Undefiant and confused, Holden nevertheless served as "the first image of middle-class youth growing up absurd," which Hayden would situate at the psychological center of the Port Huron Statement.[37]

The dynamism inherent in youthful revolt, one historian has claimed, can best be defined as "a mystique . . . that fused elements of Marlon Brando's role in *The Wild One,* James Dean's portrayal in *Rebel without a Cause,* J. D. Salinger's Holden Caulfield in *Catcher in the Rye,* the rebels of *Blackboard Jungle,* and the driving energy and aggressive sexuality of the new heroes of rock 'n' roll into a single image. The mystique emphasized a hunger for authenticity and sensitivity." But something is askew here, for Holden is too young to have felt the Dionysian effects of rock 'n' roll, which erupted about three years after he left Pencey Prep. A "sex maniac" only in his head, he hardly represents "aggressive sexuality" either. *The Wild One, Rebel without a Cause,* and *Blackboard Jungle* are "goddam movies," which Holden professes to hate, because "they can ruin you. I'm not kidding" (p. 136). His own tastes are emphatically literary, ranging from *The Great Gatsby* and *Out of Africa* to Thomas Hardy and Ring Lardner. Even if the bland official ethos of the 1950s ultimately failed to repress the rambunctious energies the popular arts were about to unleash, Roland Marchand understands that the "mystique" he has identified would not be easily radicalized. Indeed, it could be tamed. Conservative consolidation was a more predictable outcome: "If the problems of a society are embedded in its social structure and are insulated from change by layers of ideological tradition, popular culture is an unlikely source of remedy. It is far more likely to serve needs for diversion and transitory compensation . . . [and] solace."[38] Such dynamism could not be politicized.

The deeper flaw with interpreting *The Catcher in the Rye* as a harbinger of revolt is the aura of passivity that pervades the novel. Alienation does not always lead to, and can remain the antonym of, action. Salinger's own sensibility was definitively pre- (or anti-) Sixties. His "conviction that our inner lives greatly matter," John Updike observed in 1961, "peculiarly qualifies him to sing of an America, where, for most of us, there seems little to do but to feel. Introversion, perhaps, has been forced upon history" rather than the other way around. Therefore "an age of nuance, of ambiguous gestures and psychological jockeying" could account for the popularity of Salinger's work.[39]

Describing Holden as "a misfit in society because he refuses to adjust" and because he lacks the self-discipline to cultivate privacy, one young literary critic of the fifties was struck by "the quixotic futility" of the protagonist's "outrage" at all the planet's obscenities, by his isolation. Holden seems to have sat for psychologist Kenneth Keniston's portrait of uncommitted youth: those who have the most to live for but find no one to look up to; those who are the most economically and socially advantaged but feel the deepest pangs of alienation.[40] Jack Newfield ('60) was a charter member of SDS but remembers Hunter College as mired in an apathy "no public question seemed to touch." His fellow students "were bereft of passions, of dreams, of gods. . . . And their *Zeitgeist*—J. D. Salinger—stood for a total withdrawal from reality into the womb of childhood, innocence, and mystical Zen." Holden's creator, evidently, had captured the spirit of the Silent Generation.[41]

It may not be accidental that David Riesman, whose most famous book was a veritable touchstone of social analysis in the era, assigned *The Catcher in the Rye* in his Harvard sociology course on Character and Social Structure in the United States. He did so "perhaps," a *Time* reporter speculated, "because every campus has its lonely crowd of imitation Holdens." Indeed, Holden demonstrates the characteristics of anomie, which is associated with "ruleless" and "ungoverned" conduct, that Riesman had described in *The Lonely Crowd;* the anomic are "virtually synonymous with [the] maladjusted." Though Salinger's narrator does not quite exhibit "the lack of emotion and emptiness of expression" by which "the ambulatory patients of modern culture" can be recognized, he does display a "vehement hatred of institutional confines" that was bound to make his peers (if not his psychoanalyst) uneasy.[42] One reviewer, in true Fifties fashion, even blamed Holden himself for his loneliness, "because he has shut himself away from the normal activities of boyhood, games, the outdoors, friendship."[43] It is true that Holden hates schools like Pencey Prep, where "you have to keep making believe you give a damn if the football team loses, and all you do is talk about girls and liquor and sex all day, and everybody sticks together in these dirty little goddam cliques" (p. 170). But Holden remains confined to his era, unable to connect the dots from those cliques to a larger society that might merit some rearrangement. Nor does the novel expand the reader's horizons beyond those of the narrator; it does not get from pathos to indignation.

For *The Catcher in the Rye* is utterly apolitical—unlike its only rival in arousing the ire of conservative parents. Steinbeck's fiction directs the attention of susceptible young readers to exploitation of the weak and the abuse of power. But a serious critique of capitalism would not be found in Salinger's text even if a full field investigation were ordered. Certainly Holden's fantasy of secluding himself in a cabin in the woods is scarcely a prescription for social activism: "I'd pretend I was one of those deaf-mutes. That way I wouldn't have to have any goddam stupid useless conversations with anybody. If anybody wanted to tell me something, they'd have to write it on a piece of paper and shove it over to me. They'd get bored as hell doing that after a while, and then I'd be through with having conversations for the rest of my life" (pp. 257–258). Such passages will hardly alarm those wishing to repudiate or erase the 1960s, which is why *The Catcher in the Rye* does not belong to the history of dissidence.

Growing Up Absurd (1960) sports a title and a perspective that Holden might have appreciated, but Paul Goodman does not mention the novel. Published at the end of the tumultuous, unpredictable decade, Theodore Roszak's *The Making of a Counter Culture* (which *Newsweek* dubbed "the best guide yet published to the meaning . . . of youthful dissent") likewise fails to mention Salinger, though Holden certainly personifies (or anticipates) "the ethos of disaffiliation that is fiercely obnoxious to the adult society." In 1962 the editor of a collection of critical essays on Salinger—the future editor-in-chief of *Time*—found American campuses innocent of activism: "'Student riots' are a familiar and significant factor in European politics. The phenomenon has no equivalent in the United States."[44] That generalization would soon be falsified. But it should be noted that authors who have fathomed how the 1950s became the 1960s (like Morris Dickstein, Fred Inglis, Maurice Isserman, James Miller) ignore the impact of Salinger's novel.

Because any reading of the novel as a prefiguration of the 1960s is ultimately so unpersuasive, an over-reaction has set in. Alan Nadel, for example, has fashioned Holden into a Cold Warrior, junior division. "Donning his red hunting hat, he attempts to become the good Red-hunter, ferreting out the phonies and the subversives, but in so doing he emulates the bad Red-hunters," Nadel has written. "Uncovering duplicity was the theme of the day," he adds, so that "in thinking constantly about who or what was phony, Caulfield was doing no more than following the instructions of J. Edgar Hoover, the California Board of Regents, *The Nation* [*sic*], the Smith Act, and the Hollywood Ten. . . . Each citizen was potentially both the threat and the threatened." After all, hadn't Gary Cooper, testifying before HUAC, defined Communism as something that was not "on the level"? Nadel equates Caulfield's "disdain for Hollywood" with HUAC's, nor could the young prostitute's mention of Melvyn Douglas have been accidental—since Congressman Richard Nixon had run against Helen Gahagan Douglas, and her husband was himself "a prominent Hollywood liberal." Nadel concludes that "the solution to Caulfield's dilemma becomes renouncing speech itself." Having named names, he realizes: "I sort of *miss* everybody I told about. . . . It's funny. Don't ever tell anybody anything," he advises; that is, don't be an informer. "If you do, you start missing everybody" (pp. 276–277). The narrator "spoke for the cold war HUAC witness," Nadel argued, "expressing existential angst over the nature and meaning of his 'testimony.'"[45] Such an interpretation is far-fetched:

Holden is no more interested in politics than his creator, and he's considerably less interested in sanctioning conformity than were the Red-hunters.

Citizens who abhor the 1960s commonly deplore one of its most prominent legacies: the fragmentation into "identity politics," the loss of civic cohesion. Those worrying over this sin also will not find it in Salinger's book, which promotes no class consciousness, racial consciousness, or ethnic consciousness of any sort. Sol Salinger had strayed so far from Judaism that he became an importer of hams and cheeses;[46] and his son left no recognizably Jewish imprint on his fiction. Nor does his novel evoke the special plight of young women and girls. That omission would be rectified about two generations later, when Eve Horowitz's first novel appeared. Her young narrator and protagonist is not only female but emphatically Jewish, and she longs to meet her own Holden Caulfield. Jane Singer recalls: "I hadn't known any males who were as depressed as I was in high school, except for maybe Holden Caulfield, and I didn't really know him." As she's packing to leave Cleveland for Oberlin College, she muses, "besides clothes and shampoo and *The Catcher in the Rye,* I couldn't think of anything else to bring."[47] In her account of growing up female, Horowitz may have wanted to correct the imbalance David Riesman identified in 1961, when, attempting to explain the United States to a Japanese audience, he had commented on the inscrutable popularity of Salinger's novel: "Boys are frustrated because they aren't cowboys, and girls are frustrated because they aren't boys." The sociologist noted that "women have been the audience for American fiction and for movies. There are no girls' stories comparable to *Catcher in the Rye*. Yet girls can adapt themselves and identify with such a book, while a boy can't so easily identify with a girl."[48] In the literary marketplace, Riesman speculated, readers aren't turned off or away if the central characters are male but only if they are female. How many Boy Scouts and Explorer Scouts have been moved by reading *The Bell Jar?*

The Curse of Culture

Another way to understand the power of Salinger's novel to generate controversy is to recognize its vulnerability to moralistic criticism. From wherever the source—call it Puritanism, or puritanism, or Victorianism—there persists a tradition of imposing religious standards upon art or of rejecting works of the imagination because they violate conventional ethical codes. According to this legacy, books are neither good nor bad without "for you" being added as a criterion of judgment. This entwining of the aesthetic and the moralistic was obvious as prize committees struggled with the terms of Joseph Pulitzer's instructions that the novels to be honored in his name "shall best present the whole atmosphere of American life." But until 1927, the novels selected more accurately conveyed "the wholesome atmosphere of American life."[49] That eliminated Dreiser. Had the subtle revision of

Pulitzer's own intentions not been overturned, virtually all great writers would have been categorically excluded. Nabokov comes quickly to mind. His most famous novel was given to the good family man Adolf Eichmann, then imprisoned in Israel, but was returned after two days with an indignant rejection: "*Das ist aber ein sehr unerfreuliches Buch*"—quite an unwholesome book. *Lolita* is narrated from the viewpoint of an adult, a pervert whose ornate vocabulary made the novel unintelligible to young readers, and so censors passed it by to target *The Catcher in the Rye*. It is a measure of Salinger's stature among other writers that, though famously dismissive of many literary giants, Nabokov wrote privately of his fellow *New Yorker* contributor: "I do admire him very much."[50]

But the reviewer for *The Christian Science Monitor* did not: *The Catcher in the Rye* "is not fit for children to read"; its central character is "preposterous, profane, and pathetic beyond belief." Too many young readers might even want to emulate Holden, "as too easily happens when immorality and perversion are recounted by writers of talent whose work is countenanced in the name of art or good intention."[51] Here was an early sign of trouble. Nor was respectability enhanced by the novel's first appearance in paperback, for it was offered as pulp fiction, a genre that beckoned with promises of illicit pleasure. The common 1950s practice of issuing serious books in pulp meant that "dozens of classic novels appeared in packages that were cartoonish, sordid or merely absurd." The aim of such marketing, Julie Lasky has suggested, was to grab "the attention of impulse shoppers in drugstores and bus depots; slogans jammed across the four-inch width of paperbound covers compressed the nuances of prizewinning authors into exaggerated come-ons." The 1953 paperback edition of Salinger's novel, for example, assured buyers that "this unusual book may shock you . . . but you will never forget it." The illustration on the cover depicted a prostitute standing near Holden and may have served as the only means by which some citizens judged the book. The cover so offended the author that it contributed to his move to Bantam when his contract with Signet expired. By then, the pulping of classics had largely ended in the wake of hearings by the House of Representatives' Select Committee on Current Pornographic Materials. But the availability of such cheap editions of books ranging from the serious to the lurid drew the curiosity of censors as well as bargain-hunters. The vulnerability of Salinger's novel testified to the aptness of Walter Lippmann's generalization that censorship "is actually applied in proportion to the vividness, the directness, and the intelligibility of the medium which circulates the subversive idea." Movie screens, he wrote in 1927, therefore tend to be more censored than the stage, which is more censored than newspapers and magazines. But "the novel is even freer than the press today because it is an even denser medium of expression."[52] At least that was the case until the paperback revolution facilitated the expansion of the syllabus.

Of course, the paperback revolution was not the only cultural shift affecting the reception of the novel. The career of *The Catcher in the Rye* is virtually synchronous with the Cold War, and Holden Caulfield takes a stand of sorts: he calls himself "a pacifist" (p. 59). For men slightly older than Holden in 1949–1950, military conscription was more or less universal, yet he predicts that "it'd drive me crazy if I had to be in the Army. . . . I swear if there's ever another war, they better just take me out and stick me in front of a firing squad. I wouldn't object." Indeed he goes further: "I'm sort of glad they've got the atomic bomb invented. If there's ever another war, I'm going to sit right the hell on top of it. I'll volunteer for it, I swear to God I will" (pp. 182, 183). Barely a decade later, Stanley Kubrick's pitch-black comedy *Dr. Strangelove* (1964) would confront nuclear terror by showing Major "King" Kong (Slim Pickens) doing precisely what Holden vows he will step forward to do. With such images in mind, one interpreter has thus boldly claimed that "the fear of nuclear holocaust, not the fear of four-letter words[,]" sparked controversy about *The Catcher in the Rye*.[53]

Salinger's novel may thus also be about history veering out of control, about the abyss into which parents could no longer prevent their offspring from staring, about the impotence to which a can-do people was unaccustomed. "The lack of faith in the American character expressed in the *Catcher* controversies," Professor Pamela Steinle has argued, "is rooted not in doubts about the strength of adolescent Americans' character but in recognition of the powerlessness of American adults—as parents, professionals and community leaders—to provide a genuine sense of the future for the adolescents in their charge." According to Steinle, the novel indicts "adult apathy and complicity in the construction of a social reality in which the American character cannot develop in any meaningful sense beyond adolescence." Nor does the novel warrant any hope that the condition can be remedied. The story is, after all, told from a sanitarium in California—a grim terminus given the common belief that the West offers a second chance. No wonder, then, that John Seelye, who ended his own revised version of *The Adventures of Huckleberry Finn* with Huck's bleakest pessimism ("I didn't much care if the goddamn sun never come up again"), could read Salinger's book "as a lengthy suicide note with a blank space at the end to sign your name."[54]

The advantage of Steinle's argument is that she situates the controversy over *The Catcher in the Rye* where it actually took place, which is less in the pages of *Ramparts* than at school board meetings. In such settings, the novel was branded by parents as a threat to their control and heralded by teachers as a measure of their professional autonomy and authority. But the disadvantage of Steinle's view is the scarcity of direct evidence that nuclear fears fueled the debate. Neither those who condemned *The Catcher in the Rye* nor its defenders made the specter of atomic catastrophe pivotal.

Neither the moral nor the literary disputes were ventilated in such terms. Compared to Holden's far more pronounced resistance to maturation, compared to more immediate targets of his scorn, the Bomb hardly registered as a concern among objections to the novel.

But if "the essence of censorship," according to Lippmann, is "not to suppress subversive ideas as such, but to withhold them from those who are young or unprivileged or otherwise undependable,"[55] then Steinle's emphasis upon parental assertion of authority is not misplaced. In a more class-conscious society, the Old Bailey prosecutor of the publisher of *Lady Chatterley's Lover* could ask in his opening address to the jury, in 1960: "Is it a book that you would even wish your wife or your servants to read?"[56] But in the United States, overt conflicts are more likely to take generational form; and the first of Lippmann's categories deserves to be highlighted. Some of the books that have aroused the greatest ire place children at the center, like Richard Wright's *Black Boy*, Anne Frank's *Diary of a Young Girl*, and of course *The Adventures of Huckleberry Finn*; and despite the aura of "cuteness" hovering over Salinger's work, it emitted danger by striking at the most vulnerable spot in the hearts of parents. Nor could it have escaped the attention of alert readers that Holden's emotional affiliations are horizontal rather than vertical. His father, a corporate lawyer, is absent from the scene; and his mother is present only as a voice speaking from a dark room. The only relative whom the reader meets is Phoebe, the younger sister (and a mini-Holden).[57]

The contributor's note Salinger submitted to *Harper's* in 1946 was his credo: "I almost always write about very young people";[58] and the directness with which he spoke to them had much to do with his appeal—and with the anxiety that his literary intervention provoked in the internecine battle between generations. The effectiveness of his empathy posed a challenge to parents who invoked their right to be custodians of the curriculum, and the "legions of decency" may have sensed "a unique seductive power" which Salinger's biographer claims *The Catcher in the Rye* exudes. Even if the less sensitive or eccentric of its young readers might not try to assume Holden's persona, at least teenagers could imitate his lingo. A book that elicits such proprietary interest—succeeding cohorts believing in a special access to Salinger's meaning—was bound to arouse some suspicion that conventional authority was being outflanked.[59] Salinger's adroit fidelity to the feelings and experiences of his protagonist was what made the novel so tempting a target. Perhaps *The Catcher in the Rye* has been banned precisely because it is so cherished; because it is so easily loved, some citizens love to hate it.

Steinle has closely examined the local controversies that erupted over the book in Alabama, Virginia, New Mexico, and California as well as the debates conducted in such publications as the *PTA Magazine* and the *Newsletter on Intellectual Freedom* of the American Library Association. She discovered a "division . . . over whether to prepare adolescents for or to protect them from adult disillusionment. . . . In the postwar period . . . recognition of the increasing dissonance between American ideals and the realities of social experience has become unavoidable, and it is precisely this cultural dissonance that is highlighted by Salinger's novel."[60] Its literary value got lost in the assertion of family values, in a campaign that must be classified as reactionary. "They say it describes reality," a parent in Boron, California, announced. "I say let's back up from reality. Let's go backwards. Let's go back to when we didn't have an immoral society."[61] When so idyllic a state existed was not specified, but what is evident is the element of anti-intellectualism that the struggle against permissiveness entailed. Here some of the parents were joined by Leonard Hall, the school superintendent of Bay County, Florida, who warned in 1987 against assigning books that were not state-approved because, he sagely opined, reading "is where you get ideas from."[62]

Attempts at vindication were occasionally made on the same playing field that censors themselves chose. Though Holden labels himself "sort of an atheist" (p. 130), he could be praised as a saint, if admittedly a picaresque one. One educator discerned in the protagonist a diamond in the rough: "He befriends the friendless. He respects those who are humble, loyal, and kind. He demonstrates a strong love for his family" (or for Phoebe anyway). Besides enacting such New Testament teachings, "he abhors hypocrisy. He values sex that comes from caring for another person and rejects its sordidness. And, finally, he wants to be a responsible member of society, to guide and protect those younger than he."[63] But a character witness is not the same as a literary critic, and such conflation seems to have gained little traction when the right of English teachers to make up reading lists was contested. If Holden's defense rested on a sanitized version of his character, then the implication was that assigned books with less morally meritorious protagonists might be subject to parental veto. Such a defense also assumed that disgruntled parents were themselves exegetes who had simply misread a text, that community conflicts could be resolved by more subtle interpretations. There is no reason to believe, however, that the towns where the novel was banned or challenged overlapped with maps of misreading. But such communities *were* places where parents tried to gain control of the curriculum, which is why *The Catcher in the Rye* would still have been proscribed even had it been re-read as a book of virtues.

For the objections that were most frequently raised were directed at the novelist's apparent desire to capture profuse adolescent profanity in the worst way. In the *Catholic World*, reviewer Riley Hughes disliked the narrator's "excessive use of amateur swearing and coarse language," which made his character simply "monotonous."[64] According to one angry parent's tabulation, 237 instances of "goddamn," 58 uses of the synonym for a person of illegitimate birth, 31 "Chrissakes," and one incident of flatulence constituted what was wrong with Salinger's book. Though blasphemy is not a crime, *The Catcher in the Rye* "uses the Lord's name in vain two hundred times," an opponent in Boron asserted—"enough [times] to ban it right there."[65] The statistics are admittedly not consistent. But it is incontestable that the text contains six examples of "fuck" or "fuck you," though here Holden is actually allied with the censorious parents, since he does not swear with this four-letter word himself but instead tries to efface it from walls. He's indignant that children should be subjected to such graffiti. Upon seeing the word even in the Egyptian tomb room at the Metropolitan Museum of Art, however, Holden achieves a melancholy and mature insight that such offenses to dignity cannot really be expunged from the world: "You can't ever find a place that's nice and peaceful, because there isn't any" (p. 264).[66]

What happened to *The Catcher in the Rye* wasn't always nice and peaceful because it took a linguistic turn. Though historians are fond of defining virtually every era as one of transition, it does make sense to locate the publication of Salinger's novel on the cusp of change. The novel benefited from the loosening of tongues that the Second World War sanctioned, yet the profanity in which Holden indulges still looked conspicuous before the 1960s. Salinger thus helped to accelerate the trend toward greater freedom for writers but found himself the target of those offended by the adolescent vernacular still rarely enough recorded in print. During the Second World War, the Production Code had been slightly relaxed for *We Are the Marines*. This 1943 *March of Time* documentary was permitted to use mild expletives like "damn" "under stress of battle conditions." Professor Thomas Doherty adds that, "in the most ridiculed example of the Code's tender ears, Noel Coward's *In Which We Serve* (1942), a British import, was held up from American release for seventeen words: ten 'damns,' two 'hells,' two 'Gods,' two 'bastards,' and one 'lousy.'"

Only three years before publication of Salinger's novel, homophonic language was inserted into Norman Mailer's *The Naked and the Dead* at the suggestion of his cousin, Charles Rembar. A crackerjack First Amendment attorney who would later represent such clients as Fanny Hill and Constance Chatterley, Rembar proposed the substitution of *fug* (as in "Fug you. Fug the goddam gun") partly because the president of the house publishing the novel feared his own mother's reaction. The U.S. Information Agency was nevertheless unpersuaded and banned Mailer's book from its overseas libraries. As late as 1952, the revised edition of *Webster's Unabridged* offered a simple but opaque definition of masturbation as "onanism; self-pollution."[67] The next year President Eisenhower delivered a celebrated plea at Dartmouth College: "Don't join the book-burners. . . . Don't be afraid to go into your library and read every book." His amendment is less cited—"as long as that document does not offend our own ideas of decency." Though the war in which Mailer and Salinger fought allowed some indecorous terms to go public, the

1960 Presidential debates included the spectacle of Nixon seeking to trump
another ex-sailor by promising the electorate—after Harry Truman's salty
lapses—to continue Ike's restoration of "decency and, frankly, good language"
in the White House.[68]

In this particular war of words, Salinger was conscripted into a cause
for which he was no more suited than any other. If he was affiliated with any
institution at all, it was the *New Yorker,* which initially published most of his
Nine Stories as well as the substance of his two subsequent books. In that magazine even the mildest profanity was strictly forbidden, and editorial prudish-
ness would have spiked publication of excerpts from the final version of what
became his most admired work. It may be plausible, as one scholar circling the
text has noted, that "the radical nature of Salinger's portrayal of disappointment with American society, so much like Twain's in *Huck Finn,* was probably as much of the reason that *Catcher* (like *Huck*) was banned from schools
and colleges as were the few curse words around which the battle was publicly
fought."[69] But such ideological objections to Salinger's novel were rarely raised,
much less articulated with any cogency; and therefore no historian of the reception of this book should minimize the salience of those "few curse words."

Could *The Catcher in the Rye* have avoided the turbulent pool into which
it was so often sucked? Could the novel have been rescued from primitive
detractors and retained an even more secure status in the public school curriculum? One compromise was never considered. It is the solution that Noah
Webster commonly applied to dictionaries and spelling books, that Emerson
recommended to Whitman for *Leaves of Grass,* and that Lewis Carroll intended to enact with a volume entitled *The Girl's Own Shakespeare:* expurga-
tion. Had Holden's lingo been sanitized in accordance with the legacy of
Dr. Thomas Bowdler, the moral (or moralistic) resistance to Salinger's novel
would have evaporated. Bowdlerization constitutes what its leading student
has called "literary slum clearance," but it also cordons off the censors. Of
course Holden would not have been Holden with expletives deleted. The
guileless integrity of his language makes him so memorable and therefore the
novel so distinctive. Richard Watson Gilder had inflicted the kindest cuts of
all on Huck's talk,[70] but by the 1950s no expurgators survived to spare Holden
from the animosity he incurred. Such an explanation may be too obvious and
all, if you really want to know. It's so simple it kills me, for Chrissake. But I
really believe it's the best explanation. I really do.

Notes

1. Adam Moss, "Catcher Comes of Age," *Esquire,* December 1981, p. 57; Jack
Salzman, ed., intro. to *New Essays on "The Catcher in the Rye"* (New York: Cambridge
University Press, 1991), pp. 6, 7.

2. Salzman, intro. to *New Essays*, pp. 6, 19 n. 16; Ian Hamilton, *In Search of J. D. Salinger* (New York: Random House, 1988), p. 136; Moss, "Catcher Comes of Age," pp. 56, 57; [Jack Skow,] "Invisible Man," in *Salinger: A Critical and Personal Portrait*, ed. Henry Anatole Grunwald (New York: Pocket Books, 1963), p. 4.

3. David J. Burrows, "Allie and Phoebe" (1969), reprinted in *Holden Caulfield*, ed. Harold Bloom (New York: Chelsea House, 1990), p. 80; Hamilton, *In Search of Salinger*, pp. 155–156.

4. Salzman, intro. to *New Essays*, p. 22 n. 46; [Skow,] "Invisible Man," p. 4; Moss, "Catcher Comes of Age," p. 57.

5. Quoted by Nadine Brozan, "J. D. Salinger Receives an Apology for an Award," *New York Times*, 27 April 1991, p. 26.

6. Stefan Kanfer, "Holden Today: Still in the Rye," *Time*, 7 February 1972, pp. 50–51.

7. J. D. Salinger, *The Catcher in the Rye* (Boston: Little, Brown, 1951), p. 171. Subsequent page references, enclosed in parentheses in text, are to this edition.

8. Shawn Levy, *King of Comedy: The Life and Art of Jerry Lewis* (New York: St. Martin's, 1996), p. 271; Peter Shaw, "Love and Death in *Catcher in the Rye*," in *New Essays*, p. 100.

9. John Fowles, *The Collector* (Boston: Little, Brown, 1963), pp. 156–157, 192, 219–220, 246; John Simon, *Private Screenings* (New York: Macmillan, 1967), p. 165.

10. Priscilla Johnson McMillan, "An Assassin's Portrait," *New Republic*, 12 July 1982, pp. 16–18.

11. Moss, "Catcher Comes of Age," p. 58; Daniel M. Stashower, "On First Looking into Chapman's Holden: Speculations on a Murder," *American Scholar* 52 (Summer 1983): 373–377; Jack Jones, *Let Me Take You Down: Inside the Mind of Mark David Chapman, the Man Who Killed John Lennon* (New York: Villard Books, 1992), pp. 7, 22, 174–179, 184; Warren French, *J. D. Salinger, Revisited* (Boston: Twayne, 1988), pp. 17, 48.

12. Richard Schickel, *Intimate Strangers: The Culture of Celebrity* (Garden City, N.Y.: Doubleday, 1985), p. 280; Lincoln Caplan, *The Insanity Defense and the Trial of John W. Hinckley, Jr.* (Boston: David R. Godine, 1984), pp. 42–43.

13 John Guare, *Six Degrees of Separation* (New York: Random House, 1990), pp. 31–35, 107.

14. Quoted by Justin Kaplan, in *Mr. Clemens and Mark Twain* (New York: Simon & Schuster, 1966), pp. 268–269.

15. Frank Trippett, "The Growing Battle of the Books," *Time*, 19 January 1981, p. 85; Mary Jordan, "Reports of Censorship in U.S. Schools Up 50%," *International Herald Tribune*, 4 September 1992, p. 5.

16. Quoted by Salzman, in intro. to *New Essays*, p. 15.

17. Quoted in Salzman, intro. to *New Essays*, p. 15; Pamela Steinle, "'If a Body Catch a Body': The Catcher in the Rye Censorship Debate as Expression of Nuclear Culture," in *Popular Culture and Political Change in Modern America*, ed. Ronald Edsforth and Larry Bennett (Albany: State University of New York Press, 1991), p. 127; L. B. Woods, *A Decade of Censorship in America: The Threat to Classrooms and Libraries, 1966–1975* (Metuchen, N.J.: Scarecrow Press, 1979), p. 82.

18. Quoted by Seth Mydans, in "In a Small Town, a Battle Over a Book," *New York Times*, 3 September 1989, p. 22; Woods, *Decade of Censorship*, p. 150.

19. "*Catcher* in the News," *Esquire*, December 1981, p. 58; Salzman, intro. to *New Essays*, p. 14.

20. Quoted by Edward B. Jenkinson, in *Censors in the Classroom: The Mind Benders* (Carbondale: Southern Illinois University Press, 1979), p. 35.

21. Jenkinson, *Censors in the Classroom*, pp. 35, 156; Jack R. Sublette, *J. D. Salinger: An Annotated Bibliography, 1938–1981* (New York: Garland, 1984), pp. 160, 162, 164–167.

22. Marvin Laser and Norman Fruman, "Not Suitable for Temple City," in *Studies in J. D. Salinger: Reviews, Essays, and Critiques*, ed. Laser and Fruman (New York: Odyssey Press, 1963), pp. 124–129.

23. Mydans, "Small Town," p. 3.

24. Mydans, "Small Town," p. 3.

25. Willie Morris," Houston's Superpatriots," *Harper's*, October 1961, p. 50; Laser and Fruman, "Community Critics . . . and Censors," in *Studies in Salinger*, p. 123.

26. Leslie A. Fiedler, *Being Busted* (New York: Stein & Day, 1969), pp. 59, 60; Edward Allen, *Mustang Sally* (New York: W. W. Norton, 1992), pp. 20–21; Anna Quindlen, "Don't Read This," *New York Times*, 1 October 1994, sec. 4, p. 23.

27. Timothy Noah, "Censors Right and Left," *New Republic*, 28 February 1981, p. 12.

28. Robert J. Clements, "Forbidden Books and Christian Reunion," *Columbia University Forum* (Summer 1963): 28; conversation with Jonas Barciauskas, librarian for theology, Boston College, 28 October 1996.

29. Warren Hinckle, *If You Have a Lemon, Make Lemonade* (New York: Bantam Books, 1976), pp. 41–42, 44–45; Robert O. Bowen, "The Salinger Syndrome: Charity Against Whom?" *Ramparts*, May 1962, pp. 52–60.

30. Robert Harris, *Fatherland* (London: Hutchinson, 1992), p. 17; Robert Darnton, *Berlin Journal, 1989–1990* (New York: W. W. Norton, 1991), p. 205.

31. Woods, *Decade of Censorship*, pp. 149–150.

32. Quoted by Mydans, in "Small Town," p. 22; "Censorship's Coming of Age," *Boston Globe*, 3 September 1993, p. 14.

33. Carol and Richard Ohmann, "Reviewers, Critics, and *The Catcher in the Rye*," *Critical Inquiry* 3 (Autumn 1976): 34–36.

34. John Seelye, "Holden in the Museum," in *New Essays*, pp. 24, 32.

35. Charles A . Reich, *The Greening of America* (New York: Random House, 1970), pp. 222–223.

36. E. L. Doctorow, *The Book of Daniel* (New York: Random House, 1971), p. 95.

37. Tom Hayden, *Reunion: A Memoir* (New York: Random House, 1988), pp. 8–9, 17–18.

38. Roland Marchand, "Visions of Classlessness, Quests for Dominion: American Popular Culture, 1945–1960," in *Reshaping America: Society and Institutions, 1945–1960*, ed. Robert H. Bremner and Gary W. Reichard (Columbus: Ohio State University Press, 1982), pp. 179, 181–82.

39. John Updike, "Franny and Zooey," in *Salinger: A Portrait*, pp. 58–59.

40. Paul Levine, "J. D. Salinger: The Development of a Misfit Hero," *Twentieth-Century Literature* 4 (October 1958): 97, reprinted in *If You Really Want to Know: A Catcher Casebook*, ed. Malcolm M. Marsden (Chicago: Scott, Foresman, 1963), p. 48; and "The Fiction of the Fifties: Alienation and Beyond," in *America*

in the Fifties, ed. Anne R. Clauss (Copenhagen: University of Copenhagen, 1978), pp. 46–49; Kenneth Keniston, *The Uncommitted: Alienated Youth in American Society* (New York: Harcourt, Brace & World, 1965), pp. 7–8.

41. Jack Newfield, *A Prophetic Minority* (New York: Signet, 1967), pp. 28–29.

42. [Skow,] "Invisible Man," in *Salinger: A Portrait,* p. 5; David Riesman, with Nathan Glazer and Reuel Denney, *The Lonely Crowd: A Study of the Changing American Character,* abr. ed. (Garden City, N.Y.: Doubleday Anchor, 1953), pp. 278–282; French, *Salinger, Revisited,* pp. 57–58; James Lundquist, *J. D. Salinger* (New York: Ungar, 1979), pp. 65–67.

43. T. Morris Longstreth, "New Novels in the News," in *Christian Science Monitor,* 19 July 1951, p. 7, reprinted in *If You Really Want to Know,* p. 6.

44. Robert A. Gross, review of *Making of a Counter Culture,* in *Newsweek,* 15 September 1969, p. 98; Theodore Roszak, *The Making of a Counter Culture: Reflections on the Technocratic Society and Its Youthful Opposition* (Garden City, N.Y.: Doubleday Anchor, 1969), p. 174n; Grunwald, intro. to *Salinger: A Portrait,* p. xxx.

45. Alan Nadel, *Containment Culture: American Narratives, Postmodernism, and the Atomic Age* (Durham, N.C.: Duke University Press, 1995), pp. 71, 75, 79, 86, 181; "Communist Infiltration of the Motion Picture Industry," in *Thirty Years of Treason,* ed. Eric Bentley (New York: Viking, 1971), p. 149.

46. "The Complete J. D. Salinger," *Esquire,* December 1981, p. 58; Hamilton, *In Search of Salinger,* pp. 13–14.

47. Eve Horowitz, *Plain Jane* (New York: Random House, 1992), pp. 52, 200, 230.

48. David Riesman and Evelyn Thompson Riesman, *Conversations in Japan: Modernization, Politics, and Culture* (New York: Basic Books, 1967), p. 171.

49. John Hohenberg, *The Pulitzer Prizes* (New York: Columbia University Press, 1974), pp. 19, 55–56.

50. Hannah Arendt, *Eichmann in Jerusalem: A Report on the Banality of Evil,* rev. ed. (New York: Viking, 1964), p. 49; Vladimir Nabokov to John Leonard, 29 September 1971, in Nabokov's *Selected Letters, 1940–1977,* ed. Dmitri Nabokov and Matthew J. Bruccoli (San Diego: Harcourt Brace Jovanovich, 1989), p. 492.

51. Longstreth, "New Novels," pp. 5–6.

52. Julie Lasky, "Savage Puritans Ripped Her Bodice," *New York Times Book Review,* 12 November 1995, p. 67; Walter Lippmann, "The Nature of the Battle over Censorship" (1927), in *Men of Destiny* (Seattle: University of Washington Press, 1970), pp. 100–102.

53. Steinle, "If a Body," p. 136.

54. Steinle, "If a Body," p. 136; Seelye, "Holden in the Museum," p. 29, and *The True Adventures of Huckleberry Finn* (Evanston, Ill.: Northwestern University Press, 1970), p. 339.

55. Lippmann, "Nature of the Battle over Censorship," p. 99.

56. Quoted by Charles Rembar, in *The End of Obscenity* (New York: Random House, 1968), p. 156.

57. The absenteeism of Holden's parents is noted perceptively by Jonathan Baumbach, in *The Landscape of Nightmare* (New York: New York University Press, 1965), p. 65.

58. Quoted by Sanford Pinsker, in *Bearing the Bad News: Contemporary American Literature and Culture* (Iowa City: University of Iowa Press, 1990), p. 29.

59. Hamilton, *In Search of Salinger*, p. 4; Moss, "Catcher Comes of Age," p. 56.

60. Steinle, "If a Body," p. 131.

61. Quoted by Nat Hentoff, in *Free Speech for Me—But Not for Thee: How the American Left and Right Relentlessly Censor Each Other* (New York: HarperCollins, 1992), pp. 374–375.

62. Quoted by Joan DelFattore, in *What Johnny Shouldn't Read: Textbook Censorship in America* (New Haven: Yale University Press, 1992), p. 109.

63. June Edwards, "Censorship in the Schools: What's Moral about *The Catcher in the Rye?*" *English Journal* 72 (April 1983): 42.

64. Quoted by Salzman, in intro, to *New Essays*, pp. 5–6; Edward P. J. Corbett, "Raise High the Barriers, Censors," *America*, 7 January 1961, pp. 441–442, reprinted in *If You Really Want to Know*, pp. 68–70.

65. Riley Hughes, "New Novels," *Catholic World*, November 1951, p. 154, reprinted in *Holden Caulfield*, p. 8; Moss, "Catcher Comes of Age," p. 56; Steinle, "If a Body," p. 129; Quindlen, "Don't Read This," p. 23; Hentoff, *Free Speech for Me*, pp. 374–375.

66. French, *Salinger, Revisited*, p. 42.

67. Thomas Doherty, *Projections of War: Hollywood, American Culture, and World War II* (New York: Columbia University Press, 1993), pp. 54, 56; Hilary Mills, *Mailer: A Biography* (New York: Empire Books, 1982), pp. 90–93; Rembar, *End of Obscenity*, p. 17n; Noel Perrin, *Dr. Bowdler's Legacy: A History of Expurgated Books in England and America* (New York: Atheneum, 1969), p. 251.

68. Quoted by Rembar, in *End of Obscenity*, p. 7; Walter L. Hixson, *Parting the Curtain: Propaganda, Culture, and the Cold War, 1945–1961* (New York: St. Martin's, 1997), p. 123; "The Third Debate," 13 October 1960, in *The Great Debates: Background, Perspective, Effects*, ed. Sidney Kraus (Bloomington: Indiana University Press, 1962), p. 397.

69. Gerald Rosen, "A Retrospective Look at *The Catcher in the Rye*," *American Quarterly* 29 (Winter 1977): 548, 557–558.

70. Perrin, *Dr. Bowdler's Legacy*, pp. 8, 105, 163, 167–172, 212, 220.

PAMELA HUNT STEINLE

The Catcher in the Rye
as Postwar American Fable

Here's for the plain old Adam, the simple genuine self against the whole
world.

—Ralph Waldo Emerson, *Journals*

J.D. Salinger's novel *The Catcher in the Rye* is one of the most significant books in American literature to appear since World War II. The center
of heated censorship debates for the past forty years and the cause of some
confusion and consternation to American literary critics, *The Catcher in the
Rye* has held the attention of popular American readership with a force that
can perhaps be best appreciated by a brief review of its publishing history.
First published in mid-July 1951 by Little, Brown and Company, *The Catcher
in the Rye* was simultaneously published as a Book-of-the-Month Club selection. By the end of July, Little, Brown and Company was reprinting the novel
for the fifth time, and by late August *Catcher* had reached fourth place on
the *New York Times* best-seller list. Signet Books brought out the first paperback edition in 1953, selling over three million copies in the next ten years.
Grosset and Dunlap brought out an edition of their own in 1952, Modern
Library in 1958, and Franklin Watts Publishers in 1967. In January of 1960,
Catcher reappeared on the *New York Times* best-seller list, this time placing
fifth among paperback books. All the while, Little, Brown and Company
continued reprinting their original edition—completing thirty-five printings

In Cold Fear: The Catcher *in the Censorship Controversies and Postwar American Character*
(Columbus: Ohio State University Press, 2000): pp. 15–28. Copyright © 2000 Ohio State
University Press.

89

by 1981. In 1964, Bantam Books brought out their paperback edition and by 1981 had reprinted it fifty-two times. All in all, the total number of copies in print by 1997 was estimated at over ten million, with sustained sales of nearly two hundred thousand copies per year.[1]

Clearly *The Catcher in the Rye* is a landmark book for the post–World War II period in its immediate and sustained popularity. However, publication and printing records alone do not necessarily indicate that a literary work has engaged or become a significant part of the cultural imagination. One might argue that *Catcher* has been so frequently printed in response to its classroom usage—reflecting an appreciation of the novel by English teachers but not necessarily the choice or interest of a voluntary readership. Another interpretation is that sales of *Catcher* have been spurred by its very presence on various censorship lists. While these perspectives certainly bear some truth, the materials of popular culture provide evidence that the success of *Catcher* is broader and of deeper significance than these explanations acknowledge.

Continuing references to *Catcher* in commercial television series and several novels illustrate that the producers of popular media assume a broad base of audience familiarity with the novel.[2] A 1977 novel by Erich Segal, *Oliver's Story*, as well as 1982 episodes of the television series *Sixty Minutes* and *Archie Bunker's Place* all referred to *Catcher* in terms of its status as a controversial text. In another television series, the long-time favorite game show *Family Feud*, as the host reviewed the "correct" answers to an audience-survey question about types of bread, he called out, "Rye," and then quipped, "As in catcher."[3]

Revealing their own esteem for Salinger's work, three authors of contemporary novels have used *Catcher* to move their plot lines forward. In his 1987 teen novel *Can't Miss*, author Michael Bowen assumed and relied on the adolescent reader's familiarity with Holden Caulfield's critique of the "phoniness" of postwar American life to enhance his development of the teenage main character.[4] In the award-winning 1982 novel *Shoeless Joe*, not only did the author, W. P. Kinsella, assume reader familiarity with *Catcher* but the tale itself was written to facilitate an imaginary dialogue with J. D. Salinger. Given the same name as one of Salinger's fictional characters, the novel's protagonist, Ray Kinsella, is a baseball fan who has a vision of a game being played in his cornfields by a literal "dream team" that includes deceased baseball legends—and the very much alive if reclusive J. D. Salinger.

Transforming his cornfields into a ballfield based on the mysterious instructions given by an imaginary ballpark announcer in Ray's vision, the second command requires the real-life presence of Salinger to "ease his pain." Convincing the fictional Salinger that he should leave New Hampshire and come to Iowa with him, Ray tells Salinger, "I've thought about you and baseball. . . . You've captured the experience of growing up in America, the same way Freddy Patek corners a ground ball. *The Catcher in the Rye* is the definitive novel of a young man's growing pains, of growing up in pain. . . . But baseball can soothe even those pains, for it is stable and permanent, steady as a grandfather dozing in a wicker chair on a verandah."[5]

Yet it is Salinger's snug capture of adolescent angst in *Catcher* that is used to soothe the growing pains of a thirteen-year-old girl in popular writer Julie Smith's 1994 detective novel *New Orleans Beat*. At a crucial point in this story, an adult "friend of the family" named Darryl attempts to reach out to a recently returned adolescent "runaway" named Sheila by giving her a book as a gift at a "welcome home" gathering. At first, the title of the book is not disclosed to Sheila—nor to the reader—and she is clearly disappointed that her special adult friend has brought her something that she sees as an impersonal and typical adult-to-adolescent present.

Begrudgingly responding, "I'm not mad. I could . . . read a book," Sheila's disappointment deepens when Darryl tells her the novel is about a boy: "'A boy?' Her (inner) voice said, What on Earth are you thinking of?" Asking her to trust him, "even though it's a book and even though it's about a boy," Darryl then tells Sheila that this book is different, that "it's going to change your life. You're going to read this and think, 'There's somebody out there who understands.'" At this moment the book's title is finally revealed, not by Darryl nor by the unwrapping of the package, but by the larger gathering of adult family members and friends who exclaim in unison before they even see the book: "Catcher in the Rye."[6]

Everyone, it seems, is assumed to understand something about *Catcher*. Exactly what or how much the reader is required to understand is more vague, ranging from the brevity of the first few examples—requiring a "household familiarity" with at least the title *The Catcher in the Rye*—to the complexity of the latter three: to fully enjoy Kinsella's novel, the reader must have some knowledge of both the basic story of *Catcher* and the questions and problems that interested Salinger himself. As both the novels and the television series are geared toward a widespread "middle-American" audience, these references reveal an assumption about *Catcher*'s place in the culture: if people haven't read it for themselves, they are at least familiar with the book's title, its status, and some sense of the story line.[7]

For many of those who have read it, *Catcher* holds an enduring appeal that some readers believe can transcend the cultural gap between generations. When critic Sanford Pinsker sought to define the characteristics of a "formative book" for his literary peers, he chose *Catcher* as his post–World War II exemplar of fiction capable of leading "double lives as cultural statements, fastened as firmly to the here and now as they are to fiction's universals." Noting that formative books have their greatest impact among adolescents, engaging these readers "at a point when options loom larger than certainties, when an admonition to 'change your life' can still have teeth,"

Pinsker recalled his own youthful response to *Catcher* as a reader "hooked" on Holden Caulfield's "talking" voice.[8]

Similarly, critic Adam Moss, reflecting upon his early reading of *Catcher*, wrote in 1981 that it had become "one of those rare books that influence one generation after another, causing each to claim it as its own."[9] Five years later, the casual remarks of a department store cosmetician in her mid-thirties confirmed and further personalized Moss's point when she commented to me that "*The Catcher in the Rye* was the key thing that got he [her then thirteen-year-old son] and I really talking about reading and how you don't always have to read 'junk.'"[10] Finally, it seems *Catcher* is not only a "formative" book to be shared across generations but a text that is capable of actually transforming its reader, leading Julie Smith to conclude her *Catcher* scene in *New Orleans Beat* with this claim: "Anybody who reads this book . . . can talk any way they want . . . because you can't stop anybody after they've read it, can you? They come out a whole different person, don't they?"[11]

The question then becomes, What is this book, this story that catches the attention and often the affections of so many? Simply told, *The Catcher in the Rye* is the tale of a sixteen-year-old boy, Holden Caulfield, who is flunking out of his third prep school and suffers a breakdown of sorts when he leaves school early to spend three days on his own in New York City. Holden is the narrator of the story, which is told in retrospect from a sanitarium in California, and Salinger maximizes the impact of the narrative by adhering meticulously to the teenage vernacular of the late 1940s–early 1950s. The resulting text is peppered with mild obscenities as Holden expresses his disappointment and, often, disgust with much of the postwar adult world.

Holden's definitive sense of American life is that it is largely "phony"—a term he applies repeatedly throughout the tale to various contemporary definitions of success, ranging from the realms of corporate achievement, conventional marriage, social status, and "belonging" to physical attractiveness, Hollywood glamour, and athletics. The implied "craziness" of his perspective is enhanced by the fact that Holden is well on the way to such success himself if only he would accept it. The novel ends as it begins: with Holden in the sanitarium, expected to return to "normal life" in the near future yet with little indication as to how he will manage the return to normalcy, much less whether he desires to do so.

On the surface, then, *Catcher* appears to be a rather mundane novel with its greatest potential audience among teenagers: the audience most likely to identify with Holden, to find the novel's use of adolescent vernacular familiar, and to appreciate the critique of contemporary adulthood. It is not readily apparent why this particular novel has gained the lasting affection as well as engendered the vehement hostility of adult readers to the degree that they have been willing to debate over it for the past forty-odd years. While other contemporary novels may have found a similarly split audience (Vladimir Nabokov's *Lolita* comes to mind), they have neither spurred such lengthy controversy nor enjoyed the sustained popularity of *Catcher*. It is only by looking more closely at Salinger's carefully drawn characterization of Holden Caulfield and listening through the vernacular and the obscenities that one can isolate the eloquent critique that Salinger presents, catching his audience unaware. The argument is one in the long-standing "determining debate" of American thought and writing that has been given coherent definition in R. W. B. Lewis's *The American Adam*.

• • •

In 1955 R. W. B. Lewis put forward his analysis of and argument for a "native American mythology." Pointing out that the salient (and assumedly universal) characteristic of cultural maturation was the generation of a "determining debate over the ideas that preoccupy it: salvation, the order of nature, money, power, sex, the machine, and the like," Lewis believed that such debates were a crucial forum in which "a culture achieves identity not so much through the ascendancy of one particular set of convictions as through the emergence of its peculiar and distinctive dialogue."[12]

Lewis located the American debate in the voices of "articulate thinkers and conscious artists" of nineteenth-century America, and the resulting mythos he isolated was what he called the "American Adam": "the authentic American as a figure of heroic innocence and vast potentialities, poised at the start of a new history."[13] While much of *The American Adam* was devoted to definition and description of this mythological hero as he appeared in American fiction, the heart of Lewis's argument lay in his insistence that this cultural mythology was a motivational source toward human good and, as well, in his mourning of the absence of such a mythology in mid-twentieth-century America: "A century ago, the challenge to debate was an expressed belief in achieved human perfection, a return to the primal perfection. Today the challenge comes rather from the expressed belief in achieved hopelessness. . . . We can hardly expect to be persuaded any longer by the historic dream of the new Adam."[14]

Looking at contemporary American literature from his 1955 vantage, Lewis identified three novels in the post–World War II period as examples of "the truest and most fully engaged American fiction after the second war": *Invisible Man* by Ralph Ellison, *The Adventures of Augie March* by Saul Bellow, and *The Catcher in the Rye* by J. D. Salinger. Lewis saw each of these novels as among the very few to continue the Adamic fictional tradition of solitary experience and moral priority over the waiting world. He applauded the efforts of these mid-twentieth-century writers as they "engender[ed] from within their work the hopeful and vulnerable sense of life that makes experience and so makes narrative action possible," yet who did so by "creat[ing] it from within, since they can scarcely find it any longer in the historic world about them."[15]

Here, Lewis's recognition of the intersection between his own formulation of the "American Adam" as a once dominant yet recently shrinking force in American culture and the story of Holden Caulfield is the first clue as to the source of cultural tension created by *The Catcher in the Rye*. A story of traditional appeal and yet a contemporary oddness, both fit and lack of fit with the historic dialogue are evident when *Catcher* is examined in light of Lewis's argument.

The classic characterization of the American Adam was the nineteenth-century image of a "radically new personality, the hero of the new adventure," "happily bereft of ancestry," and free of the taint of inherited status to stand alone, "self-reliant and self-propelling, ready to confront whatever awaited him with the aid of his own unique and inherent resources." As the nineteenth century drew to a close, this characterization was modified as American literature reflected concurrent perceptions of social and environmental changes in American life: the movement of the "frontier" from forest to barren plain, and ultimately to closure. The American Adam, no longer situated in an Edenic world, found himself instead "alone in a hostile, or at best a neutral universe." Nevertheless, Lewis claimed that the Adamic character remained intact throughout the first half of the twentieth century, "for much of that fable remained . . . the individual going forth toward experience, the inventor of his own character and creator of his personal history."[16]

Bearing these characterizations in mind, at this point I introduce to you Holden Caulfield, as J. D. Salinger did in the first page of *The Catcher in the Rye:*

> If you really want to hear about it, the first thing you'll probably want to know is where I was born, and what my lousy childhood was like, and how my parents were occupied and all before they had me, and all that David Copperfield kind of crap, but I don't feel like going into it, if you want to know the truth. In the first place, that stuff bores me, and in the second place, my parents would have about two hemorrhages apiece if I told anything personal about them. . . . Besides, I'm not going to tell you my whole goddam autobiography or anything. I'll just tell you about this madman stuff that happened to me around last Christmas.[17]

In Holden's statement of introduction, his position as a solitary individual in the Adamic tradition is not only evident but reinforced by the contrast to English literary tradition ("that David Copperfield kind of crap"). The initial assumption is that the mid-twentieth-century reader *wants* to know the family and position of a central character—an assumption that is immediately challenged as irrelevant to the telling of the story itself and as contrary to middle-class expectations of personal and family privacy. Hence, Salinger's introduction of his central character provided an opening defense for the Adamic narrative as well as an implicit jab at the movement of contemporary readers away from that very tradition.

Defense of the Adamic tradition is not surprising in light of Holden's apparent literary lineage. Searching for a fictional representative for his American mythos, "unambiguously treated" and "celebrated in his very Adamism,"[18] Lewis chose James Fenimore Cooper's Natty Bumppo: hero of *The Deerslayer* and, it seems, a direct if unacknowledged ancestor of Salinger's Holden Caulfield. In a central scene in *The Deerslayer,* Natty Bumppo's name is changed as the consequence of his fight with a Huron warrior. In their struggle, Natty kills the warrior, but Cooper characterizes it as a chivalrous battle, ending with the dying man telling Natty that he should now be known as "Hawkeye" instead of the boyish "Deerslayer."[19] In this pivotal moment, Natty takes on the heroic status of the American Adam: "born with all due ceremony during an incident that has every self-conscious quality of a ritual trial . . . Deerslayer earns his symbolic reward of a new name."[20]

If the notion of rebirth is characteristic of the American Adam, it is crucial to the overlapping American narrative of "regeneration through violence" in which acts of violence and destruction are seen as fair practice when they purportedly allow a morally strengthened consciousness to emerge.[21] And it is in keeping with both traditions, then, that early on in *Catcher,* Holden Caulfield purchases a red hunting cap that his prep school roommate calls a "deer-shooting cap." "Like hell it is," Holden retorts, and then clarifies to the reader of his narrative, "I took it off and looked at it. I sort of closed one eye, like I was taking aim at it. 'This is a people shooting hat,' I said. 'I shoot people in this hat'" (22).[22]

Further along, Holden battles an older and stronger classmate to protect the reputation of a female friend and finds himself on the losing end of the fight. Searching for his cap in defeat, Holden comes face-to-face with himself, and it is this critical moment of self-recognition that will lead to his leave-taking of Pencey Prep:

> I couldn't find my goddam hunting hat anywhere. Finally, I found it. It was under the bed. I put it on, and turned the peak around to the back, the way I liked it, and then I went over and took a look at my stupid face in the mirror. You never saw such gore in your life. I had blood all over my mouth and chin and even on my pajamas and bathrobe. It partly scared me and it partly fascinated me. All that blood and all sort of made me look tough. I'd only been in about

two fights in my life, and I lost both of them. I'm not too tough.
I'm a pacifist, if you want to know the truth. (45)

If the first passage recalls the heroic tradition of Cooper's *Deerslayer*
(Holden donning the symbolic garb of the deer hunter and further identifying
himself by his hawkeyed aim), then the second passage can be seen as a suggestion for a new errand for the Adamic hero: that of pacifism except when
called to the protection of innocents. His ritual battle endured, Holden's rever-
sal of the hunting cap brings to mind the cap of a baseball *catcher*. Holden is
thus implicitly renamed and it is a name he will later explicitly claim.

Just as the moment of trial and rebirth was the creation of Lewis's
Adamic character, it was his survival through a later "fall" from grace that
brought the character to heroic status. Although the consequences of such
a fall would entail some suffering, the fall itself offered an opportunity for
learning necessary to the character's growth in moral understanding and conscience to fully heroic stature. In the writing of the elder Henry James, for
example, the hero "had to fall, to pass beyond childhood in an encounter with
'Evil,'" and "had to mature by virtue of the destruction of his own egotism."
The very act of "falling" opened the path to moral perfection, a state viewed
by James as achievable "not by learning, only by *unlearning*."[23]

Considered within this framework of the "fortunate fall," Holden's experiences after he leaves Pencey Prep can be seen as necessary to his devel-
oping moral stature: from his introduction to the seamy side of New York
City life via bar flies, stale cabs, hotel pimps and prostitutes to his confrontation with Mr. Antolini. Antolini is a teacher from one of Holden's past prep
schools, "the best teacher I ever had" (174), and Holden turns to him for both
moral support and physical shelter. Holden's visit to his home, however, is
abruptly terminated when Holden interprets Antolini's consoling caresses as
a homosexual advance.

Holden flees Antolini's apartment, disillusioned and less innocent than
when he arrived; but before he can depart, Antolini makes a prediction as to
Holden's future: "I have a feeling that you're riding for some kind of a terrible,
terrible fall. But I don't honestly know what kind," Antolini warns Holden.
"It may be the kind where, at the age of thirty, you sit in some bar hating everybody who comes in looking as if he might have played football in college."
Fearing Holden will compromise himself in conforming to normative social
roles and expectations, Antolini describes a future of miserable scenarios in
which Holden might "pick up just enough education to hate people who say,
'It's a secret between he and I,'" or become a businessman "throwing paper
clips at the nearest stenographer" (186).

Holden grasps Antolini's depiction but rejects and amends some of his
predictions. Telling him, "you're wrong about hating football players and all.

You really are. I don't hate too many guys," Holden asserts his own compassionate perspective: "What I may do, I may hate them for a little while . . . but it doesn't last too long, is what I mean. After a while, if I didn't see them . . . I sort of missed them" (187). Thinking Holden still doesn't understand him, Antolini tries to clarify the future of quiet desperation he fears for Holden:

> This fall I think you're riding for—it's a special kind of fall, a horrible kind. The man falling isn't permitted to feel or hear himself hit bottom. He just keeps falling and falling. The whole arrangement's designed for men who, at some time or other in their lives, were looking for something their own environment couldn't supply them with. Or they thought their environment couldn't supply them with. So they gave up looking. They gave it up before they ever really even got started. You follow me? (187)

In truth, Holden is already struggling against the fall from the idealism that Antolini assumes to accompany the loss of childhood innocence, but Holden is trying as well to maintain *the perception of hope* that is crucial to the struggle itself. It is in this sense that Salinger, in his development of Holden as a hero, perhaps unwittingly draws attention to a paradox within the tradition of the American Adam: heroic status is attained by gaining moral strength through "falling," yet the future role of the hero is to *prevent* (in actuality or figuratively) others from taking the same fall. Hence, in the passage that gives tide to the novel, Holden's new-found purpose in life is to be "the catcher in the rye":

> Anyway, I keep picturing all these little kids playing some game in this big field of rye and all. Thousands of little kids, and nobody's around—nobody big, I mean—except me. And I'm standing on the edge of some crazy cliff. What I have to do, I have to catch everybody if they start to go over the cliff—I mean if they're running and they don't look where they're going I have to come out from somewhere and *catch* them. That's all I'd do all day. I'd just be the catcher in the rye and all. (173)

Although he wishes to prevent the fall of others, Holden cannot "catch" himself from his own fall—indeed, the "catcher in the rye" itself is a fantasy. The world of childhood innocence may exist outside of adult society but the inescapable process of maturity will eventually find all children becoming adult "insiders," participants in the larger social context, willing or not. In this sense, Holden's wish to remain "outside" the corrupting influences of adult society is again consistent with the mythos of the American Adam. The very heroism of the Adamic character rests on his ability to participate

in and improve upon "society" even as he manages to sustain the moral cer-
titude of his a priori innocence, a paradoxical stance that requires no small
amount of skill on the part of the writer to maintain reader credibility.

Salinger manages this paradox through Holden's fearful sensation of
"disappearing." In the duality of inside/outside relations, the outside "self"
still depends upon the recognition of *other insiders* to validate one's very sense
of existence. When Holden decides to leave Pencey Prep School—an action
consistent with his outsider status—he painfully acknowledges his need for
recognition of his leave-taking by those who remain "inside" Pencey:

> What I was really hanging around for, I was trying to feel some
> kind of good-by. I mean I've left schools and places I didn't even
> know I was leaving them. I hate that. I don't care if it's a sad good-
> by or a bad good-by, but when I leave a place I like to *know* I'm
> leaving it. If you don't, you feel even worse. (4)

When the necessary "good-byes" are not forthcoming, Holden leaves
in a state of limbo, neither insider nor outsider, and the perception of loss of
self is palpable as Holden reports that he feels as if he is "disappearing" every
time he crosses a road. This sensation is repeated toward the novel's end when
Holden again takes flight in a state of near-total anomie in which he fears
that he might "never get to the other side of the street" and would instead
"just go down, down, down, and nobody'd ever see me again." In his desperation, Holden makes believe that he is talking to his dead brother, Allie, and
manages to barely maintain his sense of identity through a series of incanta-
tions to Allie, pleading "don't let me disappear" (197–198).

Readers of the novel could construe Holden's sensation of "disappearing" as well as his reliance on his dead brother's support as evidence of incipi-
ent insanity rather than an imaginative preservation of self. Holden himself
refers to his behavior as "crazy" and "madman stuff" throughout the novel. Yet
this craziness is not only the consequence of Holden's alienation from society
but also the very expression of that alienation. The only recourse Holden fore-
sees is to "reappear" inside society, in a wholly different circumstance. In an
extended fantasy sequence, he envisions himself structurally and functionally
inside society while remaining outside in any meaningful sense:

> I'd start hitchhiking my way out West. . . . I'd be somewhere out
> West where it was very pretty and sunny and where nobody'd know
> me and I'd get a job. I figured I could get a job at a filling station
> somewhere, putting gas and oil in people's cars. I didn't care what
> kind of job it was, though. Just so people didn't know me and I
> didn't know anybody. I thought what I'd do was, I'd pretend I was

one of those deaf-mutes. That way I wouldn't have to have any
goddam stupid useless conversations with anybody. (198)

In his fantasy of moving West, Holden is attempting a further "new
beginning," in which he will protect his innocence and idealism by physically
moving out and away from the inauthenticity of adult society. A course of action that is familiar in American frontier experience, the idea of escaping into
the wilderness of the "untracked American forest" is endemic to the American Adam and requires the creation of a fictional environment in which "the
world always lies before the hero, and normally, like Huck Finn, he is able to
light out again for the 'territories.'"[24]

Holden, however, is not in the midst of the "untracked American forest"
but rather in the urban "jungle" of the mid-twentieth century. Salinger's use of
this environment emphasizes the coldness of modern institutions and the lack
of meaning in contemporary language, as evidenced through his continuing
imagery of graffiti and obscenities scrawled over hard exterior surfaces. Time
and again, Holden attempts to erase or rub out the obscenities from the walls
of a railway station, a museum, and a school. Holden reads these obscenities
as expressions of hostility that represent not only the loss of innocence but the
perversion of that innocence. When Holden finds "Fuck You" scrawled on the
wall of the school attended by his sister, Phoebe, it drives him "damn near crazy"
to think that first the "little kids would see it" and "then finally some dirty
kid would tell them—all cockeyed, naturally—what it meant," causing them to
"*think* about it and maybe even *worry* about it for a couple of days" (201).

Consequently, when Holden confronts his own mortality, the perception
of hope so crucial to the continuation of the American Adam is dashed by his
recognition of the postwar cultural conditions of anonymity and alienation:

That's the whole trouble. You can't ever find a place that's nice and
peaceful, because there isn't any. You may *think* there is, but once
you get there, when you're not looking, somebody'll sneak up and
write "Fuck you" right under your nose. Try it sometime. I think,
even, if I ever die, and they stick me in a cemetery, and I have a
tombstone and all, it'll say "Holden Caulfield" on it, and then what
year I was born and what year I died, and then right under that it'll
say "Fuck you." I'm positive, in fact. (204)

Here, Holden's realization of the apparent futility of attempting to
make his individual life fully distinctive, and the absurdity of trying to prevent the loss or perversion of innocence, does not stop him from continuing
to try to erase the obscenities he personally confronts. In a revision of the
Adamic plot that reflects the paradoxical sentiments of disillusionment and

optimism prevalent in postwar America, Salinger requires his readers to entertain notions of Holden's defeat and demise only to salvage Holden's heroic status by emphasizing the relentless hopefulness of his actions.[25] Signifying the survival of Holden's optimism, Holden's repeated erasures of the obscene scrawlings take the form of what critic Ihab Hassan has termed the "rare quixotic gesture"—an eloquent act of hopefulness by the absurd yet heroic American character. Arguing that the "unmistakably American flourish" of the quixotic gesture is rooted in the "quest of American adolescents . . . for an idea of truth," Hassan believed that such actions were gestures "at once of pure expression and of expectation, of protest and of prayer, of aesthetic form and spiritual content," and finally, "behavior that sings."[26]

While the rubbing out of obscenities is the most self-conscious (and self-defeating) effort in *Catcher,* the very fantasy of being the "catcher in the rye" is itself a notion of quixotic hopefulness. Holden's account of his "madman" days ends with an expression of joy and momentary return to innocence as he watches his young sister, Phoebe, riding a carousel in the rain at his encouragement. Phoebe has just returned Holden's red hunting cap, placing it on his head and effectively acknowledging the temporal nature of his identity as "the catcher" when she tells him "you can wear it for a while."

Noting upon reflection that his hunting cap "really gave me quite a lot of protection, in a way," Holden sits in the rain and gets soaked watching Phoebe. It is a moment worth the drenching for Holden, who finds himself feeling "so damn happy, if you want to know the truth. I don't know why. It was just that she looked so damn *nice,* the way she kept going around and around, in her blue coat and all." Concluding by telling the reader, "God, I wish you could've been there," Holden's narrative here implies that while the *preservation* of innocence might indeed be impossible, the appreciation of that innocence is enough to restore the sense of hope (212–243).

Catcher closes with Holden's summary of his final state of convalescence—although whether he is recovering from a mental breakdown or physical exhaustion is unclear. Not surprisingly, the tale ends on a hopeful if enigmatic note as Holden first tells the reader that "if you want to know the truth, I don't know what I think about it. I'm sorry I told so many people about it." In the very next sentence, however, Holden goes on to acknowledge, "All I know is, I sort of miss everybody I told about. Even old Stradlater and Ackley, for instance. I think I even miss that goddam Maurice," leading Holden to warn the reader, "Don't ever tell anybody anything. If you do, you start missing everybody" (213–214). Hence, if Holden at last remains outside society, it is with an enriched sense of his kinship with those *inside*—an affinity ironically recognized through his struggle to distinguish himself from them.

In *The Myth of Sisyphus,* Albert Camus writes of the absurd hero: "The struggle itself toward the heights is enough to fill a man's heart. One must imagine Sisyphus happy."[27] And so do I see Holden Caulfield, as both absurd hero and one ultimately happy at his task, balancing between actions of individual responsibility and engagement in a social community, a hero in the tradition of one of America's central fables. That the postwar context in which *Catcher* was conceived and read is itself a quixotic construction is the subject of the next chapter: a consideration of the perceptions of post–World War II intellectuals that the American errand had gone awry if not failed, and their wish to somehow sustain that selfsame sense of innocence.

NOTES

1. I am indebted to Adam Moss's compilation of the publishing history of *Catcher* in "Catcher Comes of Age," *Esquire*, Dec. 1981, 56–57, and Michael Kennet's summary "Searching for Salinger," *Boston Globe*, 3 Sept. 1997, sect. C1. Some confusion crops up as to the initial copyright date for *Catcher*. Two incidents that appear in *Catcher* were published earlier as segments in two short stories by J. D. Salinger: "I'm Crazy" in *Collier's* (Dec. 1945), and "Slight Rebellion Off Madison" in the *New Yorker* (Dec. 1946). Nevertheless, the first date for the novel as a complete work is July 1951, published by Little, Brown and Co. (New York).

2. The television series are *Sixty Minutes* (CBS), air date 1 Nov. 1982; *Archie Bunker's Place* (CBS), air date 21 Feb. 1982; *Family Feud* (ABC), air date 19 Oct. 1983. The novels are Michael Bowen's *Can't Miss* (New York: Harper and Row, 1987), Erich Segal's *Oliver's Story* (New York: Harper and Row, 1977), W. P. Kinsella's *Shoeless Joe* (Boston: Houghton Mifflin, 1982), and Julie Smith's *New Orleans Beat* (New York: Ivy Books, 1994). These examples came to my attention in the course of everyday experience rather than through an intentional survey—and many more were recounted to me that I did not formally verify.

3. *Family Feud*, host Richard Dawson. For a discussion of the assumed audience and intent of *Family Feud*, as well as its history as a highly successful television game show, see Mark Crispin Miller's essay "Family Feud" in *New Republic*, 18–25 July 1983, 23–27.

4. Bowen 202. In fact, the reference to *Catcher* here is so abbreviated that an unfamiliar reader would likely be more confused than drawn into further identification with Bowen's character: "She sounded like something out of *The Catcher in the Rye*. He gave her a benign smile. '*Phony* is a word I'm not particularly fond of, Rook.'"

5. Kinsella 72. See also 26–34, 51–60, 73–78, and 219–224. In the film version of the novel, *Field of Dreams* (1989), J. D. Salinger is dropped as a character; however, the play on "catcher" and the treatment of baseball as a Zen experience remains focal.

6. Smith 174–175.

7. Further evidence that *Catcher* is assumed to be a part of cultural knowledge exists in its inclusion in the popular 1980s board game Trivial Pursuit (copyright 1981 Horn-Abbot; distributed in the U.S. by Selchow and Righter, Co.). See the Genus edition, card no. 955, "Arts and Literature" category: Q. "What book does Holden Caulfield appear in?" A. "*The Catcher in the Rye*."

8. Sanford Pinsker, "*The Catcher in the Rye* and All: Is the Age of Formative Books Over?" *Georgia Review* 1986 (40): 953–967. Of note, Pinsker identifies Kinsella's *Shoeless Joe* as a contemporary contender for "formative book" status.

9. Moss 56.

10. Interview with Monica Bullock, 10 Feb. 1986, Orange County, Calif.

11. Smith 175.

12. R. W. B. Lewis, *The American Adam* (Chicago: University of Chicago Press, 1955), 1–2.

13. Ibid., 1. Lewis's reliance on a select body of literature for his analysis combined with his willingness to then generalize that analysis to "a native American mythology" of "our culture" reflects 1950s intellectual assumptions about cultural holism and the value of elite literature. Often referred to as the "myth-symbol-image" school of cultural analysis, this perspective has received just criticism since the late 1960s for its lack of distinction between dominant and subcultural realms of production, familiarity, and adoption of such a mythology. Rather than wholly discounting Lewis's work on the basis of these criticisms, I find *American Adam* to be instructive on two counts: as a primary source for understanding 1950s intellectuals and for his definition of the American Adam itself. Essentially, Lewis's analysis of the American Adam as both mythology and character type remains accurate, if needing a broader range of cultural materials for evidence. Similarly, Lewis's interpretation of that mythology is not so much inaccurate as lacking in address to the question of how such a mythology functions as an ideology, and for whom. Contemporary scholars would perhaps not overlook broader sources nor fail to see the usefulness of the American Adam mythology in attempted justification of otherwise arbitrary, socially constructed inequalities in American life. I have little difficulty, for example, in recognizing the American Adam, alive if unwell, in the 1980s spate of *Rambo* films, literature, and consumer items, and could readily argue the ideological usage of the American Adam mythology in these materials. If Lewis suffered from the "intellectual blinders" of his own time of scholarship, it would be further nearsightedness to disavow what he did elucidate.

14. Lewis 9–10.

15. Ibid., 197, 198.

16. Ibid., 5, 111.

17. J. D. Salinger, *The Catcher in the Rye* (New York: Bantam Books, 1964), 1. Further citations appear parenthetically in the text.

18. Lewis 91.

19. See James Fenimore Cooper, *The Deerslayer* (1841; Albany: SUNY Press, 1987), 124–129.

20. Lewis 104;

21. See Richard Slotkin, *Regeneration through Violence* (Middletown, Conn.: Wesleyan University Press, 1973), and also Richard Drinnon, *Facing West: The Metaphysics of Indian-Hating and Empire-Building* (New York: New American Library, 1980).

22. Of note, this section of the novel is interpreted by Alan Nadel in *Containment Culture* as evidence that Holden Caulfield is a fictional McCarthyite: "Donning his red hunting hat, he attempts to become the good Red-hunter, ferreting out the phonies and subversives" (71). See my introductory discussion of my disagreement with Nadel's interpretation.

23. Lewis 55, 57.

24. Ibid., 100.

25. Necessary even to his limited consideration of post–World War II writers, this alteration of the classic mythos is what Lewis termed "the matter of Adam: the ritualistic trials of the young innocent, liberated from family and social history or bereft of them; advancing hopefully into a complex world he knows not of; radically affecting that world and radically affected by it; defeated, perhaps even destroyed . . . but leaving his mark upon the world, and a sign in which conquest may later become possible for survivors" (127).

26. Ihab Hassan, *Radical Innocence: Studies in the Contemporary American Novel* (Princeton, N.J.: Princeton University Press, 1961).

27. Albert Camus, *The Myth of Sisyphus,* trans. Justin O'Brien (New York: Vintage Books, 1959), 90.

DAVID CASTRONOVO

Holden Caulfield's Legacy

The *Catcher in the Rye* is, of course, more than a novel. A lightning rod for
a new sensibility, a wisdom book for postwar students, a behavior manual
for the age of impulse, it has had a life apart from the literary world and
cultural significance and staying power beyond its literary value. Inferior in
quality to the greatest consciousness shaping works of American modern-
ism—among them, *The Great Gatsby, The Sun Also Rises, Invisible Man*—it
nevertheless has the power to distill states of mind, spark identification, and
live beyond its covers. Like certain songs or movie characters, it has become
a part of the shared experience of a vast number of people in the second half
of the twentieth century. People know the book who haven't read it with
any care; others—like nineteenth-century people who had heard about Mr.
Pickwick or Anna Karenina—have heard the news of Holden Caulfield just
by being alive. There are websites devoted to the novel; people live by it
and, although we live in an un-Arnoldian age, it is probably one of our last
remaining literary touchstones—youth and resentment and joy and angst, in
book rather than CD, TV, or net form.

It came out in 1951, not exactly an *annus mirabilis* for American literature, but not such a bad year, either. *From Here to Eternity* was also published
and became a bestseller. The gap between the two books is the gap between an
older world of naturalism—with its careful chronicling of injustices and hard

New England Review, Volume 22, Number 2 (Spring 2001): pp. 180–186. Copyright © 2001
David Castronovo.

luck and hard living and an entirely new rendering of the American situation: the distance between Jones's war in the Pacific and Salinger's peace and prosperity is hardly the crucial point; *Catcher* has a language, texture, and view of what counts that places it firmly in America's future; *From Here to Eternity* belongs with the classics of the past. 1951 was not a notable year for cultural change in America, either. Rock 'n' roll, Brando's motorcycle in *The Wild One*, Dean's red jacket in *Rebel Without a Cause*—the spring blossoms of the coming age of antinomianism—were nowhere in sight. What was plentifully available? Endless anti-communist screeds, anxieties about conformity, books about Social Problems, music that was sentimental and kitschy or part of the wit and heart of old Tin Pan Alley (the obnoxious kid Stradlater in *Catcher* whistles themes from "Song of India" and "Slaughter on Tenth Avenue"), liberal arts students who wanted jobs and not ideologies. Salinger's book was the first embraceable book to appear after the war: the first book with an idiom and an attitude of its own, something that made young people newly aware of themselves. The novels that were still coming out about the war didn't quite do the job for these new readers. They needed their own book, one that spoke to the younger brothers who were just kids at the time of the war. They also needed a book that didn't employ the locutions of the Depression, the rhetoric of the left and right, or the language of the war years, whether the staunchly patriotic slogans of the majority or the disaffected idiom of the isolationists among the intellectuals.

At first blush, Salinger's novel, a younger brother's account of himself, seems like a reinvention of a familiar story in earlier twentieth-century literature: like *Winesburg, Ohio* or *Look Homeward, Angel* or even Hemingway's Nick Adams stories, it's about a lonely young boy who thinks there is something wrong with the world, something essentially dead and phony and disgusting about the arrangement of things. But once linked with these books, *Catcher* detaches itself, for the most part because it isn't a story about development. Holden Caulfield has no unfolding destiny, no mission, not even the dramatic moments of Nick or his avatars in battle or Eugene Gant overcoming his mother's influence. Holden is a drifter whose life story is a muddle, a series of pathetic, comic, poignant incidents that are altogether unlike the destiny-building moments of the earlier books. Salinger turns against the "David Copperfield crap" and most other patterns as well. The book is anti-literary in a new way: its pages are filled with babbling rather than talk that builds to a climax; impressions that are overtaken by afterthoughts, comic contradictions, half-recognitions, and canceled insights. While sharing the basic subject of Hemingway and Anderson—lonely youth—Salinger invents a mode of his own: a managed incoherence, an attractive breakdown of logic that appeals to the confused adolescent in all of us. Sweeping denunciations are followed by abject apologies—only to be followed by other ridiculous pronouncements.

Holden the muttering self fires off Holdenism after Holdenism. Try one of these: "I'm quite illiterate, but I read a lot." Or, "I hate the movies like poison, but I get a bang imitating them." Or, "A horse is at least human, for God's sake." Or, "The show wasn't as bad as some I've seen. It was on the crappy side, though." Or, "Listen. What's the routine on joining a monastery?"

Holden's idiom is the novel's glory, the property that has appealed to audiences for fifty years. A blend of explosive denunciation and heart-on-sleeve sentiment, it maintains a high tension for a little over two hundred pages. Since Salinger employs only the thinnest of plots—a linking of loosely connected incidents in Holden's downward journey—the rambling, ranting, and rhapsodizing are the main events. The idiom takes over as Holden's speech becomes the central conflict. How will he react next? We lurch from aperçu to aperçu, epigram to epigram—all of them drawing on carefully chosen contrasts: the boy's rendering of his world employs popular culture and classic literature, upper-middle-class taste and a thorough knowledge of urban tackiness, refinement and grossness, tender solicitude and harsh condemnation. The book is charged and energetic to the end because it never quite settles into a consistent point of view: as exasperating as this may be for readers who want character logic and clear motivation, the scattered remarks and volatility of the prose have taken hold. Its unreasoned judgments have also dug deep into our consciousness and connected with the unexplainable part of our lives. Can we account for every aspect of our own irritation, repulsion, contempt? Are there clearly drawn correlatives for Holden's disgust, anger, and disillusionment? Do we have any evidence that the people he mocks are quite as pathetic as he would have it? Ackley with his pimples and bragging about sex, Stradlater with his dapper appearance and swagger, Sally Hayes with her hard edged practicality and her little ice-skating skirt, the out-of-towners Marty and Laverne at the Lavender Lounge with their grammar errors and their gawking at celebrities? Are they enough to warrant what is magnified into what we see as Holden's contemptu mundi? If you have followed the crazy reasoning, listened to Holden's standards—sincerity, kindness, dignity—you will follow such judgments. These people are pathetic, either phonies or flops.

Holden's discontents and diatribes are infectious because we all have our irascibility and fastidiousness, and Salinger has managed to play on us by summoning up the perfect, grating details. Like Browning or Dickens, he has an extensive inventory of annoyances and human weaknesses, stupid locutions and exasperating habits. The book is a treasury of the ludicrous, and its absurdities remain fresh a half century later. Take Pencey's headmaster with his forced jokes and his toadying to rich parents; or the man at Radio City who says of the Rockettes, "that's precision"; or Sally Hayes conspicuously embracing a gray-flanneled acquaintance as if they were "old buddyroos." Recall some Dickens characters—despite Holden's self-conscious impatience with *David Copperfield*—and you will be in the same literary territory: Peckniff with his "moral throat," Fagin's "my dear," Pumblechook with his hectoring. Like Dickens, Salinger has a masterful command of pretensions. At the Wicker Bar Holden observes the singer, "Old Janine": "And now we like to geeve you our impression of Vooly Voo Fransay. Eet ess the story of a leetle Fransh girl who comes to a beeg ceety, just like New York, and falls in love wees a lettle boy from Brookleen." He captures the manner of Carl Luce, a blasé intellectual, with dead-on accuracy: "He never said hello or anything when he met you. The first thing he said when he sat down was that he could only stay a couple of minutes."There's no place quite like *Catcher* for savoring the cant and swill of contemporary life: "Newsreels. Christ almighty. There's always a dumb horse race, and some dame breaking a bottle over a ship, and some chimpanzee with pants on riding a goddamn bicycle."

But once you have had your fill of Holden denouncing anything and everything, you naturally wonder what it all amounts to. Does Salinger deliver any real insight, any recognition? Is it all clever schtick or carefully managed nastiness? Are the mots a kind of superior talk radio? Pure spleen hasn't much staying power; negativism, as Cyril Connolly once remarked, dates quickly. But *Catcher* mixes its cynicism and irascibility with a rich brew of sentiment and idealism, a child-like faith that life contains more than pretensions and phoniness. In some ways it is more a wisdom book than a novel, a collection of pronouncements about living well and discovering useable truths. After thundering at the world, it offers compact packages of insight. Holden, the comic instructor incapable of running his own life, proposes exempla for his listeners: he's the half-cracked advisor who gets our attention by the strange slant of his doctrines. The most affecting doctrine of course is that of the Catcher in the Rye: this teaching—which twists Robert Burns's line from "meet" to "catch"—is a typical Holdenism; half-informed, but totally emphatic, it produces meaning in the midst of confusion. It takes a highly recognized poem, mixes childish naïveté with the poetry and mangles the original sense. The result is a curious restatement of the New Testament exhortation to be thy brother's keeper: your mission in life is to catch little children before they fall off the cliff. No sooner do you see the odd simplicity and innocence of the doctrine's packaging than you recognize its powerful connection with other such statements in world literature. Salinger, by redesigning a sentiment about love and mercy and the innocence of children, takes a modest but quite definite place in the romantic movement; his imagery—either in the figure of the individual child (Phoebe Caulfield or the little boy who sings a snatch from "Comin' Through the Rye") or the vision of crowds of children endangered—is strongly reminiscent of Blake's language in *Songs of Innocence and Experience*. His moment of pure joy at first reminds us of Blakean joy. Looked at from a Blakean point of view, it's the all-but-incoherent utterance of the innocent, for example the voice in "Infant Joy": "I happy am / Joy is my name.— / Sweet joy befall thee!" But the more specific insight of *Catcher* is a lesson out of Wordsworth.

The doctrine of *Catcher* is presented in Salinger's characteristic spatterdash, free-associational way. In a scene with Phoebe, he enunciates his position, but does so by raking through the past and stumbling inadvertently on truth: the emotional truth of the *Catcher* "comes" to Holden—as it has to romantic poets, particularly to the Wordsworth of "Resolution and Independence"—after he has reviewed the spectacle of himself, rejected that self and the world that made it, and by chance discovered truth embodied in the quotidian, in the unproclaimed and unproclaiming world of everdayness; that truth is distilled in the actions of the nuns collecting for their order at the station, in the schoolteacher who mercifully covers the body of a young suicide, and in the sacred actions of Holden's dead brother, Allie. Like Wordsworth, Salinger favors the didactic colloquy as a prelude to emotional awakening. A teacher—without a schoolroom, of course—prepares the pupil for the recognition. Along the same lines, the leech gatherer in Wordsworth, an old man who endures despite poverty and the harshness of the environment, has a few direct, simple words—"apt admonishment" for a narrator who is depressed and caught in a web of self-absorption; he has his message, his example, his acceptance of life. Salinger's Phoebe Caulfield has her corresponding childish insights to offer an older brother caught in a similar emotional crisis.

Like Wordsworth, Salinger prefers a symbolic action or a dramatic scene to reasoning or mere words. Holden listening to Phoebe's childish jabbering and the narrator of "Resolution and Independence" listening to the old man's sparse advice: each character is more influenced by the personal situation than by the particular words. And each work is carried by spectacle and scene rather than by specific doctrine. Talk is important, but reasoned explanation will not yield insight. *Catcher*'s last dramatic scene shows Phoebe riding the carrousel in Central Park, reaching for the gold ring. The depiction includes Holden's reaction, a joyous response, something that cannot be accounted for logically or through an examination of motive: "I felt so happy all of a sudden, the way old Phoebe kept going around and around. I was damn near bawling, I felt so happy, if you want to know the truth." In its way this is our recent literature's most memorable equivalent of Wordsworth's great awakening scenes: the discovery of joy and heightened understanding and the capacity for close identification with others who are experiencing instinctual pleasure or fulfillment or satisfactory endurance. "By our spirits are we deified," Wordsworth put it. The awakening is like John Stuart Mill's famous recognition scene in his *Autobiography:* Mill's own depression lifted when he discovered the inner sense of Wordsworth's poetry. "What made Wordsworth's poems a medicine for my state of mind was that they expressed, not mere outward beauty, but states of feeling, and of thought colored by feeling, under the excitement of beauty." Hard as it is to think of human feeling as a news item at the turn of the millennium—after nearly two hundred years of writers, poets, singers, and attitudinizers prying out the meaning of emotions—it seems new to us when Salinger is the investigator. Holden watching his sister has given contemporary American literature a moment like that of "Resolution and Independence" and that of Mill emerging from his despondency: the melancholy observer awakens to the joy of life by observing another's deep involvement in some form of release or reclamation. Mill calls the process of his awakening through poetry "the culture of the feelings." In reading Wordsworth's poems, he recollects, "I seemed to draw from a source of inward joy, of sympathetic and imaginative pleasure, which could be shared in by all human beings." When Holden Caulfield was so happy he felt like "bawling," he wanted to pass on the elation—"God, I wish you could've been there." Be it said that the source of newfound joy—the culture of the feelings—is a child on a carrousel, not a series of poems. Renewal in the twentieth century is the raw experience of being in the midst of life, colliding with joy and not wanting to account for why or wherefore; Mill's highly analytic account of renewal through the cultivation of feelings assumes a world where the individual moves easily among books and abstract ideas and ordinary experiences.

The mystery of emotional awakening is Salinger's main obsession in the book; his fear is that the discovery he has made—the connection between the innocent wise child and joyous renewal—will in some way be mocked or cheapened or otherwise devalued. Or generalized about or analyzed. He also fears himself and his all-too-human inclination to traduce his own vision. Afraid to publish, afraid of the sentiment that he himself has dispersed, he has become an elderly Holden, AWOL from the responsibility to give an account of himself; in Salinger's case he has bitterly resisted the responsibilities of authorship as we generally recognize it, including the obligation to be heard periodically. *Catcher*—since its publication—has been its author's holy book, never to be defiled by stage, screen, or other profane translations. As any reader of Ian Hamilton's book on Salinger will easily recognize, the protectiveness of this author for his property is something that goes well beyond our ordinary understanding of author's rights. And the book itself provides its own self-absorbed defense against cheapness and meanness; hardly a sentence passes without the narrator's making sure that he is not falling into the ways of the world. Holden wants to immunize himself against corny rhetoric by employing every kind of hard-boiled phrase and cynical dismissal that the publishers of 1951 will permit. The scenes of pure joy and transcendence come in the main near the end of a book that has taken devastating aim at the cheap emotionalism, histrionics, sappy effects, warm and fuzzy recognition scenes in movies, books, and life. The author has his own defensive tactics—whatever it takes to keep the sacred texts from being defiled.

Salinger's idea of joy and renewal should be seen against the backdrop of Hollywood schlock; it's the awkward, hand-designed, and naive sentiment that stands out against the formulaic and corny. Askew and spontaneous, the story line is far from the calculated mass product that Holden remembers from the movies. Contrast it, for example, with his favorite love-to-hate movie, a travesty of renewal about an Englishman who suffers from amnesia after the war. Holden tells us that the character Alec staggers around on a cane until he meets a "homey babe" who wants to rejuvenate him, share her love of Dickens—as well as get help in her floundering publishing business, help badly needed since her cracked-up surgeon brother has been spending all the profits. The complications—involving Alec's ducal status and his other girlfriend—are hilariously related by Holden, whose own complications have none of the factitious neatness of this sort of plot. "Anyway it ends up with Alec and the homey babe getting married. . . . All I can say is don't see it if you don't want to puke all over yourself." Hollywood in this case is the culprit, but elsewhere human feeling is mangled by the cant of prep school teachers, New York sophisticates, phony intellectuals, doting upper-middle-class parents, even earlier writers. Dickens's David Copperfield crap is the best hint of all about Salinger's ambition to achieve his own breakthrough. True to the great project of romanticism, *Catcher* throws off the meretricious past, purifies its spirit with a new diction, tone, and objects of attention. The decorum of earlier literature disappears, along with the dignity and seriousness and measured speech of modernist heroes like Jake Barnes or Jay Gatsby. In the carrousel scene, the rain pours down and mixes with the strains of "Smoke Gets in Your Eyes" and "Oh Marie" and the spectacle of Holden in his hunting hat. No Frederic Henry here. The ludic, manic mode can't and won't account for a hero, refuses to unpack clear causes or offer careful delineations. The literary tradition is something to get a kick out of—the way Holden does from Hardy's Eustacia Vye—but not something to talk about much, or follow in much detail. When Salinger taught writing at Columbia, he was disdainful of the whole notion of classroom analysis of works. Just read them. We murder to dissect. We even murder to account for or scrutinize.

This contempt for disciplined analysis and careful tracing of literary filaments from the past does not mean the book doesn't champion other kinds of personal discipline. The central doctrine of the book—that each of us has a Catcher in the Rye lodged within—implies a strict code for living. In its ramshackle way, *Catcher* is a conduct book for the age of anxiety and conformity. No section of the book is without its precepts, prohibitions, and practical tips for cant-free living. It is, in this sense, one of the first manuals of cool, a how-to guide for those who would detach themselves from the all-

American postwar pursuit of prosperity and bliss. Holden the drop-out and outsider speaks like some crazed, half-literate Castiglione as he discourses on everything from clothing and bearing to the appropriate responses of a cool person in any situation. The following precepts are crucial:

—Ignore the messages of mass media. ("The goddamn movies. They can ruin you.")
—Be "casual as hell."
—Avoid any air of superiority or trace of competitiveness.
—Value digressions more highly than logical arguments.
—Never use the word "grand."
—Scorn routine sociability.
—Observe the margins of life: the remarks of children, the conduct of nuns; ignore the main acts. (The guy who plays the kettle drums at Radio City Music Hall is more important than the "Christmas thing" with "O Come All Ye Faithful.")

After fifty years these teachings remain a central element of our culture. Young people and their fearful elders know that coolness is the only way. Formal discourse, sequential thinking, reverence for the dignified and the heroic: these acts closed by the 1960s. The voice of Holden played a part in shutting them down. Its tone—directed against prestige and knowingness—is as cutting today as it was in 1951: "I could see them all sitting around in some bar with their goddamn checkered vests, criticizing shows and books and women in those tired, snobby voices." Cancel the checkered vests and you're right at home at the millennium.

But for all its durability, does *Catcher* continue to make sense to the mature mind? Is it infantile and simplistic, reductive and negative, expressing the attitude of a kid who is soon to get the therapy he needs? One can only say that the scorn for conventions and the search for joy are a part of the ongoing romantic project that started in the eighteenth century. Exasperating, irrational, and dangerous as these pursuits have sometimes proven, they show no signs of coming to an end. Salinger's ardor and disdain have a bracing quality of their own, inferior to that of the great romantic artists but nevertheless still important at a time when we need to resist our own age of reason, its monoliths and abstract ideas of human progress. With its horror of groupthink of all kinds—be it remembered that, like George Orwell, the Salinger of *Catcher* has nothing good to say about politics, power blocks, commercial modernity, or any orthodoxy—the book is free of the worst tendencies of the late 1940s. Like Orwell, too, Salinger has profound respect for the decencies, pleasures, and truths that can be found anywhere. But unlike Orwell, Salinger is an anti-enlightenment weaver of fantasies and denouncer of hard-headed thinking. If truth be told, his Blakean celebration of joy and wonder foreshadowed the wooliness of the beatniks and hippies and would become flabby and sententious even by the time of the Glass family stories of the late 1950s. While Franny and Zooey's complaints about civilization are preachy and humorlessly tiresome, though, Holden's negativity remains wonderfully fresh in its inconsistency. He remains a bearer of a permanent truth: that you can't fake an affectional life; that you must live through absurdity, indignity, and pain in order to get a small return of happiness.

JOHN McNALLY

The Boy That Had Created the Disturbance: Reflections on Minor Characters in Life and The Catcher in the Rye

The Bread Loaf Writers' Conference is the granddad of writing confer-
ences, initially suggested by Robert Frost and then founded in 1926. The
conference is an institution in American letters, an eleven-day orgy of,
among other things, poetry and fiction workshops and readings. The readings by both novice and well-known writers are held twice daily inside the
Little Theater, a large barn with bleacher seating.

I attended the conference in August of 1999, and on the night that
esteemed poet Ed Hirsch was to read, nearly all of the seats in the Little
Theater were taken. I was sitting in one of the top bleachers at the far back of
the theater with a few of my new friends. Gathered in the row in front of us
were the Bread Loaf fellows—writers fresh with their first published books, a
handsome and diverse group of men and women with nothing but the promise of more fortunes ahead of them. In short, the envy of Bread Loaf.

As is the case at most poetry readings, the audience responded to Ed
Hirsch's work with soft grunts of affirmation, the usual ooooooohs and ahhhhhs,
and the appreciative head bobbing. Then, during a moment of silence, a preg-
nant pause between stanzas in one of Hirsch's poems, my friend D. G. leaned
sideways and let rip the loudest fart I'd ever heard. To give some seismographic
sense of its magnitude, I need to take you, dear reader, outside of the Little
Theater, where D. G.'s friend Michael was stationed. Michael was smoking

With Love and Squalor: 14 Writers Respond to the Work of J. D. Salinger, edited by Kip Kotzen
and Thomas Beller (New York: Broadway Books, 2001): pp. 104–116. Copyright © 2001 Kip
Kitzen and Thomas Beller.

a cigarette and waiting for the reading to end. He was several hundred feet away, a wall separated him from us, and yet he clearly heard the resounding blast, too. Not only did he hear it, but he had his suspicions as to where it had originated. For a man *outside* to have heard it, you can only imagine the shock and disgust *inside* the theater. Several dozen people had turned around, hoping to catch the offender. The only person, it seemed, who *didn't* hear it was Ed Hirsch, the poet. Without missing a beat, Hirsch carried on with his poem, reading the next stanza.

I was thirty-three years old that year, my title at the conference was "scholar," and yet I was doing all that I could not to laugh. I stared Zenlike out one of the barn's windows, into the Vermont darkness, emptying my head of all thought; but then I caught D. G.'s reflection in the window, his face contorted from holding back his own laugh, and then I heard him snort, and I couldn't help it: I snorted in return. Lan Samantha Chang—a fiction fellow in the row in front of us—turned around to shoot D. G. a look, but a wave of fumes must have hit her entire row at that exact moment, and all the fellows—soon-to-be Pulitzer Prize–winner Jhumpa Lahiri among them—pitched forward. Poor Lan even gagged.

Months later, D. G. sent an e-mail to me. He signed it, *The Boy That Had Created the Disturbance at the Ed Hirsch reading.*

Edgar Marsalla is "the boy that had created the disturbance" in J. D. Salinger's *The Catcher in the Rye.* Marsalla was sitting in the row in front of Caulfield in the chapel, and during a speech by one of the school's donors, Marsalla "laid this terrific fart" that "damn near blew the roof off." "It was a very crude thing to do, in chapel and all," Caulfield says, "but it was also quite amusing."

But after damn near blowing the roof off with his terrific fart, Edgar Marsalla never returns to *The Catcher in the Rye.* He enters the book, creates a scene, then leaves—the fate of a minor character.

In his book *Aspects of the Novel,* E. M. Forster calls them flat characters. According to Forster, "Flat characters were called 'humours' in the seventeenth century, and are sometimes called types, and sometimes caricatures. In their purest form, they are constructed round a single idea or quality."

Our days and nights are crowded with flat characters—people who, like Edgar Marsalla, enter our lives, make a scene, then leave—but it's the scene they make, large or small, that we remember them by, and by which we define them. (I did not know D. G. before Bread Loaf, and if I had never seen him again afterward, I would always think of him at that Ed Hirsch reading bent over, red-faced and snorting, actually convulsing from trying not to laugh—the perennial grade-school prankster.)

Salinger is a master at the minor (or flat) character, and *The Catcher in the Rye* is full-to-bursting with these folk. There are over fifty-five such characters in the novel—over fifty-five!—many of whom never appear more than once, many of whom, in fact, never actually appear in the book at all, floating ghostlike through the dark recesses of Holden Caulfield's mind. If they *do* appear, they do so as bit players, characters of little or no long-lasting consequence to either Holden or the novel's plot. And yet without these minor or flat characters, *The Catcher in the Rye* would evaporate in our hands. *Poof:* No more book. To excise these characters would be literary genocide, for what we have in *The Catcher in the Rye* is an entire population. My own copy of *The Catcher in the Rye* is a beat-to-hell hardback in its sixty-third printing, an ex-library copy with a protective Mylar cover. Reading the book once again, I placed yellow Post-It notes at the introduction of each minor character, and by the time I finished reading it, the book had become bloated with yellow stickies, names and attributes curling into view. The book had become a tenement, and the characters were peeking out from the pages.

Salinger uses characters the way a pointillist uses paint: stand back and you'll see a portrait of Holden Caulfield. But it's more than that, really, because the *way* that Holden sees these characters says a lot more about Holden Caulfield than it says about any individual character, the cumulative effect of which is that we see, by the end of the novel, not only a portrait of Holden but a blueprint of his psyche as well, his vision of the world.

For my money, this is the beauty of the book. There's much to be said about the *voice* of the novel, but frankly the voice gets a little old in places, and Holden's tics (all of his "and all"s at the end of sentences, or calling everyone "old" so-and-so) start to grate on me, especially once Salinger starts piling them on, sentence after sentence. These tics become a literary affectation, a device to *create* Holden's voice, but devices in and of themselves often call more attention to the creator than the created. The minor characters, however, are gems who don't linger on the scene long enough to grow stale.

There are so damn many characters in *The Catcher in the Rye* that the book becomes a profile of personality prototypes, but what makes the characters unique isn't a set of abstract characteristics. More often than not, Salinger provides us with a gesture, and it's this gesture that pumps blood into the heart of the character, bringing him or her to life. The gesture is so precise, so *perfect*, that we recognize it—we know what sort of person would behave this way—and it becomes difficult to read the novel without matching Salinger's characters to real people we know.

When I read about Ackley, the kid who lives in the room next to Holden's at Pencey, and how when he's done looking at the photo of Sally Hayes, he puts it back in the wrong place, I can't help thinking about this guy I knew in graduate school who was pathological about putting things back in the wrong place, and how it drove me mad. In Barnes and Noble, for instance, he'd take a book off the shelf, and while talking to me, he'd stuff the book back *anywhere* but where it belonged. Whenever I mentioned it to him, he'd get defensive. "Oh, *sorry*," he'd say, and then he'd start huffing and snorting for a while, making a big show of putting everything back in its correct place for the rest of that particular visit. That's Ackley. Holden says, "He did it on purpose. You could tell." You *could* tell. Absolutely. Holden's right.

Even when Holden offers a sweeping generalization about a group of people, the generalization is so fresh and acute that it quickly gloms onto the face of a flesh-and-blood person—one of the many minor characters from our own lives—and then through the act of literary transference, that group takes on a distinct personality and becomes a minor character in its own right, albeit a *cumulative* minor character. Early in the novel Holden says of Pencey, "The more expensive a school is, the more crooks it has—I'm not kidding." The *biggest* crook I've known was a graduate of one of the most expensive schools in the country, so when Holden makes his proclamation, the Pencey quad, its dormitories, and its classrooms instantly fill up with this mumbling, snickering little shithead whom I knew. Well, actually, he wasn't the biggest crook I've known, but he was certainly the most consistent and the most annoying, in large part because he had obviously come from a family with money, and because most of what he did was so petty that you felt guilty calling him on it—or you simply couldn't believe he'd done what he'd done. He'd be standing in front of a parking meter and he'd ask if you had a quarter. When you handed him the quarter, he'd stuff it into his pocket and then start walking away from the meter, striking up a conversation to make you forget that he'd taken your quarter. Or he'd eat with you at a restaurant and then leave just before the waiter delivered the bill. Or he'd try to pay for his beer with the tip you left for the bartender. Or he'd steal books from your house, tucking them inside his coat when you weren't in the same room,

What I'm saying is this: you know these people. Salinger has imbued his novel with enough *types* that surely part of the reason for *The Catcher in the Rye*'s endurance isn't simply what's there on the page but what we, as readers, bring to the page. It's exactly what I tell my students *not* to do when they're talking about one another's stories in class—"Don't critique a story based on your own life experiences or how you, personally, could relate to it . . . don't superimpose your own experiences onto the story . . . the story must work on its own, with or without your life experiences"—and yet Salinger causes me, to some extent, to reconsider the issue. After all, isn't that part of Salinger's unique genius, his ability to make the reader say, page after page, "Oh, yeah, I relate to Caulfield," or "I know a guy just like Ackley"? Salinger's genius is his ability to create the universal out of the individual. I didn't go to a prep school, after all. I attended piss-poor public schools in the Chicago area's working-class neighborhoods, so on the surface I have nothing in common with Holden and his cast of characters. But it doesn't matter. An Ackley is an

Ackley is an Ackley, and I know Salinger's Ackley as well as I know my own Ackley.

Keeping with Forster's theory that flat characters are "created round a single idea or quality," Salinger uses the single-brushstroke approach to characterization—one sentence, one *swipe* of his brush, and there you have it. We're given a detail or an action or something that the character says, and it's enough to nail the bastard for good. "That's exactly the kind of guy he was," Holden says of Ernest Morrow, who likes to snap his classmates' asses with wet towels, and with each subsequent brushstroke for each new character, the implication is that *this is the sort of person he or she is.*

- The old, bald bellboy with the comb-over.
- Faith Cavendish, former burlesque stripper, who "wasn't exactly a whore or anything but that didn't mind doing it once in a while."
- Sunny, the spooky, skinny prostitute.
- Dick Slagle, who'd say snotty things about Holden's Mark Cross suitcases but then hope that people thought that they were *his* suitcases.
- Louis Shaney, the Catholic kid from Whooton, always looking for an opening to mention the Catholic church in town in order to gauge if Holden was a Catholic, too (Catholics are like that, you know).
- Sally Hayes's mother, who'd do charity work only if "everybody kissed her ass for her when they made a contribution."
- Gertrude Levine, Holden's partner during the museum field trips, whose hands were "always sticky or sweaty or something."
- The woman who cried all through the movie but wouldn't let her own kid go to the bathroom. ("You take somebody that cries their goddam eyes out over phony stuff in the movies, and nine times out of ten they're mean bastards at heart.")
- Holden's "stupid aunt with halitosis," who kept saying "how peaceful" Allie looked in the coffin.
- James Castle, who wouldn't take back what he said about a conceited kid. (Of course, he jumped out of a window and killed himself, but there you have it: bullheadedness at the expense of everything.)
- Richard Kinsella, whose lip quivered when he made a speech.

We do this when we talk about the minor characters in our own lives—it's the shorthand of characterization—but in spontaneous conversation we're more likely to fumble, throwing out too many defining characteristics, waiting for the light to go on in our listener's eyes. *Take my grade-school gym teacher. This was Chicago, the South Side, and he had that surfer look going, you know: blond hair baked to straw from the sun, a big-ass Magnum P.I. mustache, but he was sort of a pedophile, too—always making the seventh-grade girls bend over so that he could stare at their asses . . . You know the type, right?* And if that doesn't nail him down, I might say, *Okay, here's the high-point of this guy's life. He had a tryout for the Rams in the seventies. A tryout, for chrissake. You know the kind of guy I'm talking about, right? A tryout, and he's still talking about it. THAT kind of guy.*

We become Mitchell Sanders in Tim O'Brien's "How to Tell a True War Story": " . . . I could tell how desperately Sanders wanted me to believe him, his frustration at not quite getting the details right, not quite pinning down the final and definitive truth." What we're doing is contradictory, really: we want to nail down the single truth about an individual, and yet we want to capture the universality within that individual that will allow our listener to see both at the same time, the specific person we're talking about as well as the *type* of person. This is the Salinger trick—peering at a character through a microscope with one eye and a telescope with the other eye.

Logic dictates that if our own lives are filled with minor characters, then we must occasionally play the role of minor character in others' lives. And what sort of a minor character are we? What is our single brushstroke? I have to tell you. It's usually not pretty.

Here's a true story. Our family moved around a lot when I was a kid, so I frequently changed schools. In the third grade—my first year in a new grammar school—I had the misfortune of throwing up during class. My stomach took me by surprise, and after I had vomited, I set off a chain reaction among the other weak-stomached students around me. At least three other kids followed suit and vomited, too. A year later, my parents and I moved again—it had nothing to do with me puking—and I attended yet another grade school. Several more years passed, though, before I rejoined my former third-grade classmates in high school, and one guy from that class came up to me in the cafeteria and said, "Hey, I remember you. You're the kid who threw up so much that it covered his entire desk."

Jesus! I thought. *Is this how everyone remembers me? The Kid Who Vomited So Much It Covered His Entire Desk? Will this be my lasting legacy?*

This kid who came up to me in the cafeteria, he didn't seem to remember anything else about me except that I was new to that school, that I had voluminously blown chunks, and that I moved shortly thereafter. No doubt he had worked out his own chain of logic and believed that my leaving the school had to do with my embarrassment at puking, and I have no doubt that after I had moved away he told his theory to anyone who would listen, creating the myth of The Boy Who Vomited So Much It Covered His Entire Desk. Like Holden, this kid was creating his own vision of the world by choosing what (and what *not*) to remember, and his memories, in this instance, certainly said more about him than they did about me. Of course, I didn't realize any of this at the time, and I doubt it would have helped me if I did. Here's where real life and fiction part ways. In real life, we are the protagonist of our own ever-unfolding story, and we must suffer the consequences of how people remember us. In fiction, we play the role of implied friend to the protagonist, and if I were to write a story titled "The Boy Who Vomited So Much It Covered His Entire Desk," I wouldn't write it from my point-of-view. No, I'd choose the other kid—a natural protagonist—because he's the one who, if I were the reader, I'd prefer to pal around with. He's the one telling stories, after all. He's the one painting a distinct view of the world (*his* view), and my role in the story was that of the flat character, a minor character in *his* life.

Maybe this is why I don't write heavily autobiographical short stories. Maybe I'm too passive to play the lead. It's true, though, that when I write stories, the character with whom I most relate, nine times out of ten, is the narrator, particularly if my narrator is younger than I happen to be. I relate to them because I hand over to them my best characteristics. *Here, try this on for size.* Or perhaps what I'm doing is giving them characteristics I *wish* I possessed. As a result, they are more charming than me, more lively, and often funnier. They are like me but not me. They are who I'd *like* to have been, I suppose. The minor characters in my stories are often the heavies. They, too, can be funny, but frequently they are pathetic or sinister or, well, downright creepy. They are, by and large, a sad lot. They're *not me.* Let me repeat: They are not me.

Or are they?

The fact is, we don't like being minor characters. Rarely when we read do we see ourselves as the minor characters. Everyone relates to Holden Caulfield, but no one says, "Hey, I'm that bald guy with the comb-over!" Or, "Hey, I'm that guy who likes to snap people's asses with towels!" Is it that the real-life people who represent these minor characters don't read and so are never privy to seeing themselves in print? Or is it that they *do* read but see only their heroic side? We're all, each of us, the protagonist, right? We're all David Copperfield, Holden Caulfield, Harry Potter. Or is that when we run across ourselves as flat characters, we *do* recognize ourselves but hope that no one else will? "Okay, sure, I'm the guy who liked to snap people's asses, but surely no one will see *me* in *him*." Are some people inherently inclined to be minor characters in life? Or is it just a matter of point-of-view: we see the guy with the comb-over and we think, *Ah, the sad-sack . . . the poor bastard,* but in truth the guy with the comb-over has his own triumphs and failures, however large or small, and he is, in fact, no less a minor character than Holden Caulfield, who, after all, is a failure of sorts too, and could easily become a minor character from, say, Ackley's point of view?

And what of Salinger himself? He's been called a great—if not the great-est—minor writer of the twentieth century. He has, by virtue of his meager output, relegated himself to literature's minor leagues. But there is that other issue, too, the issue of his privacy, his exile. Writing output aside, Salinger has chosen a path that easily lends itself to pigeonholing by the media (*those phonies!*) and by all those people who devour what the media spits out about him. In other words, he has made it easy for people to paint him with a single brushstroke, for people to shrink him to a single word, a single characteristic. Mention Salinger's name to someone who's never read him, who's never been charmed by Holden's voice, who's never met those fifty-plus characters in *The Catcher in the Rye* or any other character in any of his books—mention his name, and what are you likely to hear?

Oh, yes, him: the recluse.

BIBLIOGRAPHY

Bergson, Henri Louis. *Laughter: An Essay on the Meaning of the Comic.* Los Angeles: Green Integer, 1998.

Bonhoeffer, Dietrich. *Letter and Papers from Prison.* New York: Simon & Schuster, 1997.

Cronin, Gloria L., and Ben Siegel, eds. *Conversations with Saul Bellow.* Jackson: University Press of Mississippi, 1994.

Didion, Joan. "Finally (Fashionably) Spurious." In *Salinger: A Critical and Personal Portrait,* edited by Grunwald, Henry Anatole. New York: Pocket Books, Inc., 1962: pp. 84–86.

Freud, Sigmund. *General Psychology Theory.* New York: Simon & Schuster, 1998.

Hamilton, Ian. *In Search of J. D. Salinger.* New York: Vintage Books, 1989.

Kazin, Alfred. "Everybody's Favorite." In *Salinger: A Critical and Personal Portrait,* edited by Grunwald, Henry Anatole. New York: Pocket Books, Inc., 1962: pp. 47–57.

Leenaars, Antoon A., ed. *Suicidology: Essays in Honor of Edwin S. Schneidman.* Leonia: Jason Aronson Publishers, 1993.

McCarthy, Mary. "J. D. Salinger's Closed Circuit." *Harper's Magazine,* October 1962.

Maltsberger, John T., ed. *Essential Papers on Suicide.* New York: New York University Press, 1996.

Maynard, Joyce. *At Home in the World.* New York: Picador USA, 1998.

Salinger, J. D. *The Catcher in the Rye.* New York: Signet Books, 1953.

———. *Franny and Zooey.* Boston: Little, Brown Books, 1961.

———. *Nine Stories.* Boston: Little, Brown Books, 1953.

———. Raise High the Roof Beam, Carpenters *and* Seymour: An Introduction. Boston: Little, Brown Books, 1963.

Salinger, Margaret. *Dream Catcher.* New York: Washington Square Press, 2000.

Schneidman, Edwin S. *The Suicidal Mind.* Oxford: Oxford University Press, 1996.

JANE MENDELSOHN

Holden Caulfield: A Love Story

The winter I was eleven, we were still living in New York City. I say still because my mother and I were moving to Canada the next year to live in a city called Toronto, which sounded about as far away from New York, where I had lived my entire life and where my father would continue to live, as any place I could possibly imagine. It was a sad winter for me, especially over Christmas vacation, when there wasn't much distraction. I probably watched a lot of TV, but I had already watched so much TV in the first eleven years of my life that I was approaching the human limit. It might have snowed, I have a vague memory of a blizzard, but that would only have made the city more beautiful and me more sad. My sadness itself was mildly interesting—I told my friends that I was leaving next year as if I were going off to a sanitarium—but I couldn't devote an entire Christmas vacation to it. (I was only eleven.) So I read, probably with the television on, a lot of books.

I read whatever I could find in the apartment: *A Member of the Wedding, Dr. Spock's Baby and Child Care,* Agatha Christies, and it was somewhere in there, that winter while it was maybe snowing outside, that I first met Holden Caulfield. Saw the hat, heard the voice. Stood with him at one end of the corridor at Pencey while he called out "*Sleep tight, ya morons!*" with tears in his eyes. Turns out, I never went to boarding school and never ran away from anywhere, didn't stay in a hotel by myself until I was out of college, and never

With Love and Squalor: 14 Writers Respond to the Work of J. D. Salinger, edited by Kip Kotzen and Thomas Beller (New York: Broadway Books, 2001): pp. 104–116. Copyright © 2001 Kip Kitzen and Thomas Beller.

walked to the lagoon in Central Park at night, but I never stopped looking for Holden Caulfield. I looked on the steps of the Museum of Natural History, by the bandstand in the park, in taxis. Where I really searched for him was among the boys I knew; I was always finding the lost ones, the ones I could squint at through some haze of coffee steam and sarcasm until they became the guy in the red hunting hat. Somewhere in the back of my mind, where it's always maybe snowing and the television's on low, I still believe that any day now I'll be running away with Holden.

I say all this because I'm probably not the only one. For me and I would guess a lot of other people, Holden Caulfield set the tone for a certain kind of long-lasting literary crush. It seemed impossible that I could ever fall out of love, that I could ever outgrow Holden. His voice provided an inner soundtrack that played in the background of my every romantic misadventure. It's a scratchy, funny, knowing and know-nothing riff that makes you dream each new frog will turn into a prince but lets you know, with a cutting remark that sends you back on yourself, that you have, in fact, just kissed a toad. In Holden's world, no one ever has to fall out of love because romantic love is always unrequited or impossible.

Rereading the book as an adult, I realized that all of the objects of Holden's affection were unavailable. Who are they? Jane Gallagher, the girl of his memories now going to football games with someone else (it didn't hurt my own crush that her name was Jane); his dead brother, Allie; his little sister, Phoebe, who loves him but is too young to understand his teenage angst (she loses patience with him for not liking anything); and the Museum of Natural History ("I loved that damn museum"). In Holden's world, love is wrapped up like a mummy. His failing history essay is about the Egyptians, what they used "when they wrapped up mummies so that their faces would not rot," and his visit to the Metropolitan Museum culminates in his showing two little kids the way to the mummies. I don't want to make too much of the fact that Holden seems really to be looking for his own Mummy, or Mommy, who has been very distracted, or perhaps even dead to him since Allie died, but then again why not? I think this is at the heart of the book.

In Holden's world, you can't go back to childhood—that's locked up in the Museum of Natural History, where Holden doesn't make it past the front steps—but you can't grow up either because growing up means becoming a phony. You can't really fall in love because real love with a real person might be less than perfect (this is the adolescent's dilemma), but you can't really do anything but look for love. It's a world in which if you really want to know the truth you can just get on a train and ride out west to a ranch. Of course, when you get there, the ranch might turn out to be Hollywood, or a psychiatric hospital. So maybe it's better just to keep looking for romance, not truth—to keep failing in love forever.

• • •

So how did it happen? When did I start to fall out of love with Holden? It began, maybe, with the rumors about Salinger, old J. D., as Holden might call him, the tales that were later solidified in books that I couldn't bear to read. There was the affair with the Yale freshman when he was so much older; the orgone box; the drinking his own urine. If you really want to know the truth, I just didn't want to hear about it. What does it matter, anyway? Who cares about writers? It's the work that counts, right? But still, something seeped in, some stale smell of reality, or worse, depravity, that had always hung around Holden but that was more like a sharp cologne breezing off his preppy shoulders in the book, while in real life it just stank.

Maybe it was those stories that led me to pick up *The Catcher in the Rye* again a few years ago, when I was writing a screenplay about a teenage girl. Maybe this was the beginning of the end. Right away, I thought I'd found what I remembered: that voice, cocky and insecure, reckless and afraid, filled with jaded longing and innocent wisdom. There, on the second page, were two lines that summed up everything I had been feeling as I struggled to get my thoughts across in screenplay form: "If there's one thing I hate, it's the movies. Don't even mention them to me." At a time when I was working out my own feelings about the relationship between film and fiction, I found Holden's protestations funny and touching. All that ambivalence, the love-hate that gives the book its happy-sad tone, its aura of playful melancholy, I felt it conjured so much more than adolescence, but also American life, the stupid beautiful movie of it all. (Of course, Holden is actually obsessed with the movies—witness his death scene at the hotel—but he sees through the myths. This is what spoke to me while I was trying to reconcile what I loved about movies—the gorgeous surfaces, the layering of sound and image, the dreamlike power of enacting events—with what I loved about books: the interiority, the ability to radically, and inexpensively, compress and expand time, the feeling of traveling through consciousness, the intimacy. I never did figure out how to get my ideas across in screenplay form, and eventually I ended up turning my script into a book. But that's another story.) Hey, I thought, this is great. Here I am, back with the snow and the TV on, everything comfy and witty and poignant and familiar.

So imagine my surprise as I began to read further, and, with the so-called wiser perspective of adulthood, I discovered that *The Catcher in the Rye* isn't really a book about a smart-funny-preppy New York teenager running around town by himself for a few days and looking for romance or at least understanding, but that it was a book about a *suicidal* smart-funny-preppy New York teenager. It was *all about death*.

•••

My revelation came slowly. I just started noticing all the references to death, and many specifically to suicide. It's pretty innocuous at first. There's the "It killed me" on page two about D. B. being in Hollywood, and then, at the bottom of the page, the talk about the football game: " . . . you were supposed to commit suicide or something if old Pencey didn't win." On page four Holden tells us that he "got the ax," and by page five that "you felt like you were disappearing." Still only on page five, Mrs. Spencer asks Holden, "Are you frozen to death?" and the next thing you know he's being ushered into Spencer's room, where the old man appears to be lying, practically, on his death bed.

I didn't make too much of this, but then the references really started piling up, like, say, dead bodies. On page nine, Holden talks about his gray hair; on page eleven, about the mummies; on fourteen, about a remark Spencer makes, "It made me sound dead, or something." On page seventeen, "That killed me" reintroduces the recurring phrase that I eventually counted at least thirty-five times, and by page twenty, "You were a goner." On page twenty-two, Holden says of his hunting hat: "This is a people shooting hat . . . I shoot people in this hat." And so on, and so on.

I couldn't believe what I was reading. I'd remembered that Allie's death figured in the book, that some of Holden's mental state was a response to his loss, but I hadn't realized the magnitude of it, the scale and depth and burden of his despair. For the first time it occurred to me perhaps why Holden's hunting hat is red: because Allie had red hair. And I saw new meaning behind Holden's comment that "I act like I'm thirteen." Although he's sixteen when the book takes place, he was thirteen when Allie died. I'd never understood Holden's urgent desire to know where the ducks went in the winter when the pond froze, but now I got it; he wanted to know where Allie had gone, and where he could find his mourning and unavailable mother.

Holden's mother. Mrs. Caulfield. There's somebody I'd thought about for maybe one second. I'm not even sure I could have told you whether she appeared in the book. Turns out she does, in the scene where Holden returns home and talks to Phoebe. Actually, right before Holden comes home, he imagines his own funeral and feels especially sorry for his mother because "she still isn't over my brother Allie yet." In the middle of his conversation with Phoebe, (during which Phoebe says several times that "Daddy'll kill you" when he finds out that Holden's been expelled again), their parents come home. Holden hides in the closet and his mother questions Phoebe about the cigarette smell in the room; "Now tell me the truth," she says. I could hear her saying that a million times, to the point where naturally Holden would begin his confessions with the line "If you really want to know the truth." He's talking, in a sense, to his mother.

Of course the kind of truth Holden's mother is asking for isn't Holden's brand of truth. He cares about emotional truth, and perhaps this is what resonates so strongly for kids when they first encounter the book, the recognition that there's a difference between the two kinds of truth and that negotiating between them marks the beginning of the end of childhood. The first half of the novel reads like a descent into the truth at the center of Holden's solitude. His journey from school to the hotel to hiding from his mother to the lonely encounter with the prostitute culminates in the punch from Maurice and Holden's acting out a death scene from the movies: "I sort of started pretending I had a bullet in my guts," he says. He pictures himself staggering around, plugging Maurice, and having Jane come over and bandage him while holding a cigarette for him to smoke. It's a sendup of everything phony that Holden hates, but a revealing display of his true feelings at the same time, his gunfight fantasy, he's *concealing* the fact that he's been shot; in reality, he's been trying to hide his despair. At the end of his B-movie reverie, whether or not we want to know it, he finally tells us the truth: "What I really felt like, though," he says, "was committing suicide."

Holden's admission marks the halfway point of the book. He spends the second half trying to find someone to talk to about his feelings, someone who really wants to know the truth. He tries the chilly Sally, the condescending Luce, the gentle, intelligent Phoebe, who responds with all her love but who's too young and innocent to see that he's desperate, and finally, his ex-teacher Mr. Antolini, who lectures Holden and then proceeds to make a pass at him. And why does Holden seek out Mr. Antolini? Because he was the one who finally picked up that

> boy that jumped out the window I told you about, James Castle.
> Old Mr. Antolini felt his pulse and all, and then he took off his
> coat and put it over James Castle and carried him all the way to the
> infirmary. He didn't even give a damn if his coat got all bloody.

So there it was: the boy of my dreams wasn't so funny after all. He was miserable. That killed me.

• • •

I mention all of this death stuff not as a way of saying that there should have been more teen hotlines in the 1940s, but to describe how completely different the experience of reading *The Catcher in the Rye* was for me after so many years. It was like running into an old boyfriend and realizing that not only has he lost all his hair or gained fifty pounds, but that he was *always* bald or overweight or depressed or hostile or just plain crazy, although you had no idea at the time. It was, frankly, a little unnerving, but humbling as well. I didn't actually love *The Catcher in the Rye* any less; I just wasn't in love with Holden anymore.

And I appreciated the book in a new way. In understanding its darkness, I could see it as more than a *beautifully effective* or *fully imagined* coming-of-age story, but as a work of almost gothic imagination. As Leslie Fiedler says, all of American literature is fundamentally gothic. In the end I found references to death on almost every other page, and this relentless awareness of death and the language of death, of common phrases that embody darker meanings, this language obsessively alert to itself, seems to me the sign of something closer to art than not. Thoreau said that "Writing may be either a record of a deed or a deed. It is nobler when it is a deed." I do think that *The Catcher in the Rye* is a noble book. Messed up, but noble.

So what about Holden? I'm not in love with him anymore, but do I still love him? Last week, I took my eighteen-month-old daughter to the Museum of Natural History for the first time. We saw the canoe, the whale, the dioramas. She ran around pointing at everything and squealing and the guards were all incredibly nice and the lights were soothingly dim and everything smelled musty just like I remembered and, with the exception of a few exhibits, it seemed as though nothing had changed since I'd been there as a kid, and probably since Holden had walked the halls.

Toward the end of our visit my daughter got tired and stretched out her arms and said, "Up." I picked her up and held her for a little while and then we got ready to go, and as we strolled out onto Central Park West and I felt the huge gray museum sleeping solidly behind us, I thought about Holden. I thought about his name, about how he just wanted to be held. And I thought about how physical books are, how you can hold them in your hands. When you're young and you read a book, it seems to hold you, creating a world around you, but then as you get older, you can hold onto it; your own world takes on a life of its own, bigger than any book but able to contain many worlds, many stories within it. Maybe that's what makes a book great, if you can grow up with it, never outgrow it exactly, but find a way to pick it up over the years and form a new connection.

As I pushed my daughter's stroller into the park, she started to fall asleep, and the image of the museum began to melt into the trees. But before it disappeared completely, I thought I could see Holden, the boy in the hat, the one I first fell in love with, and the boy all alone, the one I just wanted to put my arms around. I thought I could see him, waiting for me on the steps.

Works Cited

Bergson, Henri Louis. *Laughter: An Essay on the Meaning of the Comic.* Los Angeles: Green Integer, 1998.

Bonhoeffer, Dietrich. *Letter and Papers from Prison.* New York: Simon & Schuster, 1997.

Cronin, Gloria L., and Ben Siegel, eds. *Conversations with Saul Bellow.* Jackson: University Press of Mississippi, 1994.

Didion, Joan. "Finally (Fashionably) Spurious." In *Salinger: A Critical and Personal Portrait,* edited by Grunwald, Henry Anatole. New York: Pocket Books, Inc. 1962: pp. 84–86.

Freud, Sigmund. *General Psychology Theory.* New York: Simon & Schuster, 1998.

Hamilton, Ian. *In Search of J. D. Salinger.* New York: Vintage Books, 1989.

Kazin, Alfred. "Everybody's Favorite." In *Salinger: A Critical and Personal Portrait,* edited by Grunwald, Henry Anatole. New York: Pocket Books, Inc. 1962: pp. 47–57.

Leenaars, Antoon A., ed. *Suicidology: Essays in Honor of Edwin S. Shneidman.* Leonia: Jason Aronson Publishers, 1993.

McCarthy, Mary. "J. D. Salinger's Closed Circuit." *Harper's Magazine,* October 1962.

Maltsberger, John T., ed. *Essential Papers on Suicide.* New York: New York University Press, 1996.

Maynard, Joyce. *At Home in the World.* New York: Picador USA, 1998.

Salinger, J. D. *The Catcher in the Rye.* New York: Signet Books, 1953.

———. *Franny and Zooey.* Boston: Little, Brown, 1961.

———. *Nine Stories.* Boston: Little, Brown, 1953.

———. *Raise High the Roof Beam, Carpenters* and *Seymour: An Introduction.* Boston: Little, Brown, 1963.

Salinger, Margaret. *Dream Catcher.* New York: Washington Square Press, 2000.

Schneidman, Edwin S. *The Suicidal Mind.* Oxford: Oxford University Press, 1996.

DENNIS CUTCHINS

Catcher *in the Corn:*
J. D. Salinger and Shoeless Joe

One of the most interesting treatments of J. D. Salinger's work in recent years has been W. P. Kinsella's novel *Shoeless Joe*. Kinsella's first novel must be understood, at least in part, as a complex and sustained response to *Catcher in the Rye*. The Canadian author establishes a strong affinity between Holden Caulfield, Shoeless Joe Jackson, and his own semiautobiographical Ray Kinsella. Kinsella, the writer, even uses J. D. Salinger as a character in his novel, blurring the line between reality and fiction as well as the line between the legal and the illegal. Salinger's appearance in the novel should be understood, however, as more than gratuitous name dropping, or what Kinsella referred to in an interview as "audacious" risk taking (Dahlin 7). Each of his major characters, including "Jerry Salinger," faces a crisis of faith, a set of dilemmas that may be generally understood as the conflict between idealism and reality, and in this theme Kinsella was apparently responding to *Catcher*. Arthur Heiserman and James E. Miller, Jr. in "J. D. Salinger: Some Crazy Cliff," one of the first scholarly treatments of *Catcher*, suggest that readers must understand the novel in terms of this conflict between idealism and reality, and their essay sets a tone which polarized much later criticism.[1] Readers of the novel should focus not on Holden, they argue, but rather on the world in which Holden lives, concluding that the "book's last ironic incongruity" is that "It is not Holden who should be examined for a

The Catcher in the Rye: New Essays. Ed. J. P. Steed. (New York: Peter Lang, 2002): pp. 53–77.
Copyright © 2002 Peter Lang.

sickness of the mind, but the world in which he has sojourned and found himself an alien" (38). Gerald Rosen reiterates this idea and goes so far as to call *Catcher in the Rye* a "novel of the death of belief in America" (96). Kinsella seems to accept this general interpretation of *Catcher*, and he proceeds to follow Heiserman, Miller, and Rosen in examining the modern world for a "sickness of the mind," and "the death of belief." *Shoeless Joe* goes beyond *Catcher*, however, in that it offers a possible cure for this modern illness.

Although *Shoeless Joe* is a successful novel and work of art in its own right, it makes the most sense when read in the context of *Catcher in the Rye*. Kinsella's book is, at least in part, an attempt to interpret, respond to, and even redeem Salinger's most famous work by affirming and rewarding the kind of idealism exemplified by Holden. Beliefs and desires, for both Holden and Ray, form an antithetical and paradoxical relationship with harsh reality. The paradox is created in large measure as the characters recognize their own complicity in the corrupt world. Using this idea of complicity as a partial basis for his argument, John Seelye suggests that *Catcher* "provided an American counterpart to European existential texts like Sartre's *Nausea* and Camus's *The Stranger*" (24). Jack Salzman, however, believes that there is a distinct difference between *Catcher* and other more strictly existentialist texts: "Salinger's strength as a writer is not his *appreciation* of life's absurdities and ultimate paradox; rather, it is his *struggle against such appreciation*" (17, emphasis added). Both Holden and Ray reject absurdity and seek, somewhat desperately, for meaning in the chaotic, dangerous, and callous worlds in which they live. They want to be peaceful, but they constantly encounter violence. They need spirituality, but they are disenchanted by the hollowness of religion. They seek family support, but their families are largely dysfunctional. And both characters face the age-old conflict between materialism and art.

Holden's search for a meaningful world is, arguably, fruitless. In the words of Joyce Rowe, "Because Holden is never allowed to imagine or experience himself in any *significant* struggle with others . . . neither he (nor his creator) can conceive of society as a source of growth, or self-knowledge" (90, emphasis added). Ray, on the other hand, lives in a universe that is deeply meaningful, one in which social interaction can definitely lead to growth and self-knowledge, and this may be the most important difference between the two works. Ray's outwardly strange, and even bizarre behavior eventually leads to reconciliation with both his estranged brother and his dead father. He helps ex-ballplayer Archie Graham discover meaning and reason in his life of quiet service. He helps a genuine "phoney" like Eddie Scissons turn his lies into truths. With Ray's assistance, even Shoeless Joe Jackson can be redeemed from his one great mistake. Ray's universe, the world created by Kinsella in part as a response to *Catcher in the Rye*, is not governed by random chance, insoluble paradox, or simple absurdity but by events whose interconnections are so complex as to appear random, paradoxical, or absurd.

Shoeless Joe is something of a nostalgic novel, dealing with the wishes and regrets of half a dozen or so characters and allowing them each a second chance at the road not taken. The narrator of the novel, Ray Kinsella, is an ex-insurance salesman and a serious baseball fan who moves with his wife Annie and daughter Karin to Iowa, buys a small farm, and begins growing corn.[2] In a plot made familiar by the successful film *Field of Dreams* (1989), Ray is told by a mystical voice to plow under part of his cornfield and build a baseball diamond so that his father's childhood hero, Shoeless Joe Jackson, can return from the dead and play baseball again with his teammates from the 1919 Chicago White Sox. Ray builds the field, and Jackson does come. But the erstwhile farmer is soon ordered by the voice to "Ease his pain." He instinctively knows that he is being asked to take reclusive writer J. D. Salinger to a baseball game. Ray discovers an interview Salinger had supposedly given in which he regrets not having the chance to play baseball for the New York Giants on the Polo Grounds. Ray once again obeys the voice. He finds the elderly Salinger at first a reluctant victim of his enthusiasm, then later an eager participant in his odd quest. At the behest of a third voice, the two leave for Chisholm, Minnesota, home of the deceased Doctor Archie Graham. Ray and "Jerry" interview the inhabitants of the small town and learn all they can about the doctor who, in his younger years, played a single inning of professional baseball. They eventually invite the resurrected Graham back to Iowa to play on Ray's field.

In the course of this unlikely picaresque novel, Ray, like Holden, faces some of the unpleasant realities of contemporary America. He is menaced by street thugs on Chicago's South Side, held at gunpoint in Cleveland, and knocked unconscious in Boston. Back at home, Ray's real estate mogul/brother-in-law, Mark, is busy buying all the farms in Johnson County, Iowa, and sending the simple rural folk off to live in the city. Mark and his partner, Bluestein,[3] are intent on creating a gigantic "computer farm" that will be run by a single computer operator and an army of mechanized planters and harvesters. Ray's 160 acres are the only thing standing in the way of this antipastoral nightmare, and Mark holds the mortgage. To make matters even more complex, on his return home, with Salinger still in tow, Ray discovers that his estranged twin brother, Richard, a carnival hawker and owner of a dilapidated freak show, has come to Iowa to find him. In the novel's conclusion, Ray defeats Mark, keeps the farm, and reconciles relations with both his brother and his dead father, a minor league catcher and another of the ghostly baseball players. Salinger's character is allowed to visit the afterlife with the deceased players, happy, we are led to believe, in a place where publishers, reporters, and fans can never follow.

The novel received mixed reviews. William Plummer's estimation was typical:

> It's easy enough to find fault with this wonderfully hokey first novel by a Canadian short-story writer of some repute. The language sometimes melts in the hand rather than the heart, the subplots are a hasty pudding, the Salinger of the book is not smart or quirky enough to have written about Holden Caulfield or Seymour Glass. But such complaints seem mean-spirited, tin-eared, in the face of the novel's lovely minor music. (64)

Other reviewers were not as generous in their estimation. Ian Pearson calls the novel "too contrived to be seductive . . . , too sluggish to work as a madcap picaresque" (61). Most readers, however, found something worthwhile in the book, and a few found more than that.[4]

Shoeless Joe and *Catcher in the Rye* have some obvious connections. Both novels are written as first-person narratives, with voices that are warm, personal, and perhaps each book's most compelling feature. Two of the main characters in *Shoeless Joe*, Richard and Ray Kinsella, are both characters from Salinger's canon. Richard Kinsella is the boy who kept digressing during Holden's Oral Expression class in *Catcher*, and Ray Kinsella, modeled after Salinger himself, is the lead character in "A Young Girl in 1941 with No Waist at All." The most compelling shared feature of the two novels, however, is the theme of innocent idealism in conflict with harsh reality. Both novels place peaceful and more or less innocent characters in the midst of societal corruption and decay. On his way to Comiskey Field in Chicago, for instance, Ray meets two teenaged girls who warn him that he is about to be robbed. "Hey, man," one calls, "you better watch out. There's some boys in the doorway of that block up there; they's figuring to rob you" (44). The other girl adds, "We don't want to see you get in any trouble. If you got any money on you, you better cross the street" (45). Ray considers taking their advice but suddenly worries that they maybe setting him up. "What if the boys are on the other side of the road," he wonders, "and don't want to waste their time mugging a broke white man?" (45). Ray decides not to cross the road, and discovers, as he continues down the block, that the girls probably had been in collusion with the potential muggers. For Ray, the threat of being mugged in Chicago, along with a later encounter with a would-be armed robber in Cleveland, mirror Holden's experience with Maurice and Sunny, another thug-teenage girl partnership. Both Holden and Ray find themselves too innocent and naive to understand the dangerous worlds they face. Ray certainly experiences the "sickness" of American society and is all the more ready, when the time comes, to return to the rural Iowa countryside. For Holden, however, this violent world is home. There is no pastoral Iowa to which he may retreat. The closest he can come is Central Park, and the park, with its homeless ducks and graffiti-covered walls, is little comfort.

Both novels may be considered contemporary picaresques with the two protagonists on quests for a kind of fulfilment or meaning lacking in their mundane worlds. Heiserman and Miller may have been the first to dub *Catcher* a quest novel. They note, "We use the medieval term because it signifies a seeking after what is tremendous" (32). The tremendous or extraordinary thing Holden seeks is, at least in part, the chance to serve as a savior for misguided children. In the chaotic world he inhabits, his desire to save others reflects a powerful and moving kind of idealism. Holden's basic optimism may be roughly summed up in the title passage from the novel. When Phoebe asks her brother what he would like to be, Holden imagines himself standing in a field of rye, saving children from falling over a cliff (173). Holden's dream of saving children, however, is simply not possible in the world Salinger creates. The teenager is forced, instead, to become, in the words of Jonathan Baumbach, "an impotent savior" (62). Baumbach contends that "since it is spiritually as well as physically impossible to prevent the Fall, Salinger's idealistic heroes are doomed" to failure (56).

Where Holden fails, Ray succeeds. The field he creates literally saves the *souls* of several characters in the novel as they are able to come back to life and fulfil their dreams. He becomes a savior or "catcher" not in a field of rye but on a baseball field built in the middle of an Iowa cornfield. The novel's title character, Joe Jackson, loved to play baseball and was crushed by the ruling of Commissioner Kenesaw Mountain Landis that permanently suspended him from the game. The fictional Jackson compares the lifetime suspension to "having a part of me amputated, slick and smooth and painless" (14). A moment later he adds, "I loved the game. . . . I'd have played for food money. I'd have played free and worked for food. It was the game" (15). Ray's baseball field gives Joe a second chance to play ball and to be absolved of the mistakes he made the first time around. This theme of redemption certainly does not end with Joe. Ray and Salinger discover that Archie "Moonlight" Graham died years earlier, without ever returning to baseball. He had, instead, moved to his hometown of Chisholm, Minnesota, and become a poorly paid high school doctor. During their visit to Chisholm, Salinger concludes that he and Ray had been sent to Minnesota to discover "if one inning can change the world" (152). They decide to leave with that mystery still unsolved, but on the way out of town they stop to pick up a young hitchhiker. The teenaged boy turns out to be Graham, who has come back to life to fulfil his dream of playing ball with his heroes.

Graham is able to play on Ray's field, but his subplot also suggests another kind of fulfilment. Though he seems pleased with the chance to join the team, Graham soon discovers that his life as a doctor and mentor to young people was, ultimately, more satisfying than playing professional baseball. In what is probably the novel's most touching moment, Ray's daughter, Karin, falls off of the bleachers while watching a game and begins to choke on a piece of hot dog. While the other characters stand around helplessly, the young Moonlight Graham strides confidently off of the baseball field, in the process transforming into the elderly "Doc" Graham. He quickly helps the girl, saving her life and simultaneously sacrificing his chances to play ball on the magical field. He makes, in other words, virtually the same decision he had made earlier in his life: to become a doctor rather than a ballplayer. Once again, Kinsella's novel replaces apparent absurdity with reassuring meaning. Graham's decision to help Karin affirms his career choice, giving his life a sense of intentionality and usefulness which is the very essence of meaning.

Graham's character is based partly on the real Moonlight Graham, and, I would argue, partly on a similar character in *Catcher*. At the beginning of Salinger's novel, Holden visits his history teacher, Mr. Spencer, to say goodbye. Spencer, like Graham, has spent most of his adult life working at a school, and even Holden can tell that the old teacher genuinely cares about the boys. Spencer is, after all, the only teacher he visits before leaving Pencey. But the old man seems powerless to help the boy. Holden is struck throughout the interview by Spencer's age and relative poverty: "You wondered what the heck he was still living for" (6). It never crosses the young man's mind that the Spencers are apparently happily married and that they seem more or less satisfied with their lot in life. Nor does Holden really appreciate Spencer's attempts to help him. The old teacher laments, "I'm trying to help you. I'm trying to *help* you if I can" (14). "He really was, too. You could see that," Holden admits, "But it was just that we were too much on opposite sides of the pole, that's all" (14–15). Spencer's final "Good luck" is particularly annoying to Holden. "I'd never yell 'Good luck!' at anybody," he notes. "It sounds terrible, when you think about it" (16). Holden perceives Spencer's work at the school as well meaning but ultimately futile and worthless, another set of absurd acts in the trivial world he inhabits. Ray, on the other hand, comes to see Graham's life of service to young people as both good and useful. Graham had filled his life in Chisholm with quiet labor for his neighbors and his students. "There were times when children could not afford eyeglasses or milk, or clothing because of the economic upheavals, strikes and depressions," Ray reads in Graham's obituary. "Yet no child was ever denied these essentials, because in the background, there was a benevolent, understanding Doctor Graham" (123). Graham's life, a mirror image of Spencer's, is judged, finally, to be worthwhile.

Certainly the word most often associated with *Catcher in the Rye* is "phoney." Holden first applies the term to Headmaster Haas and to the returning alumnus Ossenburger as a result of the discrepancy he perceives between their public face and their private action. Holden is bothered by the fact that Haas pretends to like wealthy or handsome parents but acts, very differently toward middle-class or poorly dressed parents:

> On Sundays, for instance, old Haas went around shaking hands with everybody's parents when they drove up to school. He'd be charming as hell and all. Except if some boy had little old funny-looking parents. . . . I mean if a boy's mother was sort of fat or corny-looking or something, and if somebody's father was one of those guys that wear those suits with very big shoulders and corny black and white shoes, then old Haas would just shake hands with them and give them a phony smile and then he'd go talk, for maybe a half an *hour*, with somebody else's parents. (14)

Like Haas, Ossenburger also misrepresents himself. At chapel he gives a speech, starting "with about fifty corny jokes, just to show us what a regular guy he was" (16). The undertaker then proceeds to describe his own humility and lack of pride. Yet all of this is belied in Holden's mind by the fact that Ossenburger "made a pot of dough in the undertaking business," and drives a "big goddam Cadillac" (16).

In *Shoeless Joe*, Kinsella does not use the term "phony," but he does include one character who, like Haas and Ossenburger, utterly misrepresents himself. Eddie Scissons, the retired farmer who sells his land and equipment to Ray and Annie, first impresses Ray with his claims to be "the oldest living Chicago Cub" (42). Ray soon discovers, though, that none of Eddie's stories are true and that he never played major league baseball. For years he has lied to his friends and neighbors about a nonexistent career. Ray, nevertheless, keeps Eddie's secret. "I understand Eddie Scissons," he explains. "I know that some of us, and for some reason I am one of them, get to reach out and touch our heart's desire," while others "are rewarded with snarls, frustration, and disillusionment" (218). When the truth about Eddie is later revealed by Mark, the old man is crushed. Once again, however, Ray's field provides an answer. As Ray and the others, including Eddie, watch one of the ghostly games, they realize that "Kid Scissons" has been called in as a relief pitcher. The fans watch as Eddie's lies are made true. His dream of playing for the Cubs is enacted before their eyes. Kid Scissons plays poorly, though, and his mistakes cost the Cubs the game. The old man takes the double humiliation philosophically. Later he reveals to Ray, "I heard somebody say once, 'Success is getting what you want, but happiness is wanting what you get'" (230). He adds, "You saw what happened to me. I got what I wanted, but it wasn't what

I needed to make me happy" (230). In Kinsella's world, even phonies get the chance to be redeemed.

Perhaps the worst kind of phonies, for both Holden and Ray, are religious ones. At the same time, however, both protagonists feel a strong need for a sense of spirituality. Jonathan Baumbach dubs *Catcher* "a religious or, to be more exact, spiritual novel" (59). Holden's feelings about *organized* religion, though, are most succinctly expressed in his discussion of Jesus and the Disciples:

> I like Jesus and all, but I don't care too much for most of the other stuff in the Bible. Take the Disciples, for instance. They annoy the hell out of me, if you want to know the truth. . . . While He was alive, they were about as much use to him as a hole in the head. All they did was keep letting Him down. (99)

The Disciples' main problem, at least as Holden sees it, is their intolerance and inability to forgive: "Jesus never sent old Judas to Hell," he argues. "I think any one of the Disciples would've sent him to Hell and all—and fast, too—but I'll bet anything Jesus didn't do it" (100). Modern Christians also come under fire for their intolerance, or potential intolerance, as well as their hypocrisy. Holden worries, for instance, that the nuns he meets at Grand Central Station will "all of a sudden try to find out if I was a Catholic" (112). Other clergy, too, fall under his condemnation. "If you want to know the truth," he allows, "I can't even stand ministers. The ones they've had at every school I've gone to, they have these Holy Joe voices when they start giving their sermons. God, I hate that. I don't see why the hell they can't talk in their natural voice" (100).

Ray has similar feelings about clergy and religious folk. He makes a point of mentioning Thaddeus Cridge, the Episcopal bishop of Iowa, whose apartment after his death contained "2000 pounds of pornographic magazines and books, as well as a number of albums full of compromising photographs of Cridge and neighborhood children" (115). Ray is also quite critical of Annie's family's outward appearance of religiousness and inner reality of intolerance and prejudice:

>]The kind of people I absolutely cannot tolerate are those, like Annie's mother, who never let you forget they are religious. It seems to me that a truly religious person would let his life be example enough, would not let his religion interfere with being a human being, and would not be so insecure as to have to fawn publicly before his gods. (175)

Kinsella can rarely pass up a chance to make fun of those who profess to be religious. When Ray first comes to Iowa, the woman who is to become his

mother-in-law at first rejects him as a renter because he was not a practic-
ing Christian. He ends up getting the room, however, because "it was early
October, her Christian roomer had been cut by the football team and had
left for Georgia, after kicking a hole in his door and writing misspelled four-
letter words on the wall with a crayon" (176). Like Holden, however, Ray
feels a need for the spiritual. His answer to that need, in fact, his answer
to most of the problems faced in the novel, is baseball. He advocates the
building of roadside shrines to baseball greats, suggests that "a ballpark at
night is more like a church than a church," and, noting the fans at a game,
points out, "We're not just ordinary people, we're a congregation. Baseball
is a ceremony, a ritual" (34, 160, 84). Holden may be denied spirituality, but
Ray finds his spiritual needs satisfied by a secular game.

    Shoeless Joe resembles *Catcher* on structural and thematic levels, but Kin-
sella's use of J. D. Salinger as a character expands and complicates *Shoeless Joe's*
response to *Catcher in the Rye*. Kinsella uses the characters of Salinger and Joe
Jackson, in particular, as metaphors to explore the very nature of public life
in America and the relationship between artistry and integrity. He asks what
it means to be a "hero" in this country and questions the responsibilities of
public life. Certainly these questions resonate, both in context of Salinger's
life and in terms of his most famous work.

    Kinsella's use of Salinger as a fictional character raised more than a few
eyebrows. One reviewer suggested that for Kinsella to put his "own words
into a living person's mouth is merely presumptuous, not clever" (Pearson
59). Kinsella himself has never fully explained his incorporation of Salinger,
telling one interviewer, "I didn't know I was going to use Salinger. . . . It was
just something in the back of my head. I like being audacious" (Dahlin 7).
He added, "I can't imagine him being terribly upset. . . . He's portrayed as
a compassionate character, and, as a matter of fact, this is something I took
great pains to do" (7).[5]

    One reason for Kinsella's use of the older author may be the fairly mun-
dane fact that Salinger had recently been in the news when Kinsella wrote his
novel. In 1974, the reclusive author sued several bookstores for selling an un-
authorized, anonymously published collection of his early fiction. In November of that year, Salinger gave his first interview in over twenty years. Speaking on the phone to Lacey Fosburgh, a San Francisco reporter, Salinger said,
"There is a marvelous peace in not publishing. It's peaceful. Still. Publishing
is a terrible invasion of my privacy" (Fosburgh 1). At the end of the interview
he added, "I pay for this kind of attitude. I'm known as a strange, aloof kind
of man. But all I'm doing is trying to protect myself and my work" (69). Five
years later, in July of 1979 in Windsor, Vermont, Salinger gave an impromptu
interview to "a college-age couple" who had stopped him in the street to
ask questions. A photographer quickly took a picture of the famous author

and asked the couple what Salinger had told them. They replied that he had asked them not to discuss their conversation but noted, "He told us not to take anybody's advice, including his, and that it's very important to read"(13). Kinsella would have been working on *Shoeless Joe* at the time, and the title of the *Newsweek* article may have been another inspiration as he worked on his homage to baseball. A clever editor gave the article an unintended baseball twist when he or she named it "Dodger in the Rye."[6]

In the summer of 1980 Salinger gave yet another interview, this time to Betty Eppes, a perky tennis player and features writer for the Baton Rouge *Advocate*. A longer version of the interview was published in the *Paris Review* in the summer of 1981 and would certainly have been noticed by Kinsella as he finished *Shoeless Joe*. In that interview Salinger told Eppes that he was writing, though he had no intentions to publish, and reiterated his plea to be left in peace. His wish, however, was not to be granted. On December 8, 1980, Mark David Chapman shot John Lennon in the back as the rock star entered his New York apartment. A few months later, in February 1981, Chapman gave a statement to the *New York Times* which stressed the importance of Salinger's *Catcher in the Rye*. He claimed that the novel itself was the best statement of his intentions as he shot Lennon. It was in this highly charged context that Kinsella wrote and published *Shoeless Joe*.

Salinger's appearances in the news, however, do not fully explain his existence as a character in *Shoeless Joe*. Kinsella saw a deeper relationship between the aging literary icon and Joe Jackson. There is little doubt that Salinger is a compelling individual. His life since the publication of *Catcher* has literally rewritten the book on the division between public and private life. Salinger's decision to avoid public life over the past forty years has shrouded the man in mystery and given his works an almost mythical quality. In creating the fictional Salinger, Kinsella worked to answer two of the most basic dilemmas facing public figures: how can one be a private individual in a very public field? and how can one have integrity as a writer and, at the same time, be a producer of consumer goods? Kinsella notes the relationship between baseball players and writers in a 1987 interview:

A baseball player is only as good as his last fifty at-bats, an author is only as good as his last book. The work each does is mercilessly scrutinized by critics and the public. In both professions only the wily, the ruthlessly ambitious, and those with eyes for the absurd have long careers. (Horvath and Palmer 190)

Salinger addresses these same questions several times in *Catcher in the Rye*. Charles Kaplan noted this theme in 1956, suggesting that the novel explored what he called "the relationship between virtuosity and integrity" (43).

Joyce Rowe echos Kaplan and adds, "From beginning to end of his journey, from school to sanitarium, Holden's voice, alternating between obscenity and delicacy, conveys his rage at the inability of his contemporaries to transcend the corrosive materialism of modern American life" (78). She argues that "the bathos of American society turns out to be the real illness from which Holden suffers" (82). In *Shoeless Joe,* Kinsella agrees with and dramatizes Rowe's interpretations, but he also suggests, in the words of James E. Miller, that "Holden's sickness of soul is something deeper than economic or political ills, that his revulsion at life is not limited to social and monetary inequities, but at something in the nature of life itself" (142).

Certainly the materialism and triviality of American art are two of the most important themes of *Catcher,* Salinger returned to them several times in the course of Holden's narration. In the opening paragraph of the book, Holden sets up the dilemma between materialism and art when he mentions that his brother, D. B., has given up his literary writing career, moved to Hollywood, and become "a prostitute" by writing for the film industry (2). The primary issue for Holden in the case of his brother seems to be money and its potential effect on D. B.'s art. He makes a point of mentioning D. B.'s new Jaguar and the fact that "He's got a lot of dough, now. [though] He didn't *use* to" (1). It's important to note that Holden doesn't suggest that his brother lacks talent as a writer, acknowledging, "he wrote this terrific book of short stories," but rather laments D. B.'s willingness to write *for money.* In Holden's mind the roles of creative artist and producer of consumer goods are mutually exclusive.

Film and stage actors come to represent, in the course of the novel, the very teeth of this dilemma. "I hate actors," Holden notes. "They never act like people" (117). For Holden, the causes of bad acting (and herein lies the dilemma) are the performer's awareness of an audience and simultaneous knowledge that he or she is a famous actor. "And if any actor's really good," he explains, "you can always tell he *knows* he's good, and that spoils it" (117). Holden notes that Alfred Lunt and Lynn Fontanne, two actors he sees in a Broadway play "didn't act like people and they didn't act like actors. . . . They acted more like they knew they were celebrities and all. I mean they were good, but they were *too* good" (126). "If you do something too good," he added, "then after a while, if you don't watch it, you start showing off. And then you're not good anymore" (126).

Holden's critique applies to other kinds of performers as well. Perhaps he is most critical of Ernie, the Greenwich Village nightclub owner and piano player. As with the Lunts and D. B., Ernie's skill is not in question. "He's so good," Holden notes, "he's almost corny" (80). The problem is the audience's effect on Ernie: "I don't even think he *knows* any more when he's playing right or not. It isn't his fault. I partly blame all those dopes that clap their heads off—they'd foul up *any*body, if you gave them a chance" (84). Holden's solution to the problem is for the artist to completely withdraw from public performance. Though not practical, it gets to the heart of the problem facing all public figures. "If I were a piano player or an actor or something and all those dopes thought I was terrific, I'd hate it. I wouldn't even want them to *clap* for me. People always clap for the wrong things. If I were a piano player, I'd play it in the goddam closet" (84). Later, at a different performance, he adds, "If you sat around there long enough and heard all the phonies applauding and all, you got to hate everybody in the world" (142). Holden's "solution" exposes his basic inability to compromise on this question. For him, this issue is black and white, right and wrong. The problem of art and materialism is, like other problems in the novel, practically insoluble in Holden's world.

The one performer Holden praises is so obscure as to avoid any public recognition. He thus remains a "pure" artist. To kill time before his appointment with Carl Luce, Holden goes to Radio City Music Hall to see a movie. He arrives in time for the floor show but is disappointed by the Rockettes "kicking their heads off" and a roller skating performer: "I shouldn't enjoy it much because I kept picturing him *pract*icing to be a guy that roller skates on the stage" (137). Finally Holden notes the kettle drummer in the orchestra. "He's the best drummer I ever saw," Holden bubbles. "He only gets a chance to bang them a couple of times during the whole piece, but he never looks bored when he isn't doing it. Then when he does bang them, he does it so nice and sweet, with this nervous expression on his face" (138). For Holden, only performers like the kettle drummer, who are able to avoid public attention, remain true artists. Through these characters, Salinger gives a fairly coherent warning, all the more powerful because of his own withdrawal from the public eye, about the danger of mixing public acclaim and private art.

Once again, Kinsella's characters echo the dilemma found in *Catcher,* but there are alternatives in *Shoeless Joe* not available in Salinger's novel. Rather than focus on actors and musical performers, Kinsella deals primarily with ball players like Joe Jackson. As with the star performers Salinger depicts, Joe is the best at what he does. With a lifetime batting average of .356 and legendary play in the field, Jackson was one of the finest ever to play the game. By 1919, however, baseball was making the transition from an amateur sport to a big business, and Kinsella notes that, even at this early date, the game had fallen victim to capitalism. "The players," he argues, "were paid peasant salaries while the owners became rich" (9). Given the popularity of baseball, and the money involved, it is little wonder that the sport attracted the attention of businessmen, gamblers, and crooks. The White Sox were heavy favorites to win the 1919 World Series when gamblers[7] convinced several of the players to "throw" the contest. Eight players on the Chicago team, including Jackson, were later accused of accepting bribe money to lose. Jackson, meanwhile, batted .375 in the series, leading all hitters and knocking a home run in the last game, the only one hit by either team. The other players involved, owner Comiskey, and even the gamblers accused of instigating the "fix," all testified that Jackson was innocent of wrongdoing, but despite strong evidence in his favor, Jackson was barred for life from playing major league baseball. He died in 1951, his name still synonymous with dishonesty. In this historical figure, Kinsella finds a strong resonance with the tainted performers Holden encounters in *Catcher*. In the words of Kinsella, "Shoeless Joe became a symbol of the tyranny of the powerful over the powerless," as well as a living, breathing example of the conflict between artistic performance and materialism (Kinsella 7). Unlike D. B., Ernie, or the Lunts, however, Joe is given a second chance, an opportunity to play on Ray's field for the pure love of the game—not for the fans, and not for the money. He enjoys a kind of redemption that is simply not possible in Holden's world.

The final major connection between these two novels is their treatment of family. Family relationships are important in *Catcher in the Rye*, particularly sibling relationships. Holden's idolization of Allie, his love for Phoebe, and his regret for the lifestyle D. B. has chosen form much of the text of the novel.[8] He desperately misses Allie, calling him the most intelligent and "nicest" member of the family (38). Holden's love for his younger brother has not weakened, despite the child's death. He exclaims to Phoebe in a moment of frustration (and insensitivity), "Just because somebody's dead, you don't just stop liking them, for God's sake—especially if they were about a thousand times nicer than the people you know that're alive and all" (171). His relationship to Phoebe is also close, and his conversation with her in D. B.'s room forms the emotional core of the novel. Though Holden has yearned for someone to talk to throughout the first two-thirds of the narrative, calling a succession of friends on the telephone, this is his first *honest* conversation. When Phoebe asks him what he truly likes, he can only think of two things—Allie, and talking with her (171). Their relationship serves as the anchor that keeps him from completely abandoning his old life. After Holden makes up his mind to run away, Phoebe meets him, suitcase in hand, with firm plans to go with him. She persists in her demand to go until he changes his mind and decides to stay. Their close relationship, one of the few bright spots in Holden's life, literally saves him.

Once again, Kinsella's book echos the concerns and themes of *Catcher*, but it adds new twists. Like the other characters in the novel, Ray's brother Richard is also redeemed on Ray's farm. When Richard first comes to Iowa, he is unable to see the ghostly players or experience the magic of Ray's field. Toward the end of the novel, however, he begs Ray, "Teach me how to see" (239). His desire becomes even more heartfelt as he discovers that their father is one of the invisible players—the new catcher for the White Sox. Ray eventually realizes that the "he" of his first voice ("If you build it, he will come") refers both to Joe Jackson and to his father, John Kinsella. In an obvious pun on Salinger's title, Kinsella has Ray's father, a minor league baseball *catcher*, return from the dead to become the catcher in the corn. In the emotional climax of the novel the two sons finally work up the courage to approach their father. In a sudden epiphany Richard begins to see John, whom Ray consistently refers to as "the catcher":

> My father stops speaking and looks questioningly at Richard, who is squinting at him as though he is at the far end of a microscope.
> "He's been having a little trouble with his eyes, but I think it's clearing up," I say.
> "It's true," says Richard, air exploding from his lungs.
> "It's true," I reply.
> "I admire the way you catch a game of baseball," he says to the catcher, slowly, hesitantly, his voice filled with awe.
> As the three of us walk across the vast emerald lake that is the outfield, I think of all the things I'll want to talk to the catcher about. I'll guide the conversations, like taking a car around a long, gentle curve in the road, and we'll hardly realize that we're talking of love, and family, and life, and beauty, and friendship, and sharing. (255)

Both Richard and John are reborn on Ray's field, and the family relationships that had been permanently broken by death are magically restored.

The fact that Richard and Ray are brothers and Kinsella's inclusion of the carnival exhibit Richard owns "the world's strangest babies"—suggests one final connection between *Shoeless Joe* and *Catcher in the Rye*. Holden visits two museums in the course of *Catcher*. The first, the Museum of Natural History, contains, among other things, dioramas of Native American life. Holden is most impressed by the seemingly immutable nature of the museum.

> The best thing, though, in that museum was that everything always stayed right where it was. Nobody'd move. You could go there a hundred thousand times, and that Eskimo would still be just finished catching those two fish, the birds would still be on their way south, the deers would still be drinking out of that water hole. . . . Nobody'd be different. The only thing that would be different would be *you*. (121)

At the second museum he visits, the Metropolitan Museum of Art, Holden, along with two young brothers, views a reconstruction of an Egyptian tomb.

Here, once again, Holden notes a peaceful changelessness, explaining to the boys, "They wrapped their faces up in these cloths that were treated with some secret chemical. That way they could be buried in their tombs for thousands of years and their faces wouldn't rot or anything" (203). After the boys become scared and leave, Holden is left alone in the tomb. He notes, "I liked it, in a way. It was nice and peaceful" (204). Peter Shaw has pointed out that in both cases, Holden's museum experience "expresses his need for a moratorium on both death and love" (101). Holden yearns, literally, for the changeless peace of the tomb. Once again, though, he is denied what he seeks. The scrawled profanity in the tomb shocks him back to reality; not even the tomb is peaceful for Holden. He explains, "I think, even, if I ever die, and they stick me in a cemetery, and I have a tombstone and all, it'll say "Holden Caulfield" on it, and then what year I was born and what year I died, and then right under that it'll say 'Fuck you.' I'm positive, in fact" (204).

The tomb is certainly not a peaceful place for the players Ray helps in *Shoeless Joe*. Even in death, their yearning to fulfil their dreams continues to haunt them. Perhaps this is the core of Holden's complaint; death will not solve his problems either. Ray's field does not *suspend* love and death, but it does allow, if not the moratorium on death Shaw describes, then at least a reprieve, a chance to fulfil lost dreams. Richard's carnival trailer, on the other hand, filled with its glass cases and faded photographs, caricatures Salinger's museums and works as the antithesis of Ray's field. The attraction he owns, a pseudo-museum which claims to display "the world's strangest babies," is, in reality, a trailer with "about a dozen glass containers, like built-in fish tanks. . . . Each one contains a photograph of a deformed fetus and a small typed card describing the origins of the photo" (207–208). If Salinger's museums offer the illusion of a moratorium on death, Kinsella's "museum" suggests nothing of the kind. It puts death and decay on display and charges admission. Ray, like Holden, notes that the displays appear to have been unchanged for years, but in this case their changelessness suggests nothing so much as their total artificiality, their utter lack of life. "What did you expect," Richard's girlfriend demands, "live babies?" (208). Richard, caught in a twisted version of Holden's museum ideal, is redeemed only by Ray's renewed love and friendship and by the family ties he is able to reestablish with his father.[9] The words of the little boy Holden meets in the Met are particularly meaningful in the context of Richard and Ray's relationship: "He ain't my friend," the boy explains to Holden as his frightened sibling runs from the museum, "He's my brudda" (203).

The structure created by W. P. Kinsella in *Shoeless Joe* mirrors in surprising detail the pattern set by *Catcher in the Rye*. Kinsella, however, seems intent on *answering* the existential questions posed by the earlier novel. The world of Ray Kinsella is deeply meaningful, and it is, therefore, inherently different from the world of Holden Caulfield. In large measure, Ray is able to fulfill Holden's dream of becoming a savior. For Ray, though, the rye has been transformed into corn, and the game being played in the field is baseball. Instead of keeping children from tumbling over a cliff, Ray offers salvation to adults who have lost their way in the world of spiritual shallowness and materialism. In Holden's world, a young boy can fall out of a dorm window to a meaningless death. In Ray's world, a young girl who falls off a bleacher can be miraculously saved by a ghostly doctor, In Holden's world, Allie's death is tragic—the end of friendship and family. In Ray's world, death is not final; family relations, love, and help can extend beyond the grave. Kinsella, in short, offers answers to Holden's problems that Salinger refused to offer. In *Shoeless Joe* Salinger's existential realism is replaced by Kinsella's magical realism.

One of Holden's most basic questions plagues all of us to some degree: how can life be meaningful in the face of a chaotic, violent, materialistic, and consumer-driven modern world? Helen Weinberg called *Catcher* "totally modern in its questions," and this is significant because she believes that in "the most honest modernist vision of the spiritual quest," the results can only be "inevitable failure" (66, 79).[10] Kinsella rejects this vision of the modern world and responds to Holden's failure with a sustained trope of redemption.[11] Ray eventually redeems even the fictional "Jerry" Salinger by offering him a world untainted by the kind of corruption which surrounds Holden. The fictional Salinger's "They wall come"[12] oration near the end of *Shoeless Joe* has become one of the most famous speeches in contemporary pop culture. In a statement of born-again, secular faith, Salinger tells Ray that people will come to his small Midwestern farm to experience the peace he and the other characters have found there. "The arrivals will be couples who have withered and sickened of the contrived urgency of their lives," he explains.

> "They'll turn up in your driveway, not knowing for sure why they're doing it, and arrive at your door, innocent as children, longing for the gentility of the past, for home-canned preserves, ice cream made in a wooden freezer, gingham dresses, and black-and-silver stoves with high warming ovens and cast-iron reservoirs.
>
> "'Of course, we don't mind if you look around,' you'll say. 'It's only twenty dollars per person.' And they'll pass over the money without even looking at it—for it is money they have, and peace they lack." (252)

One of Salinger's final statements in the novel reaffirms this assurance, this testimony of faith in the face of seeming chaos. When the players invite the aging writer to return with them to the afterlife, he admits to Ray, "I thought of turning them down. . . . But then I thought, they must know; there must be a reason for them to choose me, just as there was a reason for them to choose you, and Iowa, and this farm" (263). If *Catcher in the Rye* is, as Gerald Rosen has suggested, a "novel of the death of belief in America," then *Shoeless Joe* is about its potential rebirth and the possibility of a post-postmodern renewal of faith (96).

Notes

1. The literary battle Carol and Richard Ohmann and James F. Miller, Jr. have fought over *Catcher* may be understood at least in part as an expression of this polarization. The Ohmanns suggest a (Marxist) reading focused on Salinger's very real critique of society; Miller suggests a more personal reading with understanding Holden as the aim.

2. Like the fictional Ray Kinsella, W. P. Kinsella spent several years in Iowa (as part of the University of Iowa Writer's Workshop), and he calls Iowa "the only place I feel at home" (Dahlin 7). Kinsella did sell insurance before becoming a writer, and he does love baseball. His wife's name is Annie as is Ray's wife's name, and his father is John Kinsella, an ex-minor league player who died in 1953. Kinsella lived in Iowa for several years, and chased the baseball season in an old Datsun, as does Ray in the novel. The relationship between writer and character is close enough for Alan Cheuse to suggest that "Ray Kinsella, the novel's narrator, appears to be a doppelganger of the author himself" (V2).

3. See note number 7.

4. Phil Alden Robinson, a young Hollywood director, read the novel and found a story he believed would make a great film. Later he would note, "The only reason to adapt a novel into a screenplay is because you love the novel" *(Field of Dreams; A Scrapbook)*. He secured the rights, wrote a screenplay based on Kinsella's text, and received funding from Universal Pictures. When the real J. D. Salinger heard that the film was in preproduction, he had his lawyer contact Universal to warn them against using his name or likeness. Robinson was forced to rewrite Salinger's part, and, for the first time in his life, he wrote for a specific actor *(Field of Dreams; A Scrapbook)*. It's probably not accidental that he chose James Earl Jones, an actor as different as possible from Salinger in appearance and temperament, to play the part. See Joseph Walker's essay in this collection for more discussion of the film.

5. An obvious question here is why Salinger, known for his litigiousness, did not sue Kinsella and Random House for using his name and likeness. The answer has to do, ironically, with the writer's status as a public figure. He could not sue Kinsella for copyright violation, because Kinsella did not use any material that could be copyrighted (a book, letter, etc.). He may, however, have considered suing for character defamation. The traditional definition of defamation has three components: the statement in question must have been made to a third person (i.e., published in a novel); it must be untrue; and the victim must prove that harm was done. What Kinsella wrote in the novel was patently untrue, and Salinger could likely have claimed harm on the simple grounds of invasion of privacy. A landmark defamation case stood in his way, however. In 1964, a New York public official sued the *New York Times* for defamation (*NY Times vs. Sullivan*, 376 U S 1964). The case went all the way to the Supreme Court and was eventually decided in favor of the *Times*. The court decided that being a public official invites a greater degree of scrutiny. Officials, the court declared, had to prove actual malice on the part of

the alleged defamer. In 1967, that notion was further broadened (*Curtis Publishing Company vs. Butts,* 388 US 1967) when the court found a strong correlation between public officials and other public figures. Salinger, as a public figure, would have to prove that Kinsella wrote the novel with malice, that is, that the Canadian author was out to get him. The deeply sympathetic portrayal of Salinger in the novel would suggest otherwise.

6. In the novel, Ray confronts the fictional Salinger with an interview in which he claims to have wanted to play baseball for another New York team transplanted to California: the Giants (33–5).

7. The "bankroll" for the fix was a well-known gambler named Arnold Rothstein, who put up $100,000 to pay off the players. Bluestein's name in the novel suggests that Kinsella was drawing a comparison between modern business and land development practices and illegal gambling. The author makes the connection more explicit when he later describes Bluestein as "wearing a wide-shouldered green corduroy suit that makes him look like a gangster" (241).

8. His mother and father, on the other hand, are conspicuous by their absence. Jonathan Baumbach suggests that one of Holden's main quests is for family and, specifically, for a father, someone who could guide his life. "The world," Baumbach argues, "devoid of good fathers . . . , becomes a soul-destroying chaos in which [Holden's] survival is possible only through withdrawal into childhood, into fantasy, into psychosis" (57).

9. An oddity of *Shoeless Joe* is that Ray and Richard's mother, though still living as the action takes place, is conspicuously absent. She is mentioned only once, briefly.

10. In her essay "Holden and Seymour and the Spiritual Activist Hero," Weinberg argues, in fact, that Salinger is not completely honest in *Catcher,* that he "cheats . . . on his own vision" by allowing Holden to succeed, at least partially, in his spiritual quest (64). She believes that Salinger's vision of the modern world is more honest in "Seymour: An Introduction."

11. In support of this idea, Kinsella said of his novel soon after publication, "I put in no sex, no violence, no obscenity, none of that stuff that sells. I wanted to write a book for imaginative readers, an affirmative statement about life" (Dahlin 7).

12. The line "They will come" is actually found only in *Field of Dreams,* the film version of *Shoeless Joe.*

WORKS CITED

Baumbach, Jonathan. "The Saint as a Young Man: A Reappraisal of 'The Catcher in the Rye'." *Critical Essays on Salinger's* The Catcher in the Rye. Ed. Joel Salzberg. Boston: G. K. Hall and Co., 1990. 55–63.

Cheuse, Alan. "An Outsider's Homage to Baseball Lore." *Los Angeles Times,* 23 May 1982: V2.

Dahlin, Robert. "W. P. Kinsella." *Publisher's Weekly* 221.16 (1982): 6–7.

"Dodger in the Rye." *Newsweek* 30 July 1979: 11–13.

Eppes, Betty. "What I Did Last Summer." *The Paris Review* 23.80 (1981): 221–239.

Field of Dreams. Dir. Phil Alden Robinson, Universal Pictures, 1989.

Field of Dreams: A Scrapbook, Banned from the Ranch Entertainment, 1990. (Promotional Video)

Fosburgh, Lacey. "J. D. Salinger Speaks About His Silence." *New York Times* 3 Nov. 1974: 1A.

Heiserman, Arthur, and James E. Miller, Jr. "J. D. Salinger: Some Crazy Cliff." *Critical Essays on Salinger's* The Catcher in the Rye. Ed Joel Salzberg. Boston: G. K. Hall and Co., 1990. 32–39.

Horvath, Brooke and William Palmer. "Three On: An Interview with David Carkeet, Mark Harris, and W. P. Kinsella." *Modern Fiction Studies* 33, 183–194.

Kaplan, Charles. "Holden and Huck. The Odysseys of Youth." *The Catcher in the Rye.* Ed. Joel Salzberg. Boston: G. K. Hall and Co., 1990. 39–43.

Kinsella, W. P. *Shoeless Joe.* New York: Ballantine Books, 1982.

Miller, James. "'Catcher' In and Out of History." *Critical Essays on Salinger's* The Catcher in the Rye. Ed. Joel Salzberg. Boston: G. K. Hall and Co., 1990. 140–143.

Pearson, Ian. "Fantasy Strikes Out." Rev. of *Shoeless Joe. Macleans* 95.16 (1982): 59, 61.

Plummer, William. "In Another League." Rev. of *Shoeless Joe. Newsweek* 23 Aug. 1982: 64.

Rosen, Gerald. "A Retrospective Look at 'The Catcher in the Rye'." *Critical Essays on Salinger's* The Catcher in the Rye. Ed. Joel Salzberg. Boston: G. K. Hall and Co., 1990. 158–171.

Rowe, Joyce. "Holden Caulfield and American Protest." *New Essays on* The Catcher in the Rye. Ed Jack Salzman. New York: Cambridge University Press, 1991. 77–96.

Salinger, J. D. *The Catcher in the Rye.* Boston: Little Brown Books, 1951.

Salzman, Jack. Introduction. *New Essays on* The Catcher in the Rye. Ed. Jack Salzman. New York: Cambridge University Press, 1991. 1–22.

Seelye, John. "Holden in the Museum." *New Essays on* The Catcher in the Rye. Ed. Jack Salzman. Cambridge: Cambridge University Press, 1991. 23–34.

Shaw, Peter. "Love and Death in *The Catcher in the Rye.*" *New Essays on* The Catcher in the Rye. Ed. Jack Salzman. New York: Cambridge University Press, 1991. 97–114.

Weinberg, Helen, "J. D. Salinger's Holden and Seymour and the Spiritual Activist Hero." *J. D. Salinger.* Ed. Harold Bloom. New York: Chelsea House Publishers, 1987. 63–80.

ROBERT MILTNER

Mentor Mori; or, Sibling Society
and the Catcher in the Bly

Holden Caulfield is a young man coming of age in American society in the 1950s; caught in the adolescent transition between the childhood of his past and the adulthood which awaits him, he struggles in an uncertainty which seems as prolonged as adolescence itself, against "the ineluctability of growing up, of having to assume the prerogatives and responsibilities of manhood" (55) as Jonathan Baumbach puts it. What makes Holden's experience particularly difficult is that he is keenly aware of being isolated and feeling alienated; seemingly, there is no one he can turn to for guidance, as those few he does turn to do not provide him with effective help. Possible elder mentors—his father, his brother D. B., his former teacher Mr. Antolini, even his former student advisor Carl Luce—are unavailable or, when contacted, have other agendas, while his prep school peers— Stradlater, Ackley, James Castle—offer versions of Holden's future from which he recoils. No wonder, then, that Holden reveres the time of his own childhood, represented by his little sister Phoebe and his deceased younger brother Allie, who remains frozen at the threshold of adolescence. No wonder then that the image which mirrors Holden most closely, the Holden who fears stepping off the curb for fear of disappearing, is the image of the "swell" kid who walks in the street next to the curb singing "If a body catch a body coming through the rye" (*Catcher in The Rye* 115).

The Catcher in the Rye: New Essays, edited by J. P. Steed (New York: Peter Lang, 2002): pp. 33–52. Copyright © 2002 Peter Lang.

Initial critical response in the 1950s identified Holden as being a poor role model, as in Riley Hughes' dismissal of Holden for his "formidably excessive use of amateur swearing and coarse language"(8) or in T. Morris Longstreth's alliterative pronouncement that Holden was "preposterous, profane, and pathetic beyond belief" (6). From a contemporary perspective, however, it is evident that part of Holden's difficulty arises not so much from Holden being a poor role model as much as his having no one after which to model himself. Suspended between the world of prep schools and an upper-middle-class New York lifestyle, between childhood and adulthood, Holden is adrift in a sea of peers every bit as adrift as he is. In essence, Holden's 1950s dilemma foreshadows the sibling society of the late 1990s and early 2000s.

Robert Bly has identified a sibling society as one in which adults, due to single-parenting and divorce, fueled by the media-driven emphasis on the youth culture, are less mature and responsible than their parents' generation. Conversely, and more importantly, adolescents, due to growing up in working, single-parent homes, assume more adult responsibilities; the sibling society is thus one in which "parents regress to become more like children, and the children, through abandonment, are forced to become adults too soon" (Bly *Sibling Society* 132). The result is a society in which adults and adolescent are becoming less differentiated. This problem is further complicated as people remain adolescents long past the normal adolescent period (*Sibling Society* 45). Historically, as Bly recounts, social conditions did not allow for adolescence:

> During the Middle Ages, the stage of youth was virtually ignored; a peasant child of seven joined the workforce. At Plymouth Colony, a child was considered a small adult at the age of eight. Children were asked to be aware of the group. There was no real time for adolescence then. (*Sibling Society* 45)

Not until the late 1940s and early 1950s, the era of *The Catcher in the Rye*, did adolescence became both a social presence and a cultural concept, as linguist Bill Bryson illustrates:

> So little had they [adolescents] been noticed in the past that *teenager* had entered the language only as recently as 1941. (As an adjective, *teenage* had been around since the 1920s, but it wasn't used much.) In the heady boom of the postwar years, however, America's teenagers made up for lost time. Between 1946 and 1960, when the population of the United States grew by about 40 percent, the number of teenagers grew by 110 percent. (335)

It is evident, then, that Holden's generation represents the beginning of periodic social trends in which adolescents would outnumber adults. Holden Caulfield, in his disdain for the phoniness of joining cliques and climbing the ladder of economic success, presages the emergence of the sibling society which dominates the cultural landscape of the 1960s and beyond: in lieu of accepting the cultural norm, they learn that "one way to outwit the demands of that civilization [their parent's] is to set up a sibling society" (*Sibling Society* 48). Yet, in accepting peer guidance from a society of siblings, young men come of age without the guidance of effective male role models, which Bly considers to be the basic problem the whole sibling society faces: "the socialization of young males in the absence of fathers and mentors" (*Sibling Society* 180). In the paternal society, the world of the first half of the twentieth century, there were numerous representatives of the adult community, teachers, and elders to whom the young were drawn (*Sibling Society* 237). These elders are necessary for modeling, a socialization process intrinsic to adolescence that allows young people to imitate elders and role models until their acquired responses become habitual. Among the elders, parents are the "most significant adults in the lives of adolescents," followed by siblings and non-related significant adults, such as teachers (Rice 96). In Holden's case, this applies especially to his father.

Holden's father, a corporate lawyer, is largely absent from the book, though his comings and goings are made evident. At best a "shadowy abstraction" (Rowe 89), Mr. Caulfield is described doing such mundane activities as driving the family car to a party in Norwalk, Connecticut (*Catcher in the Rye* 162–163), and flying to California for business (162), and he is even described sympathetically as lunching with Mr. Antolini to discuss how he is "terribly concerned" about Holden (186), yet he is never shown actually interacting with Holden in any way. Presented as an absentee parent, he is typical of "many contemporary fathers [who] abandon the family emotionally by working fourteen hours a day" (*Sibling Society* 36), and is representative of Bly's belief that fathers are vanishing both physically and conceptually in the sibling society. Holden's father is presented as a private person given to strong emotional responses, as early as the first paragraph in which Holden expresses that both of his parents are "quite touchy" about discussing "anything pretty personal about them," and Holden adds "especially my father" (*Catcher in the Rye* 1) to emphasize that his father is the more emphatic of the two. When Phoebe learns that Holden has been dismissed from Pency Prep, she says, and repeats three more times for emphasis, that their Daddy will kill Holden for getting kicked out of school. However, Holden's father, who could not convince his son to be psychoanalyzed when Allie died, threatens Holden with the trump card in learning self-discipline: sending Holden to military school (166), that 1950s version of juvenile delinquent boot camp for an attitude readjustment.

Holden's father is an example of the typical "Fifties male" Robert Bly examines in *Iron John*, one who "got to work early, labored responsibly, supported his wife and children, and admired discipline" (1), a type the generation into which Salinger and Bly were born in 1919 and 1926, respectively, knew well. Yet rather than be angry with or disdainful of his father, Holden seems largely ambivalent not only about his father but about the adult world in general.

Holden's mother, the other parental figure, is described as distant, distracted; she is, as Joyce Rowe observes, "too nervous and anxious herself to do more than pay perfunctory attention to her children's needs" (89). Holden expresses that she is "*nice* and all" (*Catcher in the Rye* 1) and that he feels "sorry as hell" for her because he is aware that her grief has not ended, since she "still isn't over [his] brother Allie yet" (155). The result of her continued grief leaves her "very nervous" (107), suffering from "headaches quite frequently" (178), and experiencing symptoms akin to agoraphobia: she "doesn't enjoy herself much when she goes out" (177), and despite her telling Phoebe she "won't be home until very late" (162), she returns early. This latter incident results in Holden's being caught off guard and having to hide in Phoebe's (D. B.'s) closet, and consequently Holden's mother appears only as a ghostly presence speaking from the dark, a figure which Holden can hear but not see. Concerning this absence of parental role models in the novel, Gerald Rosen has commented that

> The absence of Holden's parents (along with the absence of real religious guidance in the form of a school chaplain or family minister) is so important it amounts to a presence. . . . Holden sorely misses being able to turn to his parents in his time of trouble. . . . So Holden cannot get advice on how to leave the world of childhood from the adults around him. (162)

Because Holden's parents are unable to assist him during his transition through adolescence, his next best choice is D. B., his older brother.

D. B., however, has deserted Holden, abandoning his true artistry as a short story writer to go to Hollywood and to write for the movies, which leads Holden to label his brother a "prostitute" (*Catcher in the Rye* 2). As a middle child—both the middle boy and, after Allie's death, the middle Caulfield child—Holden looks up to his older brother who has served in the Army and who has written and published a book that Holden admires. It was D. B. who functioned as Holden's surrogate by attending Allie's funeral when Holden was still in the hospital from hurting his hand by breaking the garage windows the night Allie died, and it is through D. B.'s eyes—"D. B. told me. I wasn't there" (155)— that Holden waked his little brother. Sibling relationships between older brothers who act as role models and younger siblings who imitate them can be "vitally important" (Rice 441) in the development of an adolescent's personality traits and overall behavior. Further, these older siblings often serve "as surrogate parents, acting as caretakers, teachers, playmates and confidants" (Rice 441), a concept not unfamiliar to Salinger who presented older siblings as surrogate parents in *Franny and Zooey* as well. Buddy Glass, for example, in a letter to his younger brother Zooey, describes how he and his brother Seymour took over the education of the two youngest Glass children, Franny and Zooey, remarking how "Seymour and I thought it might be a good thing to hold back" the usual areas of conventional knowledge, such as "the arts, sciences, classics, languages"(*Franny and Zooey* 65); instead, he reminds Zooey of how "[Seymour] and I were regularly conducting home seminars" on "who and what Jesus and Gautama and Lao-tse . . . were before you knew too much or anything about Homer or Shakespeare or even Blake or Whitman, let alone George Washington and his cherry tree"(65–66). Yet, following Seymour's suicide and Buddy's relocation—similar to Allie's death and D. B.'s relocation, respectively—Franny and Zooey find themselves mentorless with absentee older siblings. Similarly, after Allie's death, D. B. relocates to Hollywood, making himself "as emotionally remote from him [Holden] as is his father" (Rowe 89). As a result, Holden feels betrayed, partly because D. B. has become a scriptwriter for money rather than an artist who writes stories and partly because it connects D. B. to the commercial world of his father, who flies to California for business of his own. Holden is left to seek other mentors who can function as surrogate older brothers or as surrogate parents.

The person to whom Holden turns is Mr. Antolini, his former teacher from Elkton Hills who now teaches English at NYU. It is noteworthy that Antolini, like Holden, has read all of D. B.'s stories and further that he has "phoned [D. B.] up and told him not to go [to Hollywood]" (*Catcher in the Rye* 181), so that Antolini speaks like an older version of Holden, telling D. B. what Holden is feeling but cannot express. Further, and despite Holden's being drawn to Mr. Antolini because he was the "best teacher I [Holden] ever had" or because "you could kid around with him without losing your respect for him" (174), that is, he could be both a child and an adult simultaneously, what is most telling about Holden's interest in his connection with Mr. Antolini is that "He was a pretty young guy, not much older than my brother D. B." (174), and Holden even asserts that Antolini was "sort of like D. B." (181). Clearly, then, with D. B. away, Antolini becomes a surrogate older brother, someone his brother's age with whom Holden can talk. In fact, just following Holden's sharing of his vision of the catcher in the rye with Phoebe, his only local living sibling, his immediate instinct is to call Antolini, his surrogate brother. Despite his inability to call Jane Gallagher when he needed to do so, Holden calls Antolini and arranges to visit with him, going quickly by cab from D. B.'s room where Phoebe sleeps to Antolini's apartment where he is greeted intimately and familially as "Holden, m'boy!" (181). Thus Antolini, the "gentle teacher—the substitute father," is the one Holden turns to "after all the other fathers of his world have failed him, including his real father" (Baumbach 56). Yet, Antolini fails him in his own way as familialism becomes unwelcome homosexual intimacy, and Holden's father figure and surrogate older brother joins the league of disappointing older males; if D. B. is the "prostitute," then Antolini is the gigolo. Which makes Carl Luce the sex counselor.

Like Antolini, Carl Luce represents a mentor brought forward from Holden's previous prep school experiences to function as a surrogate older brother, except where Antolini represents Holden's experiences at Elkton Hills, Luce represents Holden's experiences at Whooton School. Further, like Antolini, Luce has left the prep school (he has graduated) and gone on to college (as a student) at Columbia. Three years older than Holden, Carl Luce was Holden's Student Advisor at Whooton, a kind of peer-mentoring position, though in reality

> the only thing he [Luce] ever did, though, was give these sex talks and all, late at night when there was a bunch of guys in his room. He knew quite a bit about sex, especially perverts and all. (*Catcher in The Rye* 143)

In a sense, Carl Luce plays the role usually reserved for one's father or one's older brother: initiation, through talk and male bonding, into understanding the world of sexuality, an area in which Holden is floundering due to his lack of experience. Holden, recognizing that he is in need of a mentor to guide him, meets Carl Luce at the Wicker Bar, only to have his request to be guided rejected. Holden asks Luce to listen, praises his intelligence, then states in no uncertain terms that he is in need of Luce's advice, but before he can state the nature of his problem, Carl Luce cuts him off with a dismissive groan. Carl Luce has no interest in mentoring Holden; he refuses to answer any typical Caulfield questions (146) or have a typical Caulfield conversation (145), premised, apparently, upon his belief that Holden is not old enough or mature enough to benefit from his advice even should he give it, as evidenced by his asking Holden repeatedly about when he's going to grow up (141–146). Luce acts like the older brother who feels his younger brother is just too little to be talked to as a adult, a role, by the way, which Holden never plays with either Allie (in his imagined conversations) or Phoebe. And what's worse, Carl Luce's attempt to act older than his years, manifest in his dating a Chinese sculptress in her late thirties, is similar to Mr. Antolini's being married to a wife who is, from Holden's perspective, "about sixty years older" (181). This is the same "older woman" stratagem, by the way, which Holden himself parallels by offering to buy drinks for Ernie Morrow's mother (57), Faith Cavendish (65), the three secretaries from

Seattle (74), and the Hat Check Girl at the Wicker Bar (153). Additionally, Carl Luce, again like Antolini, sides with the absent Mr. Caulfield; where Antolini met Holden's father for lunch (a kind of power lunch in Holden's interest), Luce sides with Holden's father in believing that Holden needs to be psychoanalyzed (148). Luce allays Holden's concerns about psychiatry, advising him that it will help him to "recognize the patterns of [his] mind" (148), but just as Carl Luce begins to explain the concept to Holden, to actually mentor him—an extension upon his previous role as a student advisor—he suddenly changes tack, stops, and retreats: "Listen. I'm not giving an elementary course in psychoanalysis. If you're interested, call him [Luce's father] up and make an appointment" (148). Despite Luce's directive for Holden to call his father, however, Luce's personal comment is more telling: "If you're not [interested], don't. I couldn't care less, frankly" (148). Carl Luce clearly indicates that he has no personal interest in guiding or mentoring Holden; in fact, while Holden is ironically telling Luce, hand on his shoulder, what a "real friendly bastard" he is, Luce is looking at his watch and calling to the bartender for his check (148). Of course, when Carl Luce tells Holden how he was psychoanalyzed and was able, in his words, able "to *adjust* [him]self to a certain extent" (148), it is becoming clear to Holden that if psychoanalysis will leave him as distant and disinterested as Carl Luce—and his own father by proxy—then he will not be seeking out a psychiatrist. Carl Luce leaves Holden at the bar, alone, without the benefit of any mentoring or guidance.

In a world devoid, therefore, of older male role models, either father figures or older brother surrogates, Holden is left with the peer group, his sibling society, represented by the prep schools which Holden has attended: Whooton School, Elkton Hills, and Pency Prep. At Whooton School, Holden's peers include Raymond Goldfarb, with whom Holden drank Scotch in the chapel (*Catcher in the Rye* 90), in what appears to be an initiation into the adult alcohol culture which attracts Holden. He finds his other peers, Quaker Arthur Childs (99) and Catholic Louis Shaney (112), want to foist their religious agendas on him. Thus, Whooton School teaches Holden that consumption of alcohol and religious affiliation are signifiers of the adult world, with Holden choosing the former. At Elkton Hills, Holden's peers teach him more personal lessons. One of his roommates, Dick Slagle, had a "goddam inferiority complex" (108) because his inexpensive suitcases were not "Mark Cross . . . genuine cowhide" (108) like Holden's; as a result, Slagle labels Holden's suitcases "too new and bourgeois" (108), giving Holden a lesson in class distinction (the visual signifier of the object-suitcase) and class jealousy (suitcases connote both where one comes from as well as where one is going), which Holden summarizes in his observation that:

> You think if they're [roommate/peer] intelligent and all, the other
> person, and have a good sense of humor, that they don't give a damn
> whose suitcases are better, but they do. They really do. (109)

His other roommate, Harris Macklin, whistles beautifully but is "one of the
biggest bores [Holden] ever met" (123). Here the talent, whistling, is offset
by the personality deficiency of being boring. The lesson Holden learns is
summed up in Holden's comment on bores:

> Maybe you shouldn't feel too sorry if you see some swell girl getting
> married to [a bore]. They don't hurt anybody, most of them, and
> maybe they're secretly terrific whistlers or something. (124)

Hinted at, both by extension and by contrast, is that Jane Gallagher would
be better off with a bore for a stepfather than the "booze hound" (78) Mr.
Cudahy with the "lousy personality" who Holden worries might be trying
to "get wise" (79) with Jane.

Perhaps the peer who taught Holden the greatest lesson at Elkton Hills
was James Castle, who committed suicide by jumping from a window after re-
fusing to take back his statement about how conceited Phil Stabile was. Castle
functions as a emblem for integrity and truth and exemplifies the price paid by
those who adhere to those principles: Castle spoke his mind, would not retract,
and, instead of taking back what he said, jumped out the dorm window to his
death (170). Several ironies are evident here. First, Holden, at numerous times
during the novel, considers suicide in similar ways: once, when thinking about
Stradlater with Jane Gallagher in Ed Banky's car, Holden comments "I felt
like jumping out the window" (48), and second, after Maurice punches him,
Holden stated that he felt like "jumping out the window" (104), a statement he
expands upon by adding that "I probably would've done it, too, if I'd been sure
somebody'd cover me up as soon as I landed. I didn't want a bunch of stupid
rubbernecks looking at me when I was all gory" (104). This comment which
ends chapter 14 is interesting, because it is not until chapter 22 that Holden
identifies himself as one of the rubbernecks looking at James Castle when he
was gory as "his teeth, and blood, were all over the place" (170)—and echoing
the image Holden sees in the mirror after Stradlater hit him, "You never saw
such gore in your life. I had blood all over my mouth and chin" (45)— followed
by the revelation in the next chapter that it was Antolini who "took off his
coat and put it over James Castle and carried him back to the infirmary" (174).
Furthermore, James Castle died wearing a turtleneck sweater that Holden had
loaned him (170), linking the two symbolically through the use of an object
signifier. Finally, it is implied that Holden may be following James Castle in
unintentional ways, for Salinger is careful to have Holden reveal to the reader

that "All I knew about [James Castle] was that his name was always right ahead of me at roll call. Cabel, R., Cable, W., Castle, Caulfield—I can still remember it" (171). James Castle died because he believed that it was noble never to take back one's word and thus to advance the cause of truth by speaking it and standing behind it. Ironically, Antolini's quotation from Wilhelm Stekel that "The mark of the immature man is that he wants to die nobly for a cause" echoes across Castle's death, for Castle died nobly for a cause, and Holden, by implication, can either be the next in line to die for a noble cause or be the mature man who wants "to live humbly" for a cause. If Holden's primary aversion is to avoid phonies and phony situations, James Castle's death is the lesson that teaches the price of opposing phoniness with the truth.

Holden's tenure at Pency Prep provides readers of *Catcher in the Rye* with insights into Holden's most pointed lessons concerning the peer influence typical of the sibling society. Granted, there are some other students with whom Holden spends some brief yet pleasant time; he describes, for example, tossing a football around one October evening with Robert Tichener and Paul Campbell and recalling them as "nice guys, especially Tichener" (4), and he tells of going into Agerstown to "have a hamburger and maybe see a lousy movie" with Mal Brossard, who Holden clearly identifies as "this friend of mine" (36). But that's it. Robert Ackley, who goes into Agerstown with Holden and Mal Brossard, is an example of a negative older (by two years) role model; Holden describes him as being hulking and having awful hygiene, as "one of these very, very tall, round-shouldered guys—he was about six four—with lousy teeth" and "a lot of pimples" (19). Moreover, and beyond the physical descriptions, Ackley is "a very peculiar guy" who "hardly ever went *any*where," perhaps because he was a nasty guy with a terrible personality (19); a senior and a loner, Ackley is hardly a role model for Holden. In direct contrast to Ackley is Ward Stradlater, Holden's roommate at Pency, who, though he appears as "mostly a Year Book kind of handsome guy" is really "more of a secret slob" (27). Stradlater, a kind of ward of the prep school system, is a user: he uses Holden's coat (25), his Vitalis (31), his talent by asking Holden to write an essay for him (28), and, if the implications are clear, Stradlater uses—or tries to use—Jane Gallagher for his own sexual gratification (43). The "secret slob" (27) whose sexual activities are "a professional secret" (43) is both a poor role model from the peer group of the prep school sibling society and an antithetical opposite of Holden's older brother D. B., who wrote a "terrific book of short stories, *The Secret Goldfish*" (1). Further, Stradlater wears Holden's jacket—as much an object signifier as the turtleneck sweater James Castle borrowed from Holden—during his escapade in Ed Banky's car with Jane Gallagher, making him a surrogate for Holden. Ironically, Holden's physical contact with Jane is limited to holding hands (79) and kissing her "all over—*any*where—her eyes, her *nose*, her forehead, her eyebrows and all, her *ears*—her whole face except her mouth" (79) as she cries after an encounter with Mr. Cudahy, her stepfather, and his innocent and non-exploitative actions are in direct contrast to those of Stradlater or, as is implied, even Mr. Cudahy. In essence, Holden would rather be a "bore" in this sense, one who with a "swell girl" like Jane will not "hurt anybody" (124).

In contrast to, or perhaps as an extension of, the prep school sibling society, Salinger has Holden encounter several other older males or contrasting peers, again as negative role models. One peer is "George something," who attends Andover, another prep school. When he meets with Holden and Sally at the play, he "didn't hesitate to horn in on my date, the bastard," says Holden, critical of how both George and Sally identify "more places and more names" (128) they have in common, which to Holden suggests identification through cliques. But what Holden finds most bothersome, the worst part, is that "the jerk had one of those very phony, Ivy League voices, one of those very tired, snobby voices. He sounded just like a girl" (128). And because in his adolescence Holden is concerned with his own sexuality, he perceives of George as effeminate. By contrast, Holden has been introduced earlier by Lillian Simmons, D. B.'s ex-girlfriend, to the Navy guy named "Commander Blop or something," whose macho image is emphasized by Holden's comment that Blop was "one of those guys that think they're being a pansy if they don't break around forty of your fingers when they shake hands with you" (86). Other older male role models, especially as they pertain to negative male role models concerning sexual knowledge, include Eddie Birdsell, from Princeton, who gives out ex-burlesque stripper Faith Cavendish's phone number to young inexperienced boys like Holden (63) and the "Joe Yale–looking Guy" at Ernie's who is giving his "terrific-looking girl" a feel under the table while talking about a guy who tried to commit suicide (85–86), a scene which evokes both Stradlater's forcing himself on Jane Gallagher and James Castle's suicide.

On the whole, Holden is outrightly critical of the student peers he encounters at Pency Prep. In fact, Salinger has Holden identify the image of Pency Prep in the novel's second paragraph, showing how its media image contrasts the physical actuality of the school: "Pency Prep . . . advertise[s] in about a thousand magazines, always showing some hot-shot guy on a horse jumping over a fence. Like as if all you ever did at Pency was play polo all the time. I never even once saw a horse anywhere *near* the place" (2). The ad connotes class, leisure, character, and status. Deconstructing the concept of character building at Pency Prep and schools like it, Holden adds that

> And underneath the guy on the horse's picture, it always says: "Since 1888 we have been molding boys into splendid, clear-thinking young men." Strictly for the birds. They don't do any

damn more molding at Pency than they do at any other school. And I don't know anybody there that was splendid and clear-thinking and all. Maybe two guys. If that many. And they probably *came* to Pency that way. (2)

What is suggested here is that it is during a child's formative years at home that character, morals, and ethics are developed and that in the sibling society of the prep school environment, each adolescent manifests the character traits he has, each in his own way. And Holden is critical of these traits when he encounters them. Having had his coat and gloves stolen from his room, Holden decrees that Pency was full of crooks (4), an ironic comment considering that most of the students were from the East Coast upper class, a point not overlooked by Holden who adds that "Quite a few guys came from these very wealthy families, but it was full of crooks anyway. The more expensive a school is, the more crooks it has" (4). Moreover, he tells Phoebe that Pency was "one of the worst schools I ever went to. It was full of . . . mean guys. You never saw so many mean guys in your life" (167). One such mean guy is Earnest Morrow, whom Holden recalls as "doubtless the biggest bastard that ever went to Pency, in the whole crumby history of the school. He was always going down the corridor, after he'd had a shower, snapping his soggy old towel at people's asses" (54). Worse even than mean individuals, though, are the cliques that exclude, ostracize, or gang up on the weak individuals. Holden was aware that it was "this very conceited boy, Phil Stabile" and "about six other dirty bastards" (170) who drove James Castle to his death; what's worse is that the mean individuals group together into cliques, the antithesis of individuals with integrity, boys like James Castle and, by association, Holden. After ice skating, Holden tries to explain this aspect of life at "a boy's school" (131) to Sally Hayes:

> . . . and everybody sticks together in these dirty little goddam cliques. The guys that are on the basketball team stick together, the Catholics stick together, the goddam intellectuals stick together, the guys that play bridge stick together. Even the guys that belong to the goddam Book-of-the-Month Club stick together. (131)

Holden tries to suggests that this grouping activity is an affront to the individual who sees through it, telling Sally that "If you try to have a little intel-ligent—" (131), but she—having made it clear in her conversation with George during the play that she believes that cliques are part of one's social identity—cuts Holden off before he can complete his statement. Holden indicates that the only option is to completely withdraw from such a sibling society, to go to

Massachusetts and Vermont, and "live somewhere with a brook and all" (132), a vision of a place completely unlike the world of prep schools for boys in which Holden lives and from which he manages to keep getting expelled.

Christopher Brookeman's 1991 essay "Pency Preppy: Cultural Codes in *The Catcher in the Rye*" gives every indication that Pency Prep is a form of what Robert Bly would qualify as a sibling society. In considering Pency Prep as representative of single-sex boarding schools, Brookeman sees it as a place where "young future professionals of the middle and upper classes experienced an extended period of training and socialization" (59). Because students usually board, the prep school functions as "an idealized family standing in loco parentis" (61), suggesting that all students are siblings within the prep school culture of the peer group. In considering how *Catcher in the Rye* offers commentary on the changing American social character in the 1950, Brookeman points to sociologists' interest in which agencies were most influential in the socialization process, settling on the family and the peer group (63), with Salinger presenting Holden "socializing with a member or members of his peer group" (63). Most notable is Brookeman's observation regarding the result of Holden's generation being peer influenced to a greater extent than by the family influence of previous generations:

> What Salinger shows is a world in which the loafing habits of teenagers, the peer group and its culture, have become a way of life; and although Salinger does not directly moralize about his hero's condition, there is something tragic about the sadly contracted state of Holden's world from which other generations have withdrawn, leaving his own generation in its one-dimensional fate. (64)

The other generations, represented by Holden's parents and teachers, are replaced by his own generation, represented by the peer groups of the prep schools Holden attends. Further, because the peers mentor themselves, they function as a kind of sibling society, a society so pervasive that, as Brookman notes:

> A particular aspect of Salinger's treatment of the peer group and its activities is the way Holden's brothers, D. B. and Allie, and his younger sister Phoebe are more like members of his peer group than of his family. . . . This closeness to his brothers and sister is in stark contrast to the relation with his parents, who are absent, shadowy figures. (71)

What Holden seeks, therefore, is an older sibling to mentor him, initiate him into adulthood, and this age dichotomy dominates *The Catcher in the Rye*.

If one reads Holden as H(old)en, it is evident that Holden seeks someone who is older as a mentor to guide him. He refers to many characters, both
potential mentors and siblings, as "old," using the term as one of respect, familiarity, or intimacy. He uses the term appropriately to describe older males,
as in "old Spencer, my history teacher" (*Catcher in the Rye* 3), "old Thurmer"
(17), the Pency Headmaster, and "old Ossenburger" (16) after whom Hold-
en's dorm at Pency was named. Interestingly, he uses the adjective to describe many of the girls his own age, as in "Old Selma Thurmer—she was the
headmaster's daughter" (3), "old Sally Hayes" (105), and "old Jane" Gallagher
(77). Many of his peers at Pency are labeled similarly: "old Ackley" (19), "old
Stradlater" (25), and even "old Marsalla" the Pency student who farted during
Ossenburger's talk in chapel; further, Holden remembers "old James Castle"
(170) from Elkton Hills, as well as "old [Carl] Luce" (143) and the ironically
labeled "old Childs" (99) the Quaker, both from Whooton School. Holden
doesn't limit himself to this prep school peers, however, for he refers to "old
Maurice," the pimp, and "old Sunny," the prostitute (101), and even his own
younger siblings, "old Phoebe" (67) and "old Allie" (39).

In contrast to Holden's use of the word "old" as a term of specific familiarity, he is aware of his own youth. Holden states that he is prone to "act
quite young for my age sometimes," and that, in fact, "sometimes I act like
I'm about thirteen" (9), and even more so, Holden is aware that "I still act
sometimes like I was only about twelve. Everybody says that, especially my
father" (9). These ages are important, in that Holden was thirteen when Allie,
who was eleven, died; it seems that, because "Life stopped for Holden on July
18, 1946, the day his brother died of leukemia," as Edwin Haviland Miller
notes, Holden "is emotionally still the same age [thirteen]" (132). In this way,
Holden has a kind of arrested emotional development, remaining the emotional age he was when his brother died, as if remaining at this (emotional)
age could keep Allie closer to him. In addition, Phoebe, ten at the time of
the events narrated in *Catcher in the Rye,* is one year younger than Allie was
when he died. Holden is caught in this age contradiction with various peers
during the course of the novel. At Pency Prep, for example, Ackley, who was
always telling Holden that he was a kid, was angered himself when Holden
called him "Ackley kid" (*Catcher in The Rye* 21). Holden, who, when in New
York, stands to order drinks and turns his few gray hairs toward the waiters,
does so because he is all too aware that he is still a minor (70). When Holden
asks Sally Hayes to run away with him "up to Massachusetts and Vermont,"
she is quick to remind him that they are "both practically children" (132).
Meeting Carl Luce, his logical mentor, Holden is asked by Luce, when they
first meet, when he is going to grow up (144), followed by Luce's comment
that Holden's mind is immature (147). Then Antolini passes on to Holden
the Wilhelm Stekel quotation concerning maturity and immaturity (188),

implying that Holden's immaturity is the current problem. Holden is left, alone at Grand Central Station, reading a magazine article about hormones, indicating Holden's fingering interest in finding some scientific explanation for his immaturity:

> It [the magazine] described how you should look, your face and eyes and all, if your hormones were in good shape, and I didn't look that way at all. I looked exactly like the guy in the article with lousy hormones. (195)

Poor Holden: he no more matches the visual image of the mature adolescent shown in the magazine than he matches Stekel's definition of the mature man! No wonder, then, that Holden's "sense of alienation is almost complete—from parents, from friends, from society in general as represented by the prep school from which he has be expelled" (Jones 24). What completes his alienation, his own profound recognition that he is mentorless himself, occurs when Phoebe wishes to run away with him. He sees her, as if in a mirror, arriving with Holden's "crazy hunting hat on" (205) and dragging Holden's "old suitcase, the one I used when I was at Whooton" (206). In that moment, he seems to realize that he has become an older sibling mentor to his own little sister, Phoebe, much in the same way that his older brother, D. B., is a mentor to him.

A short time later, Holden, sitting on a bench by the carrousel like the other kids' parents, projects an image of himself as a surrogate parent. Having assumed the role of mentor, having moved further through the door to adulthood, Holden is able to grasp, in a near-epiphany, by watching Phoebe on the carrousel, what he himself has been going through:

> All the kids kept trying to grab for the gold ring, and so was old Phoebe, and I was sort of afraid she'd fall off the goddam horse, but I didn't say anything or do anything. The thing with kids is, if they want to grab for the gold ring, you have to let them do it, and not say anything. If they fall off, they fall off. . . . (211)

From his new perspective as older mentor, Holden can see that adolescence is a time for reaching for gold rings and that falling off while doing so is often a part of the process.

Throughout the novel, Holden's alienation and awareness of his own lack of maturity have had him seeking an *older* person to mentor him. As Robert Bly suggests, however, the sibling society "offers very little generosity or support to young men" (*Sibling Society* 129). Holden, therefore, struggles in the book because he is unable to "invest his trust in anyone who is not an image of innocence," that is, those he deems phony; as a result, he "has no guides or teachers whom he can accept" (Bloom 6). Robert Bly's concern is that in the sibling society, both with its blurred distinction between adolescents and adults and with its absence of visible adult mentors, that too many of the young—and this would include Holden Caulfield—are "forced to become adults too soon, and never make it" (*Sibling Society* 132). Hope, concludes Bly, lies in "tak[ing] an interest in younger ones by helping them find a mentor" so that "their own feeling of being adult will be augmented" (237). As such, Holden Caulfield, a "typical" adolescent of the 1950s, becomes a prototype of the troubled, aimless young men Bly sees evident in the *fin de siècle*'s sibling society. Perhaps, then, what troubled critics of *Catcher in the Rye* most was not so much what they saw evident in Holden but what they suspected in the coming tide of social disruption which he represented. Holden's "breakdown" at the end of the novel is therefore endemic of the societal breakdown, in adolescent transition currently occurring, based, in part, in the loss of effective male mentors for young men, upon the "death" of the mentor.

For Holden, his hope may be in reconnecting with his older sibling, D. B., who, by the final chapter, lives close enough to drive over to visit Holden, suggesting that Holden has been intentionally relocated (by his parents?) to be closer to his brother. On the one hand, Holden's father has had his way: Holden is working with "this one psychoanalyst guy they have here," presumably getting the therapy to deal with Allie's death, which has affected him and which he has not effectively dealt with. On the other hand, D. B. may be Holden's necessary mentor; unlike everyone else who "keeps asking me if I'm going to apply myself when I go back to school next September," D. B., who "isn't as bad as the rest of them," instead asks Holden "what I thought about all this stuff I just finished telling you about" (*Catcher in the Rye* 213). Holden's response is interesting: "I didn't know what the hell to say" (213), for Holden up until now hasn't had anyone who would just listen to him, ask his opinion, help him find the patterns of his own mind, in short, be an adult mentor who helps augment Holden's feelings of being an adult.

Works Cited

Baumbach, Jonathan. "The Saint as a Young Man: A Reappraisal of *The Catcher in the Rye*." *Modern Language Quarterly* 25:4 (December 1964): 461–472. Rpt. in *Critical Essays on Salinger's* The Catcher in the Rye. Ed. Joel Salzberg. Boston: G. K. Hall, 1990. 55–63.

Bloom, Harold. Introduction. *J. D. Salinger's* The Catcher in the Rye: *Bloom's Notes*. Broomall, PA: Chelsea House, 1996. 5–6.

Bly, Robert. *Iron John*. Reading, MA: Addison-Wesley, 1990.

———. *The Sibling Society*. Reading, MA: Addison-Wesley, 1996.

Brookeman, Christopher. "Pency Preppy: Cultural Codes in *The Catcher in the Rye*." *New Essays on* The Catcher in the Rye. Ed. Jack Salzman. Cambridge: Cambridge University Press, 1991. 57–76.

Bryson, Bill. *Made in America: An Informal History of The English Language in the United States.* New York: William Morrow, 1994.

Hughes, Riley. "New Novels." *Catholic World* (November 1951): 154. Rpt. in *Holden Caulfield.* Ed. Harold Bloom. New York: Chelsea House Publishers, 1990. 8.

Jones, Ernest. "Case History of All of Us." *Nation* 173:9 (1 September 1951): 176. Rpt. in *Critical Essays on Salinger's* The Catcher in the Rye. Ed. Joel Salzberg. Boston: G. K. Hall, 1990. 55–63.

Longstreth, T. Morris. "New Novels in the News." *Christian Science Monitor* (19 July 1951): 11. Rpt. in *Holden Caulfield.* Ed. Harold Bloom. New York: Chelsea House Publishers, 1990. 5–6.

Miller, Edwin Haviland. "In Memoriam: Allie Caulfield." *Mosaic* 15:1 (Winter 1982): 129–140. Rpt. in *Holden Caulfield.* Ed. Harold Bloom. New York: Chelsea House, 1990. 132–143.

Rice, Philip F. *The Adolescent: Development, Relationships, and Culture.* 6th Ed. Boston, Allyn and Bacon, 1990.

Rosen, Gerald. "A Retrospective Look at *The Catcher in the Rye*." *American Quarterly* 5 (Winter 1977): 547–562. Rpt. in *Critical Essays on Salinger's* The Catcher in the Rye. Ed. Joel Salzberg. Boston: G. K Hall, 1990, 158–171.

Rowe, Joyce. "Holden Caulfield and American Protest." *New Essays on* The Catcher in the Rye. Ed. Jack Salzman. Cambridge: Cambridge University Press, 1991, 77–95.

Salinger, J. D. *Franny and Zooey.* Boston: Little, Brown and Co., 1961.

———. *The Catcher in the Rye.* Boston: Little, Brown and Company, 1991.

CARL FREEDMAN

Memories of Holden Caulfield— and of Miss Greenwood

Two years ago, the fiftieth anniversary of J. D. Salinger's *The Catcher in the Rye* took place. The book is almost exactly the same age I am. To be precise, it's about three months younger: I appeared in April 1951, the novel—after a much longer gestation period—in July. Inevitably, a good many essays about it have recently been published, and, though they indicate little consensus about the exact meaning or value of the novel, they do generally agree that it is still, in some sense, an extraordinary text. At the height of Salinger's reputation—the 1950s and 1960s—his was in many ways the dominant voice in contemporary American fiction, despite his slender output, and it was not unusual for him to be discussed in tones that suggested a genius almost on the order of Shakespeare's or Tolstoy's to be at stake. His stature has long since assumed much more modest proportions. Few, I suppose, would maintain now that *The Catcher in the Rye* belongs in the absolute first rank of the modern novel: on a level, that is, with Conrad's *Nostromo* (1904) or Lawrence's *Women in Love* (1920) or Joyce's *Ulysses* (1922) or Faulkner's *Absalom, Absalom!* (1936) or Pynchon's *Gravity's Rainbow* (1973). Yet if it is, in this strict sense, a work of the second rank, it is also a novel that possesses a remarkable hold on its readers, or at least on a good many of them. There are more than a few of us for whom *The Catcher in the Rye* still feels less like a canonical book than like a personal experience, and one of the most powerful

The Southern Review, Volume 39, Number 2 (Spring 2003): pp. 401–417. Copyright © 2003 Louisiana State University.

of our lives. Though I earn a living chiefly by producing materialist criticism of literary texts (on the page and in the classroom), I think of this text mainly as a part—a phase, really—of my personal history, and of its protagonist as someone I know, or once knew: attitudes that do not necessarily exclude a properly critical approach but that by no means inevitably make for one either. Accordingly, though what follows will certainly have its critical moments, it is at least as much a memoir as a critical essay, a memoir of the Holden Caulfield I knew and of an earlier self, both of whom are now long in the past but also still with me.

But this must also be a memoir of Miss Greenwood. No, I do not mean Sylvia Plath's Esther Greenwood, protagonist of *The Bell Jar* (1963) and the most memorable, perhaps, of all the many fictional characters conceived under the direct influence of Holden Caulfield. The real Miss Greenwood was my eighth-grade English teacher and my first teacher who was also, in some important way, a friend. Not that I had gotten along badly with my earlier teachers—quite the contrary. But before Miss Greenwood a teacher was no more to be counted as a friend than was a parent, a doctor, or a rabbi. Teachers were all just adults, authority figures, and one took it for granted that they inhabited a world different from one's own. Miss Greenwood, somehow, was different. Doubtless this was at least partly because she was quite young herself, no more than a year or so out of college. It is a somewhat staggering thought that, during the time I am remembering, she was thus only slightly older than the seniors I teach today, and younger than nearly all of my graduate students. It is even more staggering to think that, if she and I were to meet today, we would be, for most practical purposes, about the same age. In the eighth grade, of course, the gulf was much wider—and yet bridgeable in a way that the age gulf between an adult and me had never quite been before.

I still have before me a fairly clear mental image of Miss Greenwood. She was thin, of about average height, with brown hair cut relatively short and a pleasant, freckled face. Her looks were not those of a bombshell or head-turner, but I expect that a fair number of men would have found her—I expect that a fair number of men *did* find her—attractive, and increasingly attractive as they got to know her better. But you would probably have had to be in love with her to call her beautiful. I was in love with her, though it is a love that I recognized as such only many years later. I am pretty sure that, at the time, I never consciously thought of Miss Greenwood in a romantic or even a sexual way, and in retrospect that seems a curious omission. After all, I was a horny, virginal fourteen-year-old boy, and I was preoccupied with sex in that intense, yearning way typical of my age and gender; but, as far as I can recall, the guest stars in my lustful fantasies tended to be either female classmates my own age or else generically "good-looking" women whose images were based on models and movie stars. Why not Miss Greenwood? She was pretty enough for the role. Perhaps I just respected her too much. Perhaps it was just that, in those more innocent days, the idea of "doing anything" with Miss Greenwood was literally beyond (conscious) comprehension.

In retrospect, however, it seems clear that nothing short of sexual love could have driven me to do what I frequently did during the eighth grade: namely, to *stay* in the school building after the final bell had rung, to use some of those precious hours of freedom between the end of school and dinner at home to talk with a teacher whose class I had been required to attend earlier in the day. Miss Greenwood was often in her classroom for a while after classes had ended, doing various chores—cleaning blackboards, arranging papers, and the like—and I got in the habit of dropping by. I would help her to the extent I could, and we would chat about various things. Some of these talks were brief—no more than ten or fifteen minutes—but others went on for an hour or even more. My house was within walking distance of the school, but sometimes, especially after one of our longer chats, Miss Greenwood would give me a lift home in the used, battered Volkswagen bug that she had recently purchased and about whose mechanical soundness she was, as I remember, a bit nervous. She took some consolation in the relatively low number on the odometer, and was mildly alarmed when I told her that odometer readings could be faked. Our relations were by no means completely informal. It was always clear that we were teacher and pupil, and certainly I never called her anything except "Miss Greenwood" (with the result that today I am not sure of her first name, though I once knew it well—Mary, perhaps?). But we were definitely friends.

Our conversations were mainly about two of our strongest common interests, politics and literature, which, as it happens, are the two main fields about which I write professionally today. We probably talked more about politics than about literature. The school year was 1964–1965, and we shared happiness and relief that, in the presidential election, Lyndon Johnson defeated Barry Goldwater so resoundingly, though Miss Greenwood, I believe, was somewhat discreet about her political preferences (doubtless a prudent habit for any schoolteacher, but especially wise since the school principal was widely thought to be a rather unbalanced right-winger). I think the first political bet that I ever made—and won—in my life was with Miss Greenwood. In January 1965, Hubert Humphrey was inaugurated as vice-president and so had to give up his seat in the Senate, where he had been the Democratic whip. Several senators competed to succeed him, with the frontrunners generally agreed to be John Pastore of Rhode Island and Russell Long of Louisiana. Miss Greenwood liked Pastore's chances—a choice she shared with most journalistic pundits and by no means a stupid one, for Pastore's political profile resembled Humphrey's own, and his northeastern liberalism seemed in tune with the (very brief) moment of triumph that American liberalism was then enjoying. But I already knew a fair bit about how the Senate worked, and I reckoned that the southerners—still the dominant force in that body, despite the huge defeat they had recently suffered when the Civil Rights Act of 1964 was passed—would prove strong enough to win the post for one of their own. As indeed they did.

Long's victory brought him a position for which he never displayed much aptitude and which he lost to Edward Kennedy four years later. But it brought me the copy that I still possess of Salinger's fourth (and, as things now seem to have turned out, last) book, the one that collected the long stories, "Raise High the Roof Beam, Carpenters" and "Seymour—An Introduction." The volume was already out in hardcover, and Miss Greenwood and I agreed that the loser of the bet would buy the winner a copy of the paperback as soon as it appeared. It was a logical choice, for there was nothing we shared more intensely than our common admiration for Salinger. I think that I vaguely knew who Salinger was even before meeting Miss Greenwood—I browsed through the current paperbacks frequently, and those Salinger paperbacks, with their covers nearly blank save for title and author, were hard to miss—but I had never read his work until Miss Greenwood recommended *The Catcher in the Rye* to me. I didn't realize at the time how typical an enthusiasm for Salinger was among intelligent college students of her generation, nor did it occur to me that, in urging me to read *The Catcher in the Rye*, Miss Greenwood was running something of a risk. Salinger's novel was one of three strictly banned throughout our public school system (Aldous Huxley's *Brave New World* [1932] and George Orwell's *Nineteen Eighty-four* [1949] were the others); and, though recommending it to a single student in an after-school chat was not, presumably, a transgression on the order of assigning it to a whole class, I'm sure she could have gotten into some trouble if, for instance, my parents had been the sort to make a fuss. Looking back, I suspect that, out of college and living on her own in a new city, Miss Greenwood was missing companions with whom she could discuss her favorite writer, and so she took a chance on me.

Her recommendation was about as successful as a recommendation can be. The book just knocked me out, as Holden himself would say. Today it seems clear to me that, technically, the main source of the novel's overwhelming power is its almost unparalleled mastery of *voice*. Except for *Huckleberry Finn* (1884)—often enough proposed as the chief precursor text of *The Catcher in the Rye*—there is not a novel in American literature, perhaps not a novel in the world, that more convincingly invents and sustains a young colloquial voice, page after page after page, with virtually not a single false note, and while managing to avoid both sentimentality and condescension on the part of the unseen author. If it is difficult to believe that Holden Caulfield is "just" a literary fabrication, it's because the reader seems to hear an entirely real human being talking to him or her for more than two hundred pages without interruption. But at the age of fourteen, of course, I was less struck by Salinger's technique than by the reality that his technique appeared to convey. Simply put, Holden seemed absolutely *right* to me—in some ways the rightest human being I had ever encountered. His world was basically similar to my own—never mind the differences between an upper-class northeasterner in the late 1940s and a middle-class southerner in the mid-1960s—and, at two or three years older than me, he was just young enough to be a peer and just enough older to seem automatically savvier and more worldly wise. Again and again Holden hit off exactly what a morass of mendacity the world had prepared for children in the process of leaving childhood behind; again and again he articulated, with painful but exuberant and wonderful accuracy, the essential inauthenticity of bourgeois American society that I myself was just beginning to be able to name.

Take Holden's roommate Stradlater, for instance: crude, obtuse, brash, outgoing, handsome, athletic, and, Holden believes, one of the few boys at Pencey Prep who actually succeeds in "giving the time" to the girls that he dates. I knew the type, and I resented the all-but-universal envy and admiration that the type attracted from his fellows. Who but Holden would have had the clear-sightedness and courage to dismiss him simply as "a stupid bastard"? And who, really knowing the type, could deny that Holden was exactly right? Or take Mr. Spencer, the history teacher who pompously and uselessly lectures Holden about his future: "Life *is* a game, boy. Life *is* a game that one plays according to the rules." I heard this sort of thing all the time, and Holden knew exactly what it was worth: "Game, my ass. Some game. If you get on the side where all the hot-shots are, then it's a game, all right—I'll admit that. But if you get on the *other* side, where there aren't any hot-shots, then what's a game about it? Nothing. No game."

Or take "this guy Ossenburger," the wealthy mortician and Pencey alumnus after whom Holden's dorm is named:

> The first football game of the year, he came up to school in this big goddam Cadillac, and we all had to stand up in the grandstand and give him a locomotive—that's a cheer. Then, the next morning, in chapel, he made a speech that lasted about ten hours. He started off with about fifty corny jokes, just to show us what a regular guy he was. Very big deal. Then he started telling us how he was never ashamed, when he was in some kind of trouble or something, to get right down on his knees and pray to God. He told us we should always pray to God—talk to Him and all—wherever we were. He told us we ought to think of Jesus as our buddy and all. He said *he* talked to Jesus all the time. Even when he was driving his car. That

killed me. I can just see the big phony bastard shifting into first gear and asking Jesus to send him a few more stiffs.

Though at the age of fourteen I had never even set eyes on a school precisely similar to Pencey, this passage seemed to sum up practically every school assembly I had ever been forced to attend; and future assemblies were made a little more bearable for knowing that at least one other person saw them for exactly what they were.

Sometimes it seemed to me that there was almost no variety of phony that Holden had not managed to spot and expose, from the insufferably pretentious pseudo-intellectual Carl Luce, an old schoolmate with whom he has an extended conversation in a bar, to the young naval officer ("His name was Commander Blop or something") he meets briefly in Ernie's nightclub: "He was one of those guys that think they're being a pansy if they don't break around forty of your fingers when they shake hands with you. God, I hate that stuff." Though most of Holden's insights are delivered in this ad hoc manner, there are a few more synoptic passages. Perhaps the best is the summary of Pencey he offers to Sally Hayes, herself an excruciating phony—the sort who appears much more intelligent than she is because she knows "quite a lot about the theater and plays and literature and all that stuff" and whom Holden finds harder to shake than most phonies because she is physically very attractive and usually willing to make out with him.

> "You ought to go to a boys' school sometime. Try it sometime," I said. "It's full of phonies, and all you do is study so that you can learn enough to be smart enough to be able to buy a goddam Cadillac some day, and you have to keep making believe you give a damn if the football team loses, and all you do is talk about girls and liquor and sex all day, and everybody sticks together in these dirty little goddam cliques. The guys that are on the basketball team stick together, the Catholics stick together, the goddam intellectuals stick together, the guys that play bridge stick together. Even the guys that belong to the goddam Book-of-the-*Month* Club stick together. If you try to have a little intelligent—"

Sally is technically correct, as Holden himself agrees, when she interrupts him to object, "Lots of boys get more out of school than *that*." But no matter—Holden has Pencey, and the world, dead to rights.

Holden's wisdom seemed all the more impressive to me because there is no trace of superiority about it. He is never the detached, self-sufficient bystander, coolly and ironically observing life from its foyer; instead, he is passionate and disappointed, always newly indignant at every fresh instance of phoniness that life offers. It is also true that he is therefore extremely un-happy—an aspect of the book that I rather glossed over in my first few read-ings. I was able to see that Holden almost never seems to be having a good time, but I was not particularly unhappy myself—allowing for the fact that hardly any fourteen-year-old can be unambiguously called happy—and I hesi-tated to attribute to such a powerfully kindred spirit the extreme degree of psychic misery that now seems to me one of the principal features of Holden's character. Or to put it another way: The almost unerring acuteness of Holden's insights, and the superb colloquial vigor with which he could express them, seemed to make for a kind of intellectual high spirits that I could not, at the age of fourteen, easily reconcile with underlying pain. To see phonies so clearly could not exactly be a recipe for happiness in a world where phonies were so numerous, but surely, I felt, truth itself had its own consolations.

Not everyone has felt such a deep affinity with Holden as I did. Some readers—most prominently Mary McCarthy—believe that Holden is too harsh in his judgments of others, that he is too much the pitiless phony-spot-ter. "I was surrounded by jerks," says Holden of his fellow patrons at Ernie's, and for some this sentence sums up almost the entirety of Holden's world view. Miss Greenwood to some extent held this opinion. Indeed, one of the things that slightly divided us in our shared passion for Salinger was that for me, then as now, Salinger was first and foremost the author of *The Catcher in the Rye,* whereas Miss Greenwood preferred his stories about the Glass family. Looking back, I suspect that this difference of opinion was largely a gendered one. Holden's outlook is intensely masculine (though never ma-cho), and I suppose that from the other side of the gender divide it might well often seem suffocatingly masculine. But this point never occurred to me at the time, and I doubt it did to Miss Greenwood either. The problem with Holden, she once said to me, is just that you get the idea he probably wouldn't like you very much—whereas Buddy Glass, Holden's successor as Salinger's principal narrator and alter ego, was Miss Greenwood's idea of a very nice guy indeed.

I now think that Holden's supposed pitilessness in judging others has been greatly exaggerated. It has become conventional to say that he likes no-body except his three siblings; and, since one of them, his younger brother Allie, is dead, and since another, his older brother D. B., seems, as an evi-dently successful Hollywood screenwriter, to be in danger of becoming a bit of a phony himself, only his kid sister Phoebe ("himself in miniature or in glory," as McCarthy insisted) would be left as an unambiguously Good Per-son, a certified nonphony, in the land of the living. But in fact Holden likes quite a lot of people: people of both sexes and of various ages, and chance acquaintances as well as old friends. He immensely likes Jane Gallagher, sort of his girlfriend but not exactly, who always kept her kings in the back row whenever they played checkers. He equally likes his old English teacher Mr. Antolini, even though he is understandably disconcerted when Mr. Antolini makes what appears to be a homosexual pass at him. He likes the nuns he meets in a sandwich bar, and he likes Mrs. Morrow, the mother of a classmate, whom he meets on a train. He even likes Selma Thurmer, the daughter of the headmaster at Pencey, despite her big nose and her falsies and her fingernails bitten bloody. He likes children in general, and so tries to rub out dirty words scrawled where children might see them; and, of course, he fantasizes about being the catcher in the rye, spending every day keeping children safely in the field of rye and away from the cliff's edge. He likes the ducks in the Central Park lagoon, and worries about what happens to them when the pond freezes solid in winter. Furthermore, Holden (unlike the Hemingway heroes with whom McCarthy so unjustly compares him) usually manages a good deal of concrete human sympathy even for those whom he cannot bring himself to like: his obnoxious, pimple-squeezing schoolmate Ackley, for instance, and Sunny, the prostitute who cheats him out of five dollars. His encounter with the latter makes for one of the book's most memorable scenes. At the end of a very long, very lonely, and frequently horny evening, Holden accepts a pimp's offer to send a whore to his hotel room. But when Sunny (who is "[n]o old bag," just as the pimp Maurice promises) actually arrives, Holden is so over-come with sadness at the thought of her life that his enthusiasm for losing his virginity evaporates into thin air and he offers to pay Sunny full price for just a few minutes of conversation.

In the eighth grade it did not occur to me to point out this deeply sensi-tive and compassionate side of Holden's character in reply to Miss Green-wood's criticism of him as too astringently judgmental. Nonetheless, her (perhaps not wholly intentional but clear enough) implication—that Holden might not like *me*—bothered me very little. It was not so much that I dis-agreed with her suggestion as that it somehow seemed beside the point. May-be Holden wouldn't necessarily like me, but so what? Holden *was* me. And indeed, Holden by no means expresses invariable liking for himself through-out the long monologue that constitutes the novel. Though most readers have, I think, failed to notice the fact, he frequently confesses to acts of phoniness on his own part. Precept, as Samuel Johnson said, may be very sincere even when practice is very imperfect, and the fact that Holden—as sturdy a moral-ist, in his own way, as Dr. Johnson—is capable of self-criticism, that he can recognize his own involvement in the whole system of phoniness from which he recoils so bitterly, only made (and makes) him all the more admirable and all the more right in my eyes.

Whatever Holden might have thought of me, though, Miss Greenwood had an explanation for why I liked Holden and *The Catcher in the Rye* so much more than her own favorite, Buddy Glass, and the stories centered on his family. She once commented that people closer to her own age—people in their late teens, I believe she meant—often liked *The Catcher in the Rye* because people that age often felt rebellious toward society (this conversation took place, remember, just as the 1960s was coming into focus as a political and cultural era). She suggested that I myself was feeling that kind of rebelliousness, at an earlier age than was typical. At the time, I recall, I felt slightly uncertain as to exactly what Miss Greenwood's attitude toward my supposed rebelliousness was, though I took her remark as basically flattering, if only for the precocity it implied. Today, especially in view of the fact that I did not, at that point, overtly fit the usual profile of the school rebel—I had never, by the eighth grade, detonated firecrackers in the school bathroom, or brought a subversive petition to class, or smoked marijuana, or even grown my hair long—hers must surely be counted as a pretty shrewd, prescient judgment of a fourteen-year-old boy who grew up to become a Marxist literary critic.

But it must also he pointed out that Holden himself is not really a rebel. True enough, his acute penetration into the life of his society could in principle supply the basis for rebellion, but Holden is never able to take the step from diagnosis to action, or even to serious planning. The only action he ever even contemplates is a strategy not of rebellion but of withdrawal: He imagines leaving civilization (like Huck Finn at the end of Mark Twain's novel, though in Holden's America the frontier has been long closed) and living somewhere out west in a cabin on the edge of the woods, pretending to be a deaf mute in order to avoid conversations with phonies. Even this is pure fantasizing, as Holden at heart always knows. Not only is Holden not a rebel, but (like Hamlet, who is in many ways almost as much Holden's predecessor as Huck is) he even has great difficulty acting meaningfully in *any* way. Etymologically, the opposite of an actor is a patient—someone who is acted upon—and it is no accident that a patient is precisely what Holden is during the time present of the novel. It is also significant that, though everyone knows that Holden tells his story from some sort of medical institution ("this crumby place," as he calls it), there has been considerable disagreement among readers as to exactly what sort of hospital it is and why Holden is there. Is it because he is threatened by tuberculosis and needs a long rest in a sanatorium? Or because he has suffered some sort of mental collapse and requires psychiatric help? The source of the confusion is that Salinger definitely allows both explanations. Holden is a mess, physically *and* psychologically.

Holden, then, might be seen as basically pathetic, someone who, despite all his advantages (intelligence, eloquence, evident good looks, family money), is essentially incapable of coping with life—hence his removal not to an isolated Thoreauvian cabin where he can practice Emersonian self-reliance, but to an expensive private hospital where a professionally trained staff is on call twenty-four hours a day to tend to his physical and emotional weaknesses. This was not, needless to say, an interpretation that occurred to me during my first reading of the novel, or my second, or even my third. But by about the fourth reading—undertaken when I was eighteen or nineteen, and so about as much older than Holden as I had been younger when in Miss Greenwood's class—I did begin to see Holden less as a hero or a kindred spirit than as a pathetic weakling. I remember some feeling of loss when I began to view him in this way, but on the whole I welcomed my changed perception: It seemed to me a more adult perception, and I considered the fact that I could now look down on Holden to be a sign of my own increasing maturity. One of the advantages of middle age, however, is that it often allows us to see how much more wisdom there usually is in even the most callow idealism of adolescence than in the superior "knowingness" of young adulthood. Yes, Holden is defeated by life, at least temporarily, and we don't know what path he will take "after" the end of the novel. He might begin to act on the insight that Mr. Antolini (quoting the psychoanalyst Wilhelm Stekel) tries to convey to him—"The mark of the immature man is that he wants to die nobly for a cause, while the mark of the mature man is that he wants to live humbly for one"—though it is also conceivable that he will gradually abandon his revulsion from phoniness and learn to "adjust" better to the latter. The incontestable point is that Holden's defeat is an honorable one, and honorable defeats are in the scheme of things more valuable than most victories. I think that I was right, at the age of fourteen, to gloss over the pain and weakness in Holden's character, for at that stage of life I probably couldn't have taken the full pressure of those things and still properly appreciated just how right Holden is.

Proust suggests somewhere that the "first edition" of a book ought to mean the edition in which one first happened to read it, and it may seem that I am now advocating a somewhat similar privileging of the first reading, at least insofar as my own first reading of *The Catcher in the Rye* is concerned. Though I do indeed maintain the essential validity of my original pro-Holden and indeed "Holdencentric" interpretation (it is noteworthy that Holden dominates his text as relatively few great characters other than Hamlet and Huck Finn have done), I am not actually proposing an emulation of Peter Pan. Growing up can have its virtues. When I first read the book, I gave little thought to the historical contexts of Holden's character, because for me Holden's "context" was simply life itself, life as I knew it. But as a professional critic and teacher, I now insist that a more specific and rigorous analysis of context can enhance rather than diminish one's appreciation of Holden.

One such context, for example, is the Second World War. As part of the revival of interest in America's last "good war" that has in recent years played such a prominent role in American popular culture, the notion that *The Catcher in the Rye* is in some sense about that war—that it is, as Louis Menand suggested in a fiftieth-anniversary essay published in the *New Yorker*, more a book of the 1940s than the 1950s—has gained a certain currency. It has some biographical plausibility. Like several of his characters—D. B. Caulfield, Seymour Glass, the unnamed American soldier who narrates "For Esmé—with Love and Squalor"—Salinger did serve in the war. He landed on Utah Beach during the fifth hour of the Normandy invasion and in the following months took part in some of the fiercest combat of the twentieth century; his daughter Margaret (author of a fascinating and remarkably even-tempered memoir called *Dream Catcher* [2000]) has said that he was among the first American soldiers to enter a liberated Nazi concentration camp. As a result of his combat experience he suffered something like a nervous breakdown—but only after the German army had surrendered—and, again according to his daughter, has remained forever after possessed by memories of the war and by a sense of his own identity as a soldier. It is often said that the truest and most sincere pacifists are combat veterans, and there may well be a direct connection between Salinger's experience of war at its most ferocious and Holden's description of himself as "a pacifist, if you want to know the truth."

But there are no combat scenes in *The Catcher in the Rye*. A brief mention of D. B.'s military service is the most explicit indication the novel gives that World War II even took place. But perhaps it is the professional writer D. B. who himself supplies the best clue to reading the book as a war novel. Holden well remembers the occasion on which Allie suggests to D. B. that at least one advantage of D. B.'s time in the army must be that it gave him a good deal of material about which to write; D. B. replies by asking Allie to compare Rupert Brooke with Emily Dickinson and then to say who ranks as the greater war poet. The correct answer, as Allie sees at once, is of course Emily Dickinson. If Dickinson is indeed the great poet of the American Civil War—and if, for that matter, Virginia Woolf's *Mrs. Dalloway* (1925), with its unforgettable portrait of Septimus Smith, is one of the great World War I novels—then in much the same way *The Catcher in the Rye* can be read as a record of the war against Hitler. One way to express the gap between Holden's shrewd perceptions and his pathetic inability to act effectively is to say that he (again like Hamlet) just takes everything a little too hard. Wealthy and privileged as his background may be, Holden's world is every bit as bad as he says it is; but nothing plainly in it, not even Allie's death from leukemia, *quite* accounts for the extreme degree of pain and loneliness and psychic dislocation that often seems to lie just beyond Holden's awesome powers of self-expression. Life appears to have a kind of wrongness for Holden that neither he nor Salinger can ever completely verbalize, and it may be that this wrongness is finally to be identified with the inexpressible barbarism of the Second World War.

Doubtless what is at issue here is not only the war in general but the Holocaust in particular, and at this point a war-centered reading of the novel may shade into an ethnic one. Again biography seems pertinent. Salinger's own ethnic make-up—of Jewish background on his father's side and Irish Catholic background on his mother's, just like the seven Glass children—was pretty unusual in his generation, and he is said to have felt severely dislocated by his mixed heritage, especially as regards his being, yet not being, Jewish. One can easily understand that, under these circumstances—and especially given the fact that during the 1920s, the 1930s, and well into the 1940s, anti-Semitism existed in the United States at levels that are practically un-imaginable today—the annihilation of European Jewry was bound to be a deeply complex and traumatic event for him, especially after seeing some of the machinery of extermination with his own eyes: "You never really get the smell of burning flesh out of your nose entirely, no matter how long you live," he told Margaret. A further complexity was that he evidently had a tense, dis-tant relationship with his father (who vainly wished that young Jerry would join the family business, a prosperous firm that imported kosher meats and cheeses), but a warm, loving one with his mother, to whom *The Catcher in the Rye* is dedicated: a situation perhaps reflected in Salinger's giving Holden an Irish surname and a home address not on the (stereotypically Jewish) Upper West Side of Manhattan, where he himself was raised, but on the (stereotypi-cally Gentile) East Side—while also, however, supplying a note of Jewishness in the name of the Caulfields' next-door neighbors, the Dicksteins.

The context of war and ethnicity—the two categories intimately and complexly linked by the mediating term of the Holocaust—thus enters the novel as a determinate absence. We do not get overt scenes of combat or extermination, but instead something like the negative imprint of the un-speakable physical violence visited upon the world during the decade or so prior to 1951, the period during which Salinger worked, on and off, toward the completion of his novel. This context may well illuminate Holden's sad-ness and mental instability, though it hardly says much about his intelligence and sensitivity. Another context, however, and one that illuminates both these sides of his character, is presented far more explicitly: the context of class rela-tions under capitalism, which constitute a different kind of violence.

Though Holden is constantly talking about the injuries of class, this dimension of the book has been astonishingly—or maybe not so astonish-ingly—ignored by journalistic and academic Salinger critics, as Richard and Carol Ohmann show in "A Case Study in Canon Formation: Reviewers, Critics, and *The Catcher in the Rye*" (perhaps the single most perceptive critical treatment of the novel to date, at least insofar as my own—fairly extensive though far from exhaustive-reading of the secondary literature goes). Class, of course, has been the great taboo subject in American discourse for more than half a century, a taboo so strong that it extends, to some degree, even into the overtly "progressive" circles of institutionalized cultural studies, where elaborate attention to race and gender is taken for granted. Still, it seems extraordinary that Salinger criticism has been able so thoroughly to erase a subject with which Salinger himself deals so overtly and so often.

Consider, for instance, Mr. Haas, the headmaster at Holden's old prep school Elkton Hills, who bears the remarkable distinction of being, in Holden's opinion, "the phoniest bastard I ever met in my life." Mr. Haas's general practice is to ingratiate himself as much as possible with the parents of his pupils, and he normally turns on as much charm as he can. But he does make exceptions:

> I mean if a boy's mother was sort of fat or corny-looking or something, and if somebody's father was one of those guys that wear those suits with very big shoulders and corny black-and-white shoes, then old Haas would just shake hands with them and give them a phony smile and then he'd go talk, for maybe a half an *hour*, with somebody else's parents. I can't stand that stuff. It drives me crazy. It makes me so depressed I go crazy.

Holden understands that, in the American upper bourgeoisie at the middle of the twentieth century, a fashionable suit and pair of shoes are *de rigueur* for a man, as a trim, elegant body is for a woman. He understands, too, that Haas cares nothing for his pupils or their parents as individuals: He is interested only in toadying up to those who unambiguously appear to be members in good standing of the class with which he identifies and toward which, probably, he aspires. Or consider—again—the successful businessman Ossenburger, who has amassed a fortune through a chain of cut-rate mortuaries ("these undertaking parlors all over the country that you could get members of your family buried for about five bucks apiece"). Holden has not, perhaps, read his Max Weber as carefully as he might have, and so fails to remark that Ossenburger's speech suggests the links between capitalist acquisitiveness and Protestant spirituality as clearly as any Weberian sociologist could wish. But he does plainly see that Ossenburger is considered important enough at Pencey to rate a cheer at the football game and a speech in the chapel simply and solely because of his ability to throw large sums of money around: "[H]e gave Pencey a pile of dough, and they named our wing after him." Holden also possesses a shrewd sense of the routine fraudulence that so typically underlies capitalist success in modern America: "You should see old Ossenburger. He probably just shoves them [i.e., the remains of his customers] in a sack and dumps them in the river."

Haas and Ossenburger, then, are especially odious because of the relative purity, so to speak, with which they incarnate the market-based relations of the capitalist class structure. Conversely, the nuns that Holden meets at the sandwich bar are admirable not so much for their religious vocation (Holden admits to being "sort of an atheist"), but because they have chosen to live outside the class system to the maximum extent feasible. It is not merely that they spend their lives teaching school and collecting money for charity. Holden, after all, has known plenty of phony teachers, and charity can be practiced by those of his own high-bourgeois background—his mother, for instance, and his aunt (who is "pretty charitable—she does a lot of Red Cross work and all"), and Sally Hayes's mother—but when such women perform good works it is with no renunciation, or even qualification, of their privileged place in the socioeconomic hierarchy. Holden's aunt may help out the Red Cross, but "when she does anything charitable she's always very well-dressed and has lipstick on and all that crap. I couldn't picture her doing anything for charity if she had to wear black clothes and no lipstick while she was doing it"—that is, if she had to abandon, even temporarily, the uniform of her class position. As for Sally's mother, she (like her daughter) craves attention as a spoiled child does, and "[t]he only way *she* could go around with a basket collecting dough would be if everybody kissed her ass for her when they made a contribution." Otherwise, "[s]he'd get bored. She would hand in her basket and then go someplace swanky for lunch." But the nuns are genuinely different: "That's what I liked about those nuns. You could tell, for one thing, that they never went anywhere swanky for lunch." Holden immediately adds that he is saddened by the nuns' inability to enjoy the swankiness that is routine for his own people—he does not sentimentalize the poverty they have chosen—but at the same time their integrity remains an inspiration in a world so heavily populated by those obsessed with scrambling up, or staying on top of, the class ladder.

Even before striking up a conversation with the nuns (who turn out to be moving from a convent in Chicago to one in New York), Holden notices that they have with them a pair of cheap suitcases, "the ones that aren't genuine leather or anything," and this observation provokes what is perhaps the most remarkable meditation on class in the novel. Holden thinks back to his roommate at Elkton Hills, Dick Slagle, who, like the nuns, had cheap suitcases, whereas Holden's own "came from Mark Cross, and they were genuine cowhide and all that crap, and I guess they cost quite a pretty penny." Holden finds Dick to be smart and funny, and the two are capable of having a good time together. But their relationship is soon poisoned by class. Dick is resentful and envious of the superior class position that the Mark Cross suitcases symbolize: He ridicules Holden's suitcases as "bourgeois" (an adjective he then extends to Holden's fountain pen and other possessions) while also pretending to other people that the Mark Cross suitcases really belong to him. Holden is baffled as to what to do. He tries stuffing his suitcases out of sight under his bed, and is perfectly willing to throw them away or even to trade suitcases with Dick, if doing so will save the friendship. But nothing avails, and within two months both boys ask to be moved. Holden sadly sums up the lesson:

> The thing is, it's really hard to be roommates with people if your suitcases are much better than theirs—if yours are really *good* ones and theirs aren't. You think if they're intelligent and all, the other person, and have a good sense of humor, that they don't give a damn whose suitcases are better, but they do. They really do. It's one of the reasons why I roomed with a stupid bastard like Stradlater. At least his suitcases were as good as mine.

On personal grounds, Holden likes and admires Dick, and despises Stradlater, but such purely personal factors are finally less powerful than the social realities of class.

So the reality Holden confronts—the reality whose phoniness he so acutely diagnoses—is not "the human condition" or "the pains of adolescence" or any of the other ahistorical clichés that have dominated Salinger criticism; it is, rather, the specific historical conjuncture of a particular time and place. What I find especially remarkable—and this is a point that even the Ohmanns, to whose excellent analysis I am much indebted, do not, I think, sufficiently emphasize—is the extent to which Holden, while perched near the top of capitalist America's class hierarchy, is nonetheless capable of understanding how much misery class relations cause. *The Catcher in the Rye* is about as far from being a proletarian novel as a novel can be, and it would sound odd to describe Salinger as a political writer. But the novel demonstrates that the standpoint of the proletariat is not the only one from which the injustices of capitalism can be glimpsed, and Holden's situation irresistibly suggests an impeccably Marxist point: namely, that any comprehensive system of oppression corrupts the quality of life for *everyone,* even for those who materially gain the most from it. In the eighth grade, of course, I was hardly capable of constructing a class analysis of a work of literature—though I strongly suspect (especially in view of Miss Greenwood's evident prescience as regards my political tendencies) that the sheer *rootedness* of Holden's outlook, the historical concreteness of his insights, did subliminally contribute to my spontaneous sense that Holden saw things as they really were. In any case, today this concreteness helps to confirm my sense that I was always justified in seeing Holden as simply right, and, though in chronological age he is only a few years older than my own daughter is now, there are important ways in which he remains for me a kindred spirit and even a hero. Miss Greenwood was clearly a far-seeing teacher—but could she have guessed anything like the actual impact on me of being introduced to J. D. Salinger?

And what, you may ask, became of Miss Greenwood herself? I have almost no idea. Not long after she taught me, she got married—becoming, after the all-but-universal fashion of the time, Mrs. Walker—and soon after that she left the school, probably because she and her new husband moved out of town. She is most likely a grandmother today—yet another staggering thought. I am tempted to try to get in touch with her, though it is not clear to me that this is feasible. How much, after all, do I have to go on? One possible—and very common—first name, two common Anglo-Saxon surnames, and the certain knowledge that, for a brief time in the mid-1960s, she taught English at Leroy Martin Junior High School in Raleigh, North Carolina. The evidence is scant, and the trail very cold. Still, I suppose a professional detective could do the job, and, given the resources of the telephone and the Internet, even an amateur might have a reasonable shot. But, beyond the question of whether the thing could be done, there is also the question of whether it would be a good idea. Such reunions sometimes produce much pleasure and even joy—such, indeed, has been my own personal experience—but one hears that sometimes they yield little but disappointment and embarrassment. It is possible that, in the aging grandmother I now imagine Miss Greenwood to be, I would plainly see traces of the skinny kid just out of college who once so enchanted my much younger self. But it is also possible that her whole manner and personality would seem utterly different and unfamiliar to me, whether because of actual changes in her, or because of flaws in my adolescent perceptions of more than three and a half decades ago, or because of the tricks that memory can play. Perhaps she would not even remember me except after detailed prompting, or—most humiliating possibility of all—not even *with* such prompting. So I remain undecided about trying to see Miss Greenwood again. One of the most startling and disconcerting things about living in a world with other human beings is the thousand and one ways they have of turning out to be different from what one had thought or assumed or expected or remembered them to be. The Miss Greenwood of this memoir may or may not (still) exist. But—and this is, of course, one of the most magical things about art—I am quite certain that for me Holden Caulfield will always, *always,* be there.

YASUHIRO TAKEUCHI

The Zen Archery of Holden Caulfield

Many have considered the deep influence of Zen Buddhism on J. D. Salinger,[1] but the perspective afforded on Salinger by Eugen Herrigel—the German philosopher who wrote on Zen and his experience of Japanese archery—has somehow escaped the attention of critics. Yet Herrigel's account of what he calls the "Great Doctrine" of Japanese archery offers substantial insight into *The Catcher in the Rye*, for the novel is intimately concerned with both Zen and hunting, two themes that converge in the Japanese art of the bow. The mystical "shooting" technique of the master Japanese archer illuminates the Zen-informed way in which Holden Caulfield is at once the catcher in the rye and the children he protects, the "shooter" of phonies and a phony himself, and finally a figure in whom binary oppositions merge in a state of transcendent aimlessness.

Salinger's short story "Seymour: An Introduction" evinces the author's direct engagement with Japanese archery. In this story, Seymour Glass's younger brother Buddy is "playing curb marbles" on the street. Seymour offers Buddy advice that is seemingly contrary to the goal of marble throwing, suggesting that he not target his opponent's marble: "Could you try not aiming so much?"[2] But Seymour's counter-intuitive advice is to be understood in light of the technique of a Japanese master archer:

English Language Notes, Volume XLII, Number 1 (September 2004): pp. 55–63. Copyright © 2004 Regents of the University of Colorado.

183

When he [Seymour] was coaching me [Buddy], from the curbstone
across the street, to quit aiming my marble at Ira Yankauer's . . .
I believe he was instinctively getting at something very close in
spirit to the sort of instructions a master archer in Japan will
give when he forbids a willful new student to aim his arrows at
the target; that is, when the archery master permits, as it were,
Aiming but not aiming. (241–242)

Salinger's understanding of Buddy's "master archer in Japan" likely reflects specifically the teachings of Kenzo Awa, the master archer who served as mentor
to Herrigel. Salinger would have been familiar with Awa through his ties to
renowned Zen master Daisetz Suzuki, to whom Herrigel was also linked.

To review the circumstances of these connections, Herrigel stayed in Japan from 1924 to 1929, teaching philosophy at Tohoku Imperial University
(now Tohoku University). After returning to Germany, he published a lecture
on Zen, "Die ritterliche Kunst des Bogenschiessens" (The Gallant Art of Archery); in 1936, the Japanese translation of which was published in the same
year.[3] Herrigel later published an expanded version of this work as *Zen in der
Kunst des Bogenschiessens* (Zen in the Art of Archery), in 1948 (three years prior
to the publication of *Catcher*). The preface to the English translation of Herrigel's book, published in 1953, was written by Zen master Daisetz Suzuki,
with whom Salinger had "become friends," according to Salinger's daughter
Margaret. In Margaret's view, Salinger was well informed on the subject of Zen
through Suzuki by the time he wrote *Catcher*.[4] Given his special interest in Zen
together with his command of German,[5] it is likely, once again, that Salinger
was familiar specifically with archery master Awa's teachings to Herrigel.

This speculation on Salinger's knowledge of Awa is particularly sugges-
tive considering the significance of hunting in Salinger's *Catcher:* the defining motif of the novel is a catcher (in a hunting hat) whose job is to catch
and save children. For many, to be sure, hunting is one thing and saving is
quite another; Trowbridge, for instance, maintains that Holden's calling his
hunting hat "a people shooting hat" reflects a hostile attitude towards others (though to be fair, Trowbridge demonstrates a shrewd understanding
of Holden's "double vision. . . . his love-hate for humanity").[6] Yet for Jesus
Christ, a frequent presence throughout *Catcher*—indeed, the novel is set during the Christmas season—these two acts, shooting/hunting/catching and
saving are synonymous. At the lake of Gennesaret, to cite a familiar Bible
story, Jesus tells the fisherman Simon to "let down your [Simon's] nets for a
draught." Though Simon has caught nothing all night, he quickly catches "a
great multitude of fishes" through Jesus's grace. Simon is frightened, but Jesus
says, "Fear not; from henceforth thou shalt catch men" (Luke 5:4–10). Thus,
Jesus plays the role of Simon's fishing master, and in this role employs the

metaphor of fishing (hunting)—and specifically the word "catch" in English-language Bible translations—to represent saving.

Salinger makes use of the hunting/catching trope not only through the catcher in the rye motif, but throughout the novel. For instance, Salinger chose Phoebe as the name for Holden's younger sister; in Greek mythology, Phoebe is a name for Artemis, goddess of the hunt and protector of children. Although Phoebe has also been the goddess of the moon and a Titan, the association of the name of Holden's sister with Artemis resonates particularly with the catcher of the novel's title, for it is Phoebe Caulfield who acts as Holden's master in the art of hunting/catching leading up to the novel's climactic carousel scene, as I have discussed elsewhere.[7] In view of this understanding of the hunting/catching trope, one senses little hostility in Holden's description of his hunting hat: "This is a people shooting hat. . . . I shoot people in this hat"[8]. Rather, one relates Holden's shooting to his dream of being a catcher in the rye.

Holden's way of "shooting" people is further illuminated by the master archer's mystical way of shooting at a target, as understood by Herrigel:

> For them [Japanese master archers] the contest consists in the archer aiming at himself—and yet not at himself, in hitting himself—and yet not himself, and thus becoming simultaneously the aimer and the aim, the hitter and the hit. . . . Then comes the supreme and ultimate miracle: art becomes "artless," shooting becomes not-shooting.[9]

This ambivalent way of shooting, shooting-but-not-shooting, accords with Seymour's advice to Buddy that he "try not aiming so much," as does a similar teaching that Herrigel relates, that "the archer should hit without taking aim, [and] that he should completely lose sight of the goal and his intention to hit it."[10] Holden's dream of catching/saving people, viewed from the perspective of the paradoxical way of Zen archery, is consonant with his strange unwillingness to touch or otherwise contact the people he wishes to catch/save. One senses the resonance of Holden's "no-shooting" way of catching/saving in his reluctance to throw a snowball at a snow-covered car and hydrant; the very act of not throwing the snowball preserves, or saves, their pristine, "nice and white" (48) condition. One also senses this resonance in his avoidance of "saying hello to" or calling up Jane (40, 42, 77, 82, 137, 151, 175, 195, 262), the embodiment of innocence (i.e. she is "nice and white") for Holden. Moreover, one senses it in his childhood memory of a rule against touching museum exhibits ("one of the guards would say to you, 'Don't touch anything, children'" [157]), which works to reinforce Holden's own desire: "certain things they should stay the way they are" (158).[11] The not-aiming of Zen archery similarly informs the admonition that Phoebe, as goddess of the hunt, directs at Holden when—desperate to connect with her as the novel approaches its climax—he tries to catch her, literally, by the arm: "keep your hands to yourself" (272), Phoebe responds. Holden thus learns that to succeed, catching must ultimately become not-catching, just as "shooting becomes not-shooting" for Master Awa.

This understanding enables a new reading of the well-known carousel scene at the close of the novel, during which Holden lets Phoebe face the risk of falling from the carousel (273–274). Leaving Phoebe to face this risk does not necessarily mean that Holden has given up his catcher dream and accepted the need to grow into adulthood, as many critics have argued.[12] It simply means he has mastered the art of hunting/catching. Thus when the goddess Phoebe returns from the carousel, she puts the red *hunting* hat on Holden's head (274) as an act of coronation.

Beyond the implications of the principle of not-aiming, Japanese archery illuminates a mysterious yet recurring phenomenon in *Catcher:* a sense of oneness between the catcher and the caught. In his 1936 lecture on archery, Herrigel describes Awa's experience of becoming one with the target. As Herrigel relates it, Awa observed that when he no longer took aim at the target, he felt the target itself drawing closer and closer, until he became one with it.[13] In other words, in shooting at the target, Awa shot himself. In *Zen in the Art of Archery,* Herrigel describes this state as "becoming simultaneously the aimer and the aim, the hitter and the hit."[14] In *Catcher,* Holden tries to shoot/catch characters who can be described as fallen in either a physical or moral sense, and with whom Holden himself is identified through a variety of literary devices.[15] The fallen constitute three groups: the dead (Holden's brother Allie and the suicide James Castle); children at risk of losing their innocence (Phoebe and Jane); and a number of "phonies," including Holden's own brother D. B., who as a screenwriter in Hollywood is a literary "prostitute" (4).

The third of these groups—the phonies—offers an intriguing example of how Holden is identified with his prey, that is, of how the catcher is identified with the caught. Some critics have already pointed out that Holden is himself a phony—that although Holden criticizes/attacks/shoots phonies he is himself guilty of the very behavior that he criticizes; for instance, French observes that "Holden obviously fails to see that his criticisms apply to himself."[16] But in a number of instances, Holden evinces a clear awareness of his own phoniness, rendering problematic the views of those who ascribe Holden's apparent hypocrisy to a lack of self-awareness resulting from "immaturity"[17] or "mental instability."[18] Rather, Holden's contradictory phoniness/anti-phoniness should be understood as a conscious reflection on Salinger's part of the oneness of the shooter and the shot, a central notion in Awa's teachings. For instance, soon after criticizing his roommate Stradlater for "snowing his date in this quiet, *sincere* voice" (64), Holden says that he "gave him [Ackley] a big, phony handshake" (65) and that he spoke "in this very sincere voice" (66). Stradlater and Holden, both speaking in a "sincere voice," practice the same phoniness. Other examples of Holden's phoniness also resist interpretation in terms of "immaturity" or "mental instability." At one point, Holden defines a "dumb" story as follows: "One of those stories with a lot of phony, lean-jawed guys named David in it, and a lot of phony girls named Linda or Marcia that are always lighting all the goddam Davids' pipes for them" (70). Soon after this, Holden asks a lady on a train if she would "care for a cigarette," and gives her "a light" (72). Beyond reflecting hypocrisy or a lack of self-insight, Holden's giving someone a light in proximity to this story equates the novel itself—Salinger's story—to the "dumb" (phony) sort of story that Holden describes. This structural gesture seems more strictly to concern Salinger's intention of identifying Holden (catcher/shooter/saver) and the phonies (caught/shot/fallen), than simply to model Holden's psychology.

An exchange of roles between Stradlater and Holden early in the novel offers the most striking example of the identity Salinger asserts between Holden and the phonies. Stradlater, in the course of getting ready for a date, asks two favors of Holden: that Holden lend him his hound's tooth jacket, and that Holden write an English composition in Stradlater's name. It soon emerges that Stradlater's date is Holden's former girlfriend, Jane Gallagher, and this means that Stradlater, in Holden's jacket ("He [Stradlater] put them [a pack of cigarettes] in his coat pocket —*my* coat pocket" [44; emphasis original]) and with Holden's Vitalis on his hair ("Old Stradlater was putting Vitalis on his hair. *My* Vitalis" [41; emphasis original]), is doing something that Holden probably should do. Soon after, Holden writes Stradlater's composition for him, using, interestingly enough, Stradlater's typewriter (51). Stradlater does Holden's job using Holden's possessions, and Holden does Stradlater's job using Stradlater's possession. Considering that Holden presumably imitates Stradlater's voice to write Stradlater's composition, and that Stradlater wears Holden's jacket, essentially disguising himself as Holden, the two characters effectively merge.[19] Stradlater, perhaps the most prominent embodiment of phoniness in the novel, and Holden, denouncer of phoniness, thus become one.

Beyond catching-but-not-catching and the identity of the catcher and the caught, the Great Doctrine of archery that Master Awa taught Herrigel offers a further insight that informs the character of Holden Caulfield: the identity of the shooter/catcher/saver and the Divine. As Master Awa explained of the Great Doctrine, "when the target and I become one, it also signifies that I become one with Buddha. . . . You [Herrigel] should aim not at the target but at yourself. Then you will succeed in shooting yourself, Buddha, and the target all at the same time."[20] Hence, Salinger may well have become aware of this spiritual, if not specifically Zen Buddhist, identification of opposites that informs Holden's character through Japanese archery. This possibility lends support to my argument that at the close of *Catcher* Salinger identifies Holden with the Jesus Christ of Carl Jung's conception, who also embodies the oneness of opposites, of fisherman (catcher) and fish (caught).[21]

The Great Doctrine and *Catcher* also take similar views of the condition that ensues upon the transcendent fusion of opposites wherein a subject as an active center of logical being evaporates. Through archery, Herrigel at last experiences such transcendence directly, an experience during which, in Awa's words, "the bowstring has cut right though you [Herrigel]"; Herrigel both shoots and is shot simultaneously. Later, Herrigel is at a loss, hardly knowing what to say about his experience: "I'm afraid I don't understand anything more at all, . . . even the simplest things have got in a muddle. . . . Do 'I' hit the goal, or does the goal hit me?"[22] Having transcended the binary oppositions which comprise our "knowledge" of the world, Herrigel cannot put into words what he has experienced. Yet this is precisely the nature of mastering the Great Doctrine, and at this point, Awa acknowledges that Herrigel has mastered the "artless art" of archery.[23] After the final, climactic rain scene of *Catcher*, in which Holden experiences oneness with his dead brother Allie, with the falling Phoebe, and with the phonies around him[24]—that is, after Holden too has been hit by his own arrow—Holden finds himself unable to understand or explain what he has experienced: "D. B. asked me what I thought about all this stuff I just finished telling you about. I didn't *know* what the hell to say. If you want to know the truth, I don't know what I think about it" (276–277; emphasis original). Finally, Holden respects the principle of the Zen adept, who "shuns all talk of himself and his progress" and "regards it [such talk] as a betrayal of Zen."[25] Reflecting on, presumably, his narration of the novel, Holden blurts, out (concludes), "I'm sorry I told so many people about it" (277).

Having achieved transcendence, Holden no longer takes aim at anything, and thus he finds it absurd for the doctor to ask if he is going to apply himself when he returns to school after recovering from the breakdown he has apparently suffered (276). For Holden, this is "a stupid question" because he has already moved beyond the stage of consciously pursuing goals, in other words, of taking aim. If Holden were to take aim—or to speak directly of his goal/target—he would miss his aim as surely as the novice archer straining at his bow. An understanding of this adds nuance to Holden's final words, the final words of the novel: "Don't tell anybody anything. If you do, you start missing everybody" (277).

Notes

1. See, for example, Bernice and Sanford Goldstein, "Zen and Salinger." *Modern Fiction Studies* 12.3 (1966): 313–324; and Dennis McCort, "Hyakujo's

Geese, Amban's Doughnuts and Rilke's Carrousel: Sources East and West for Salinger's *Catcher*," *Comparative Literature Studies* 34.3 (1997): 260–278.

2. J. D. Salinger, "Seymour: An Introduction," *Raise High the Roof Beam, Carpenters,* and *Seymour: An Introduction* (Boston: Little, Brown, 1963) 241–242.

3. Eugen Herriuel, *Nihon no Kyujutu,* ("The Gallant Art of Archery"), trans. Jisaburo Shibata (Tokyo: Iwanami, 1982) 101, 110–111.

4. Margaret A. Salinger, *Dream Catcher* (New York: Washington Square Press, 2000) 11.

5. For a discussion of Salinger's interest in German speaking writers such as Rilke and Kafka and his experience in wartime Germany, see Ian Hamilton, *In Search of J. D. Salinger* (London: Heinemann, 1988) 85–93, 108.

6. Clinton W. Trowbridge, "Character and Detail in *The Catcher in the Rye,*" *Holden Caulfield,* ed. Harold Bloom (New York: Chelsea House, 1990) 77–78.

7. Yasuhiro Takeuchi, "The Burning Carousel and the Carnivalesque Subversion and Transcendence at the Close of *The Catcher in the Rye,*" *Studies in the Novel* 34.3 (2002): 328–329.

8. J. D. Salinger, *The Catcher in the Rye* (Boston: Little, Brown, 1951) 236. Further citations will be made parenthetically.

9. Eugen Herrigel, *Zen in the Art of Archery,* trans., R. F. C. Hull (New York: Vintage, 1989) 5–6.

10. Herrigel, *Zen in the Art of Archery* 73.

11. For an extended discussion of these episodes, see Yasuhiro Takeuchi, "Salinger's *The Catcher in the Rye,*" *The Explicator* 60.3 (2002): 164–166.

12. See, for example, Warren French, *J. D. Salinger* revised ed. (Boston: Twayne, 1976) 122; and Sanford Pinsker, The Catcher in the Rye: *Innocence Under Pressure* (New York: Twayne, 1993), 94.

13. Eugen Herrigel, *Nihon no Kyujutu,* ("The Gallant Art of Archery"), trans. Jisaburo Shibata (Tokyo: Iwanami, 1982) 42–43.

14. Herrigel, *Zen in the Art of Archery* 5.

15. For an extended discussion of how Salinger conveys these identities, and in particular those between Allie and Holden and between Phoebe and Holden, see Takeuchi, "The Burning Carousel and the Carnivalesque," 326–331.

16. Warren French, *J. D. Salinger,* revised ed. (Boston: Twayne, 1976) 109–110. For similar instances, see Duane Edwards, "Don't Ever Tell Anybody Anything," *ELH* 44.3 (1977): 554.

17. French 110.

18. Edwards 556.

19. For other instances of role changes through lendings and borrowings of clothes, see Takeuchi, "The Burning Carousel and the Carnivalesque," 325.

20. Herrigel, *Nihon no Kyujutu,* 43. The English translation of this quotation is my own, from the Japanese.

21. Takeuchi, "The Burning Carousel and the Carnivalesque," 330. See also Jung, *Aion,* trans. R. F. G. Hull, 2nd ed. (Princeton: Princeton University Press, 1969) 112–113.

22. Herrigel, *Zen in the Art of Archery* 61.

23. Herrigel, *Zen in the Art of Archery* 64.

24. See Note 15.

25. Herrigel, *Zen in the Art of Archery* 10.

Chronology

1919   Jerome David Salinger is born in New York City on January 1 to Sol Salinger, a prosperous Jewish meat and cheese importer, and Miriam Jillich Salinger, a woman of Scottish-Irish descent.

1934   Enrolls in Valley Forge Military Academy in Pennsylvania.

1936   Graduates from Valley Forge Military Academy.

1938   Travels in Europe and begins writing short stories.

1939   Takes a short-story writing course taught by Whit Burnett at Columbia University.

1940   First short story, "The Young Folks," published in *Story,* the magazine Whit Burnett edits.

1941   Sells first story about Holden Caulfield to the *New Yorker* but publication is delayed until after World War II.

1942   Drafted into United States Army and attends Officers, First Sergeants, and Instructors School of the Signal Corps.

1943   Stationed in Nashville, Tennessee, achieving the rank of staff sergeant. Transferred to the Army Counter-Intelligence Corps. Short story "The Varioni Brothers" published in *The Saturday Evening Post.*

1944	Transferred to Europe with the U.S. Army Fourth Infantry Division. Lands at Utah Beach, Normandy with D-Day invasion forces and participates in the liberation of France. Serves as Security Agent for the Twelfth Infantry Regiment.
1945	Discharged from the army.
1945–1947	Publishes stories in *The Saturday Evening Post, Colliers, Esquire,* and the *New Yorker.* Writes a story about Holden Caulfield, "Slight Rebellion Off Madison," that is later incorporated into *The Catcher in the Rye.* Writes a ninety-page novella about Holden Caulfield that he withdraws from consideration for publication.
1948–1950	Publishes his major short stories in the *New Yorker,* including "A Perfect Day for Bananafish," "Uncle Wiggily in Connecticut," "Just Before the War with the Eskimos," "The Laughing Man," and "For Esmé—with Love and Squalor."
1950	Film version of "Uncle Wiggily in Connecticut," *My Foolish Heart* starring Susan Hayward and Dana Andrews, released by Samuel Goldwyn Studio. Salinger studies Indian thought at Sumitra Painter Ramakrishna Vivekananda Center in New York City.
1951	*The Catcher in the Rye* published in July. "Pretty Mouth and Green My Eyes" appears in the *New Yorker.*
1953	Moves to a country house in the remote village of Cornish, New Hampshire. Publishes "Teddy" in the *New Yorker. Nine Stories* appears in April. Meets Claire Douglas.
1955	Marries Claire Douglas on February 17. "Raise High the Roof Beam, Carpenters" and "Franny" are published in the *New Yorker.* A daughter, Margaret Ann, is born on December 10.
1957–1959	"Zooey" and "Seymour: An Introduction" published in the *New Yorker.*
1960	A son, Matthew, born on February 13.
1961	*Franny and Zooey* published.
1963	*Raise High the Roof Beam, Carpenters* and *Seymour: An Introduction* published.

1965	Publishes "Hapworth 16, 1924" in the *New Yorker.*
1967	Divorced. Lives in seclusion and refuses contact with public life.
1974	Salinger takes legal action to suppress the unauthorized *Complete Uncollected Short Stories of J. D. Salinger* in his only public statement in years.
1987	Salinger brings a lawsuit against Ian Hamilton for unauthorized use of his unpublished correspondence in *J. D. Salinger: A Writing Life.* He wins the suit, and the biography is published the following year in severely truncated form.

Contributors

HAROLD BLOOM is Sterling Professor of the Humanities at Yale University. He is the author of 30 books, including *Shelley's Mythmaking* (1959), *The Visionary Company* (1961), *Blake's Apocalypse* (1963), *Yeats* (1970), *A Map of Misreading* (1975), *Kabbalah and Criticism* (1975), *Agon: Toward a Theory of Revisionism* (1982), *The American Religion* (1992), *The Western Canon* (1994), and *Omens of Millennium: The Gnosis of Angels, Dreams, and Resurrection* (1996). *The Anxiety of Influence* (1973) sets forth Professor Bloom's provocative theory of the literary relationships between the great writers and their predecessors. His most recent books include *Shakespeare: The Invention of the Human* (1998), a 1998 National Book Award finalist, *How to Read and Why* (2000), *Genius: A Mosaic of One Hundred Exemplary Creative Minds* (2002), *Hamlet: Poem Unlimited* (2003), *Where Shall Wisdom Be Found?* (2004), and *Jesus and Yahweh: The Names Divine* (2005). In 1999, Professor Bloom received the prestigious American Academy of Arts and Letters Gold Medal for Criticism. He has also received the International Prize of Catalonia, the Alfonso Reyes Prize of Mexico, and the Hans Christian Andersen Bicentennial Prize of Denmark.

ALAN NADEL is William T. Bryan Professor of English at the University of Kentucky. His books include *Containment Culture: American Narrative, Postmodernism, and the Atomic Age* (1995), *Flatlining on the Field of Dreams: Cultural Narratives in the Films of President Reagan's America* (1997), and *Television in Black-and-White America: Race and National Identity* (2005).

SANDRA W. LOTT has directed the restructuring of the sophomore literature courses at the University of Montevallo. She has written on thematic parallels in works by women of Asian American, African American, and Caucasian American backgrounds.

STEVEN LATHAM teaches English at Montevallo High School.

SANFORD PINSKER is Shadek Humanities Professor, Emeritus at English Franklin and Marshall College. He is author and editor of more than a dozen books, including book-length studies of Philip Roth, Cynthia Ozick, Joseph Heller, and J. D. Salinger. His *The Catcher in the Rye: Innocence under Pressure* was published in 1993, and with his wife Ann he edited *Understanding* The Catcher in the Rye*: A Student Casebook to Issues, Sources, and Historical Documents*, 1999.

DENNIS McCORT is professor of German at Syracuse University. His *Going Beyond the Pairs: The Coincidence of Opposites in German Romanticism, Zen, and Deconstruction* was published in 2003.

STEPHEN J. WHITFIELD is the Max Richter Professor of American Civilization at Brandeis University. Among his books are *In Search of American Jewish Culture* (1999) and *A Companion to Twentieth-Century America* (2004), which he edited.

PAMELA HUNT STEINLE is professor of American studies at California State University, Fullerton. Her *In Cold Fear: The Catcher in the Rye Censorship Controversies and Postwar American Character* was published in 2000.

DAVID CASTRONOVO is professor of English at Pace University. His books include*Beyond the Gray Flannel Suit: Books from the 1950s That Made American Culture*, 2004 and with Janet Groth *Critic in Love: A Romantic Biography of Edmund Wilson*, 2005.

JOHN McNALLY is the Olen R. Nalley Associate Professor of English at Wake Forest University. His second novel, *America's Report Card*, was published in 2006, and he has also edited several anthologies, including *When I Was a Loser* (2007).

JANE MENDELSOHN has written two novels, *I Was Amelia Earhart* (1996) and *Innocence* (2000).

DENNIS CUTCHINS is associate professor of American literature and culture at Brigham Young University. He is particularly interested in Native American literature and film.

ROBERT MILTNER is assistant professor of English at Kent State University. He has written articles on Raymond Carver, Virginia Woolf, and Richard Hague.

CARL FREEDMAN is professor of English at Louisiana State University. His books include *Critical Theory and Science Fiction* (2000) and *The Incomplete Projects: Marxism, Modernity, and the Politics of Culture* (2002). He also edited *Conversations with Isaac Asimov* (2005) and *Conversations with Ursula K. le Guin* (2008).

YASUHIRO TAKEUCHI was associate professor at Nara Women's University Graduate School of Humanities and Sciences School of Comparative Culture. Prof. Takeuchi frequently wrote articles about Salinger.

Bibliography

Baicchi, Annalisa. "The Translation of Personality: Prismatic Dynamics of Emotive Markers." *Textus: English Studies in Italy*, 15:1 (2002 Jan–June), pp. 145–162.

Bail, Paul. "Sex, Violence, and Peter Pan: J. D. Salinger's *The Catcher in the Rye* (1951)" in *Women in Literature: Reading through the Lens of Gender*, edited by Jerilyn Fisher and Ellen S. Silber. Westport, Conn.: Greenwood, 2003. pp. 72–74.

Baumbach, Jonathan. "The Saint as a Young Man: A Reappraisal of *The Catcher in the Rye*." *Modern Language Quarterly*, 25 (1964): 461–472.

Beidler, Peter G. "An Allusion in Salinger's *The Catcher in the Rye*." *ANQ: A Quarterly Journal of Short Articles, Notes, and Reviews*, 17:4 (2004 Fall), p. 44.

———. 'What Holden Looks Like and Who 'Whosis' Is: A Newly Identified Movie Allusion in *The Catcher in the Rye*." *ANQ: A Quarterly Journal of Short Articles, Notes, and Reviews*, 20:1 (2007 Winter), pp. 51–56.

Belcher, William F., and James W. Lee, eds. *J. D. Salinger and the Critics*. Belmont, CA.: Wadsworth, 1962.

Bloom, Harold, ed. *Holden Caulfield*. New York: Chelsea House, 1990.

———. *J. D. Salinger*. New York: Chelsea House, 1990.

Blythe, Hal, and Charlie Sweet. "Falling in Salinger's *Catcher in the Rye*." *Notes on Contemporary Literature*, 32:4 (2002 Sept), pp. 5–7.

———. "Holden's Mysterious Hat." *Notes on Contemporary Literature*, 32:4 (2002 Sept), pp. 7–8.

———. "The Caulfield Family of Writers in *The Catcher in the Rye*." *Notes on Contemporary Literature*, 32:5 (2002 Nov), pp. 6–7.

———. "Holden, the Bomb, and Dr. Strangelove." *Notes on Contemporary Literature,* 34:3 (2004 May), pp. 11–12.

Bratoz, Silva. "A Stylistic Analysis of Four Translations of J. D. Salinger's *The Catcher in the Rye.*" *ELOPE: English Language Overseas Perspectives and Enquiries,* 1:1–2 (2004), pp. 95–100.

Burrows, David J. "Allie and Phoebe: Death and Love in Salinger's *The Catcher in the Rye.*" In *Private Dealings: Modern American Writers in Search of Integrity.* Eds. David J. Burrows, Lewis M. Dabney, Milne Holton, and Grosvenor E. Powell. Rockville, MD: Almquist and Wiksell, 1969, pp. 106–114.

Carpenter, F. I. "The Adolescent in American Fiction." *English Journal,* 46 (1957): 313–319.

Castronovo, David. "Holden Caulfield's Legacy." *New England Review: Middlebury Series,* 22:2 (2001 Spring), pp. 180–186.

Cohen, Hubert I. "'A Woeful Agony Which Forced Me to Begin My Tale': *The Catcher in the Rye.*" *Modern Fiction Studies,* 12 (Fall 1966): 355–366.

Coles, Robert. "Anna Freud and J. D. Salinger's Holden Caulfield." *Virginia Quarterly Review: A National Journal of Literature and Discussion,* 76:2 (2000 Spring), pp. 214–224.

Doxey, William. "*The Catcher in the Rye* Issue." *Notes on Contemporary Literature,* 32:4 (2002 Sept), pp. 1–8.

Dugan, Lawrence. "Holden and the Lunts." *Notes and Queries,* 52 (250):4 (2005 Dec), pp. 510–511.

Edwards, Duane. "Holden Caulfield: 'Don't Ever Tell Anybody Anything.'" *English Literary History,* 44 (1977): 556-567.

Freedman, Carl. "Memories of Holden Caulfield—and of Miss Greenwood." *Southern Review,* 39:2 (2003 Spring), pp. 401–417.

French, Warren. *J. D. Salinger.* New York: Twayne, 1963.

———. *J. D. Salinger, Revisited.* Boston: Hall, 1988.

Furst, Lilian R. "Dostoyevsky's *Notes from the Underground* and Salinger's *The Catcher in the Rye.*" *Canadian Review of Comparative Literature,* 5 (1978): 72–85.

Glasser, William. "*The Catcher in the Rye.*" *Michigan Quarterly Review,* 15 (1976): 432–457.

Goodman, Anne. Review of *The Catcher in the Rye,* "Mad about Children." *New Republic,* 125 (16 July 1951): 20–21.

Graham, Sarah. *Salinger's* The Catcher in the Rye.. London: Continuum, 2007.

Hale, John K. "Salinger's *The Catcher in the Rye.*" *Explicator,* 60:4 (2002 Summer), pp. 220–221.

Hamilton, Ian. *A Search for J. D. Salinger.* New York: Random House, 1988.

Hamilton, Kenneth. *J. D. Salinger: A Critical Essay*. Grand Rapids, MI: Eerdmans, 1967.

Hassan, Ihab. "The Victim: Images of Evil in Recent American Fiction." *College English*, 21 (1959–1960): 140–146.

Howell, John M. "Salinger in the Waste Land." *Modern Fiction Studies*, 12 (Autumn 1966): 367–375.

Jones, Ernest. Review of *The Catcher in the Rye*, "Case History of All of Us." *Nation* 173:9 (1 September 1951): 176.

Laser, Marvin, and Norman Fruman, ed. *Studies of J. D. Salinger: Reviews, Essays, and Critiques of* The Catcher in the Rye *and Other Fiction*. New York: Odyssey Press, 1963.

Lewis, Jonathan P. "All That David Copperfield Kind of Crap: Holden Caulfield's Rejection of Grand Narratives." *Notes on Contemporary Literature*, 32:4 (2002 Sept), pp. 3–5.

Longstreth, T. Morris. Review of *The Catcher in the Rye*. *Christian Science Monitor,* (19 July 1951).

Luedtke, Luther S. "J. D. Salinger and Robert Burns: The Catcher in the Rye." *Modern Fiction Studies*, 16 (1970): 198–201.

Lundquist, James. *J. D. Salinger*. New York: Ungar, 1979.

Marsden, Malcolm M., ed. *If You Really Want to Know: A* Catcher *Casebook*. Chicago: Scott, Foresman, 1963.

Medovoi, Leerom. "Democracy, Capitalism, and American Literature: The Cold War Construction of J. D. Salinger's Paperback Hero." *The Other Fifties: Interrogating Midcentury American Icons*. Ed. Joel Foreman. Urbana, IL: University of Illinois Press, 1997.

Mellard, James M. "The Disappearing Subject: A Lacanian Reading of *The Catcher in the Rye*." In *Critical Essays on Salinger's* The Catcher in the Rye. Ed. Joel Salzberg. Boston: Hall, 1990.

Menand, Louis. "Holden at Fifty: 'The Catcher in the Rye' and What It Spawned." *New Yorker,* 77:29 (2001 Oct 1), pp. 82–87.

Meral, Jean. "The Ambiguous Mr. Antolini in Salinger's *Catcher in the Rye*." *Caliban*, 7 (1970): 55–58.

Miller, James E. Jr. "*Catcher* in and out of History." *Critical Inquiry*, 3:3 (Spring 1977): 599–603.

Modern Fiction Studies, 12.3 (Autumn 1966). Special Salinger number.

Ohmann, Carol, and Richard Ohmann. "Reviewers, Critics and *The Catcher in the Rye*." *Critical Inquiry*, 3:1 (Autumn 1976): 15–37.

———. "Universals and the Historically Particular." *Critical Inquiry*, 3:4 (Summer 1977): 773–777.

Oldsey, Bernard S. "The Movies in the Rye." *College English*, 23 (1961): 209–215.

Peavy, Charles D. "'Did You Ever Have a Sister?' Holden, Quentin, and Sexual Innocence." *Florida Quarterly*, 1 (1968): 82–95.

Pinsker, Sanford. The Catcher in the Rye: *Innocence under Pressure.* New York: Twayne, 1993.

Rachels, David. "Holden Caulfield: A Hero for All the Ages." *Chronicle of Higher Education*, 47:29 (2001 Mar 30), p. B5.

Rogers, Lydia. "The Psychoanalyst and the Fetishist: Wilhelm Stekel and Mr. Antolini in *The Catcher in the Rye.*" *Notes on Contemporary Literature*, 32:4 (2002 Sept), pp. 2–3.

Rosen, Gerald. "A Retrospective Look at *The Catcher in the Rye.*" *American Quarterly*, 29 (1977): 547–562.

———. *Zen in the Art of J. D. Salinger.* Berkeley: Creative Art Books Co., 1977.

Salzberg, Joel, ed. *Critical Essays on Salinger's* The Catcher in the Rye. Boston: Hall, 1990.

Salzman, Jack, ed. *New Essays on* The Catcher in the Rye. New York: Cambridge University Press, 1991.

Schriber, Mary Suzanne. "Holden Caulfield, C'est Moi." In *Critical Essays on Salinger's* The Catcher in the Rye. Ed. Joel Salzberg. Boston: Hall, 1990.

Simonson, Harold P., and Phillip E. Hager, eds. *Salinger's* Catcher in the Rye: *Clamor v. Criticism.* Lexington, MA: C. C. Heath, 1963.

Smith, Harrison. Review of *The Catcher in the Rye.* "Manhattan Ulysses, Junior." *Saturday Review*, 14:28 (14 July 1951): 12–13.

Stashower, Daniel M. "On First Looking into Chapman's Holden: Speculations on a Murder." *American Scholar*, 52 (1982–1983): 373–377.

Steinle, Pamela Hunt. *In Cold Fear:* The Catcher in the Rye: *Censorship Controversies and Postwar American Character.* Columbus: Ohio State University Press, 2000.

Strauch, Carl F. "Kings in the Back Row: Meaning through Structure—A Reading of Salinger's *The Catcher in the Rye.*" *Wisconsin Studies in Contemporary Literature*, 2 (Winter 1961): 5–30.

Sublette, Jack R. *J. D. Salinger: An Annotated Bibliography 1938–1981.* New York: Garland, 1984.

Svogun, Margaret Dumais. "Salinger's *The Catcher in the Rye.*" *Explicator*, 61:2 (2003 Winter), pp. 110–112.

Takeuchi, Yasuhiro. "Salinger's *The Catcher in the Rye.*" *Explicator*, 60:3 (2002 Spring), pp. 164–166.

Takeuchi. "The Burning Carousel and the Carnivalesque: Subversion and Transcendence at the Close of *The Catcher in the Rye.*" *Studies in the Novel*, 34:3 (2002 Fall), pp. 320–336.

Takeuchi. "The Zen Archery of Holden Caulfield." *English Language Notes*, 42:1 (2004 Sept). pp. 55–63.

Vail, Dennis. "Holden and Psychoanalysis." *PLMA*, 91 (1976): 120-121.

Vanderbilt, Kermit. "Symbolic Resolution in *The Catcher in the Rye:* The Cap, the Carrousel, and the American West." *Western Humanities Review*, 17 (1963): 271–277.

Wells, Arvin R. "Huck Finn and Holden Caulfield: The Situation of the Hero." *Ohio University Review*, 1 (1960): 31–42.

Wenke, John. *J. D. Salinger: A Study of the Short Fiction.* Boston: Twayne, 1991.

Wiegand, William. "The Knighthood of J. D. Salinger." *The New Republic*, 141 (19 October 1959): 19–21.

Wisconsin Studies in Contemporary Literature, 4:1 (Winter 1963). Special Salinger number.

Zapf, Hubert. "Logical Action in *The Catcher in the Rye*." *College Literature*, 12 (1985): 266–271.

Acknowledgments

Alan Nadel. "Rhetoric, Sanity, and the Cold War: The Significance of Holden Caulfield's Testimony." *The Centennial Review,* Volume 32, Number 4 (Fall 1988): pp. 351–371. Copyright © 1988. Reprinted with permission.

Sandra W. Lott and Steven Latham. "The World Was All Before Them": Coming of Age in Ngugi wa Thiong'o's *Weep Not, Child* and J. D. Salinger's *The Catcher in the Rye." Global Perspectives on Teaching Literature: Shared Visions and Distinctive Visions.* Eds. Sandra Ward Lott, Maureen S. G. Hawkins, and Norman McMillan. (Urbana, IL: National Council of Teachers, 1993): pp. 135–151. Copyright © 1993 National Council of Teachers. Reprinted with permission.

Sanford Pinsker. "Go West, My Son." The Catcher in the Rye*: Innocence Under Pressure* (New York: Twayne, 1993): pp. 89–97. Copyright © 1993 Sanford Pinsker. Reprinted with permission.

Dennis McCort. "Hyakujo's Geese, Amban's Doughnuts and Rilke's Carrousel: Sources East and West for Salinger's *Catcher." Comparative Literature Studies* ,Volume 34, Number 3 (1997): pp. 260–278. Copyright © 1997 by the Pennsylvania State University. Reprinted with permission.

Stephen J. Whitfield. "Cherished and Cursed: Toward a Social History of *The Catcher in the Rye." The New England Quarterly,* Volume LXX, Number 4 (December 1997): pp. 567–600. Copyright © 1997 by The New England Quarterly. Reprinted with permission.

Index

207

DATE DUE			

86574

**813
JD**

**J.D. Salinger's The
catcher in the rye**